I0617228

Library Lin's

Biographies

Autobiographies

and Memoirs

Praise for
Library Lin's Biographies, Autobiographies, and Memoirs

66 A fantastic starting point for anyone interested in reading about the fascinating lives of others."

—Kate Moore, New York Times bestselling author of
The Radium Girls and The Woman They Could Not Silence

66 Serving as a trusty guide for readers who love true stories about amazing people, Library Lin has selected the most acclaimed, worthwhile, and fascinating biographies and memoirs you'd be delighted to discover in a lifetime."

—Evan I. Schwartz, author of
Finding Oz and *The Last Lone Inventor*

Praise for
Library Lin's Curated Collection of Superlative Nonfiction

66 This impressive book offers an amazing wealth of nonfiction reading recommendations on virtually every subject.... The only TBR list nonfiction fans will ever need."

—*Booklist* and *Blue Ink Review*

66 ...A thoughtful, thorough survey of the best nonfiction found in today's libraries."

—Kirkus Reviews

66 I am thrilled that my volume has earned a small place in *Library Lin's Curated Collection of Superlative Nonfiction*. Linda Maxie's compendium exudes both qualities I treasure in accomplished librarians: unbounded expertise and unstinting generosity in sharing it. Any curious reader will find her guidance to the best in nonfiction not only helpful but inspiring."

—James Mustich, author of
1,000 Books to Read Before You Die

Library Lin's

Biographies
Autobiographies
and Memoirs

Linda Maxie

Spoon Creek Press • Patrick Springs, Virginia • 2023

Library Lin's Biographies, Autobiographies, and Memoirs
© 2023 Linda Maxie. All rights reserved.

Published by Spoon Creek Press
An imprint of Spoon Creek Books, LLC
PO box 492
Patrick Springs, Virginia 24133
spooncreekpress.com
publisher@spooncreekpress.com

Contact the author through librarylin.com.

Name: Maxie, Linda, author
Title: Library Lin's biographies, autobiographies, and memoirs
Description: Patrick Springs, VA: Spoon Creek Press
Identifiers: LCCN 2023907484 | ISBN 9798985923421 (trade paperback) |
9798985923438 (ebook)
Subjects: Best books | Books and reading—United States
Classification: LCC Z1035.9 | DDC 028.9

Library of Congress Control Number: 2023907484

ISBN: 979-8-9859234-2-1 trade paperback
         979-8-9859234-3-8 electronic book

Design and composition: Dick Margulis, dmargulis.com

First printing

MANUFACTURED IN THE UNITED STATES OF AMERICA

To those who take the time to research and write books about other people so the rest of us can benefit from learning their stories. And to the brave souls who write autobiographies and memoirs so the rest of us know we are not alone.

Contents

Acknowledgments

No matter the genre, books don't just materialize from the ether. They take a lot of time and dedication. Authors need a lot of love and support. With that fact in mind, I'd like to thank the following people who have supported me in writing this book. First and always, I thank my husband, Roger Maxie, for his encouragement. He provided me with the time and the space to do my research, and he was tolerant while I obsessed over book titles. Without him, this book wouldn't exist. My editor and book designer, Dick Margulis, was indispensable in producing both of my books. His guidance is sound, and his patience is deep. I feel lucky that he has agreed to shepherd me through my projects. This book's beta readers, Linda Carr, Julie Moore, Nancy Carlson, Liz Wallace, and Randy Currier, provided terrific insights into my choices of books and the chapter groupings and entries. Their thoughtful commentary kept me from making tone-deaf choices on where to place some subjects, and their suggestions for other offerings were much appreciated. Randy provided insights into the book's value, and I will always be grateful for the time, effort, and guidance he put into his feedback. Linda, Julie, Nancy, and Liz had suggestions for improvement and served as sounding boards and emotional support. I'm grateful to Brad and Tracy Holley for the warm welcome into their busy lives. Brad's pictures for my book and business are crisp, clear, and professional. He is a talented photographer. My friend, former co-worker, fabulous English teacher, and all-around exceptional human being Jennifer Turner provided much-needed feedback when I needed it.

Three people that serve as cheerleaders for my writing efforts are my long-time buddy-pal Trenda Leavitt, my dear cousin Nancy Bryant, and my cousin-in-law Terry Rickmon. You all have no idea how much your kind comments and support mean to me. My kids, Ben and Ellen Maxie and Jack and Taylor Maxie have provided feedback and clerical, editing, and marketing help. I love you all bunches, now and always. I thank my mom, Fay Fisher, for listening and providing feedback. But above all, I thank her for reading to me when I was a child and spending our limited family budget on storybooks. To me, that's the greatest gift a parent can give a child. Barry Fisher and Michael North have provided insights into the publishing industry and the Library of Congress. They have offered intelligent guidance for my decisions. I value all their feedback. And I appreciated the tour of the Library of Congress. It was a librarian's dream come true. I thank my mother-in-law, Dot Maxie, for introducing me to excellent nonfiction books and sharing her enthusiasm for reading. And I thank my sisters-in-law, Linda Carr and Margaret Fey, for their interest and kindness. I'm obliged to Stephanie Chandler, CEO of the Nonfiction Authors Association, and Michael Scott of Great Books+Great Minds for their support. Stephanie has been encouraging from the beginning of my writing efforts, her organization has given me loads of helpful advice, and I'm grateful for the opportunities she's given me to review books. Michael's book community welcomed me as a guest blogger for this past year. His blog posts are insightful, thought-provoking, and inspiring. I think any thoughtful nonfiction reader would find a home in his group. And though I don't know either of them personally, I thank Nancy Pearl and James Mustich for inspiring my books with theirs. They gave me hope that the types of books I love most, books about books, can be done well and are appreciated in the wider world. Looking back over this list, I realize that I am, indeed, blessed.

Library Lin's

Biographies
Autobiographies
and Memoirs

Introduction

WHETHER WE LOVE THEM OR not, most of us find other people fascinating. Most of us are curious about the lives of others. After all, who *doesn't* have an intriguing story to tell? If we're facing a challenging situation, it's helpful to see what other people may have done under similar circumstances. Reading about someone else can be a vicarious adventure. I would rather read about someone surviving on the open ocean in a kayak than try it myself. Many people find biographies and memoirs the most accessible nonfiction genres to enjoy. The narrative format makes them easier to sink into.

I'm a retired librarian with years of reading recommended books on all sorts of nonfiction topics. After finishing my first book, *Library Lin's Curated Collection of Superlative Nonfiction* (*LCCN*), I was unhappy that there were so many great biographies that I couldn't include for lack of space. I arranged thousands of books by Dewey Decimal Classification (DDC) in that book, effectively creating a portable nonfiction library. But at 416 pages, the book was stuffed. Then it hit me, why not dedicate another work to books about people? And I sat down to write this one.

Biographies, autobiographies, and memoirs are popular books. But what are the differences between the three categories? Biographies cover any person's entire life, or at least what is known about their life, but someone other than the subject writes the account. The author can enjoy a close relationship with the person or have never met them. The subject of the book writes an autobiography about their life. Because they haven't died yet, the book only covers up to the point when the book was published. But like a biography, the focus is on the entire life story. Steve Martin could write a biography about Bob Hope if he wanted, but he could only write an autobiography or a memoir about himself.

Memoirs differ from biographies and autobiographies in that there is no attempt to even-handedly cover the life story from beginning to end. A memoir, like an autobiography, is written by the book's subject. But a memoir will focus on a particular event, era, or theme in the person's life. For example, some people write memoirs about their most outstanding achievements or greatest struggles. Grief is a common theme. Most people love to read memoirs they can relate to. Stories of child abuse or grief may help them feel less alone. These books tend to be quite personal in tone and feeling. And some are so well written they are celebrated as great literature.

This book is divided into chapters according to theme. Some chapters have a "Collective Biography" section at the end. Whereas a biography is the story of one person's life, a collective biography provides brief narratives of two or more people's lives. These may be people who knew one another and whose stories are intertwined. Or it may be a book that devotes each chapter to a separate person, such as a book with a chapter each on famous scientists or artists.

For *LCCN*, I scoured sixty-five lists of recommended books dating back a century. The books came from organizations like the American Library Association, publications like *Time* magazine, and book awards like the Pulitzer Prize. Most of the lists I consulted released lists of the best books of the year, from which I selected my titles. To find titles for this book, I returned to those lists and picked up works I didn't have room for in the first book. Then I went to book blogs and other sites like *Book Riot* and *Epic Reads* to find even more titles. I also consulted lists on GoodReads. Then I asked for suggestions from my friends and followers on Facebook and Twitter. I took notes wherever I found recommended biographies, autobiographies, and memoirs. Then I got busy looking up book reviews to select the most promising ones.

In my previous book, I arranged books by the DDC. But for this one, I grouped the titles broadly by theme. I didn't try to have roughly the same number of books about activists as I did about musicians, for instance. So, some chapters are much longer than others.

While I was trying to make things more convenient for you, the reader, even putting people into wide-ranging categories was complex and sometimes problematic. Take Arnold Schwarzenegger as just one example. The man has had blockbuster careers in *four* distinct areas: as a bodybuilder, as a businessman, as an internationally recognized actor, and as the governor of the state of California. Each career could land him in a different chapter. I placed him under "Stage and Screen" because that's what I think he is best known for. But there were many people with even broader ranges of accomplishment. An athlete may write novels and fight for LGBTQIA+ rights. Some people were notable in five or more fields. I did the best I could, and I recognize in some cases, I may have missed the mark.

This book contains chapters called "Black Experience," "Asian and Middle Eastern Narratives," "African Chronicles" "Indigenous Peoples," "Jewish Experiences and the Holocaust," "Latino/a and Hispanic," and "Women's Voices." I placed people in those chapters if their story's central theme relates to being from one of those places or in one of those groups. But there are many Black, Asian, Middle Eastern, African, Indigenous, Jewish, Latino/a, and Hispanic people (and women!) who aren't included in those specific chapters. Instead, I grouped them with other books with a similar focus. That is why Jim Thorpe, an indigenous person, is under "Athletes," and Katherine Hepburn, a woman, is under "Stage and Screen."

People are mixtures of good and bad. I decided early on that judging these people was not my role. Some have recently found themselves on the wrong side of public opinion. Rather than classify people based on mistakes, I placed them under what they are most known for. For lawbreakers and people who harmed or killed many, I put them in "Law and the Prison System." And not everyone in that chapter qualifies as a lawbreaker. Some are there simply because a big part of their story involves arrest or incarceration. In other words, my chapters and my groupings are not perfect. I'm only partially satisfied with them myself.

Another chapter that may be confusing is "Popular Culture and Comedians." I opted to put comedians and stage magicians here rather than under "Stage and

Screen." This was a somewhat arbitrary decision, but it made more sense to me. The only exception I made is that Groucho Marx, who starred primarily in movies, was placed in the "Stage and Screen" chapter.

If you have difficulty finding someone in a place that makes sense to you, please consult the index on page 261. If there is a title for the person you are looking for in this book, you can find it there.

Finally, I do not claim that every excellent biography ever written is included in this book. I omitted some titles because they were already in my first book, and I wanted to avoid repeating myself. If you are curious whether a person is in the first book, check the appendix on page 257. This appendix does not have every biography included in the first book. But if someone can be found there but not here, it tells you who and the page to find them.

Some good biographies were left out because I didn't know about them—excellent books sometimes never win prizes or land on anyone's "best books" list. And you may be surprised to find no books on someone you judge to be a top performer in their field. There may be biographies in some cases, but it's possible they aren't highly recommended reads. I only included titles that others have read and truly enjoyed.

This book is not meant to be the final word on great books about people. Instead, like *Library Lin's Curated Collection of Superlative Nonfiction*, it's meant to be a *starting* place. Please use these lists to get yourself thinking about additional people you'd like to read about. Read other books by the authors in this book if you enjoyed their writing. Find other authors who have written about the people included here. Every author can bring out information about someone others may have missed.

The main thing is to start. Read. Have fun. Enjoy yourself. I wish you many happy hours of discovery!

Linda Maxie
Aka "Library Lin"

1

African Chronicles

Waris Dirie

Waris Dirie, *Desert Flower*, 1998.

Somali model Waris Dirie tells of how, as a young teen, she walked away from her impoverished home in the African desert. Making her way to Mogadishu, she ultimately worked as a servant in London before becoming a supermodel and human rights ambassador.

Abdi Nor Iftin

Abdi Nor Iftin, *Call Me American: A Memoir*, 2018.

Somali native Abdi Nor Iftin admired America from childhood. He learned English from listening to Michael Jackson and watching movies. His nickname in Mogadishu was Abdi American, but that became a hazard in 2006 when the Islamist group al-Shabaab took power. He began sending secret dispatches to NPR, but as things grew increasingly dangerous, he was forced to flee to Kenya. When he won an annual visa lottery, he began a harrowing trip to the U.S. He writes this memoir from his home in Maine.

Hisham Matar

Hisham Matar, *The Return: Fathers, Sons and the Land in Between*, 2016.

Acclaimed novelist Hisham Matar writes of his trip to Libya to try to discover the circumstances surrounding his father's disappearance. His father served on the Libyan delegation to the United Nations when Hisham was a child. Years after their return to Libya, the Qaddafi regime accused his father of being a reactionary, and the family fled the country. But eight years later, his father was kidnapped in Cairo and was thought to be in a notorious prison. The prisons are empty now, but Matar returned, hoping to find his father alive.

Mark Mathabane

Mark Mathabane, *Kaffir Boy: The True Story of a Black Youth's Coming of Age in Apartheid South Africa*, 1986.

In this classic memoir, Mark Mathabane talks of growing up in South Africa's most notorious ghetto, where he lived with gang wars and police harassment. Yet he escaped and got an education with a scholarship at an American university. His story is one of triumph over hatred and oppression, becoming an author and lecturer.

Nega Mezlekia

Nega Mezlekia, *Notes from the Hyena's Belly: An Ethiopian Boyhood*, 2000.

During the 1970s and 1980s, Ethiopia was suffering from famine and embroiled in a civil war. Ethiopian writer Nega Mezlekia grew up in this fraught environment. He said, "We children lived like the donkey, careful not to wander off the beaten trail and end up in the hyena's belly." Religious differences between Christians and Muslims played a part in the collapse, but so did conflicts between Western European and communist governments for influence on the nation.

Dogon Mondiant

Dogan Mondiant, *Those We Throw Away Are Diamonds: A Refugee's Search for Home*, 2021.

In this memoir, Dogan Mondiant wishes to speak both of and to refugees everywhere. His experience as a refugee began when he was only three years old. One day, he and his Tutsi family were at home in the Congo when his father's friend, a Hutu, arrived carrying a machete and told the family they would all be killed within hours. They fled to the forest and made their way to Rwanda and a tent city where they lived for more than twenty years. But they were still victims of violence. When Mondiant later returned to the Congo in a desperate attempt at a better life, he was forced to become a child soldier. When he later went to college, he hid his past out of shame. Now he is speaking out.

Mende Nazer

Mende Nazer and Damien Lewis, *Slave: My True Story*, 2002.

One night in 1993, Arab raiders came to Mende Nazer's Nuba village. They killed the adults and took thirty-one children to sell into slavery. Mende was only twelve when she was sold to an Arab family in Khartoum, Sudan's capital. They fed her leftovers, had her sleep in a shed, and abused her physically, mentally, and sexually. Seven years later, she was sent to work for a diplomat working in the U.K. From there, she made her escape that same year.

Trevor Noah

Trevor Noah, *Born a Crime*, 2016.

In apartheid South Africa, being the child of a White Swiss father and a Black Xhosa mother was to be the product of illegal activity. So, Noah, whose life was a crime, was kept indoors when he was very small so the government could not imprison his mother and thus separate her from her child. When the apartheid government was abolished, Noah was allowed to shine. Then he and his mother set about experiencing the lives they had been denied. This book tells the astounding story of Noah's remarkable journey from a hidden child to international fame on *The Daily Show*. It is also a tribute to his mother.

Clemantine Wamariya

Clemantine Wamariya, *The Girl Who Smiled Beads: A Story of War and What Comes After*, 2018.

When the Rwandan genocide began, Clematine Wamirya, aged six, escaped with her fifteen-year-old sister, Claire. The two stayed on the run for six years, wandering through seven African countries, foraging for food, hiding, and seeing things no child should see. They did not know the fate of their parents. They were granted asylum in the U.S. at the end of six years and wound up in Chicago. Wamariya writes of their struggles and successes in this searing memoir.

2

Asian and Middle Eastern Narratives

Mohammed Ashraf

Aman Sethi, *A Free Man: A True Story of Life and Death in Delhi*, 2011.

How did Mohammed Ashraf, a resident of Delhi, fall from being a biology student and electrician's apprentice to a homeless day laborer? Aman Sethi examines the persistence of crushing poverty in one of the world's largest cities. Yet, despite hardships and setbacks, Ashraf perseveres.

Osama Bin Laden

Peter Bergen, *The Rise and Fall of Osama Bin Laden: The Biography*, 2021.

Osama Bin Laden was the son of a billionaire, yet he and his family lived like poor people. He loved his wives and children but ruined them. He was a religious zealot willing for thousands to die for his cause. While he had the loyalty of many, his bodyguards turned against him in the end. While Bin Laden himself is now gone, his legacy lives on. Journalist Peter Bergen narrates his story from its promising beginning to jihadists who follow in his wake.

Jung Chang

Jung Chang, *Wild Swans: Three Daughters of China*, 1991.

Chinese-born British writer Jung Chang tells the story of three generations, first Chang's grandmother, who was a warlord's concubine, next her mother, who was a devoted young communist in Mao's China, and then Chang herself, who worked as a peasant, steelworker, and electrician. Her family's story is entirely inseparable from the history of twentieth-century China.

Isabel Sun Chao and Claire Chao

Isabel Sun Chao and Claire Chao, *Remembering Shanghai: A Memoir of Socialites, Scholars and Scoundrels*, 2018.

Daughter Claire Chao and her mother, Isabel Sun Chao, returned to Shanghai after leaving it behind when Mao came to power. In Isabel's youth in the 1930s and 1940s, her family had lived a life of privilege and power. So, when she left her family to travel to Hong Kong at age eighteen, she didn't realize she would never see them again. On their return, the Shanghai family she and Claire explore is full of dark secrets.

Janine Di Giovanni

Janine Di Giovanni, *The Morning They Came for Us: Dispatches from Syria*, 2016.

U.S.-born correspondent Janine Di Giovanni first went to Syria in May 2012 to cover the peaceful uprising there. But she continued to return as the hostilities morphed into one of the most brutal conflicts in recent history. She discusses her experiences covering the war and the personal stories of Syrians, young, old, rich, and poor, who have endured the horrors.

Shin Dong-hyuk

Blaine Harden, *Escape from Camp 14: One Man's Remarkable Odyssey from North Korea to Freedom in the West*, 2012.

Journalist Blaine Harden tells the story of Shin Dong-hyuk, who was born and raised in one of North Korea's prison camps. He was raised to view his mother as competition for food, guards used him from a young age as an informant, and he witnessed his family's execution. Few of the 150,000–200,000 people in these political camps escaped, yet Shin did.

Tetsuko Kuroyanagi

Tetsuko Kuroyanagi, *Totto-chan: The Little Girl at the Window*, 1981.

Internationally recognized Japanese actress, talk show host, and children's book author Tetsuko Kuroyanagi remembers her childhood attending school in Tokyo during World War II in a school that used old railroad cars for classrooms. She shares the joy of attending this school and how its headmaster believed that children should be allowed to have fun and freedom, which influenced Kuroyanagi all her life. She has served as a champion of causes for the deaf and hearing impaired as the head of the Totto Foundation, named after the protagonist of her book *Totto-chan: The Little Girl at the Window*. In addition, Kuroyanagi was a UNICEF Goodwill Ambassador in 1984.

Le Ly Hayslip

Le Ly Hayslip, *When Heaven and Earth Changed Places: A Vietnamese Woman's Journey from War to Peace*, 1989.

Born in Ha-La in central Vietnam, Le Ly Haslip was only twelve when American soldiers landed by helicopter in her village. The youngest of six children in her Buddhist family, she was recruited by the Americans as a child spy and saboteur. By age sixteen, she had been starved, imprisoned, and raped; and she lost her family. Yet she retained her belief in the goodness of humanity. Twenty years after escaping to America, she returned to Vietnam and relived horrible moments interspersed with joyful reunions.

Souad Mekhennet

Souad Mekhennet, *I Was Told to Come Alone: My Journey Behind the Lines of Jihad*, 2017.

As a German journalist of Arab descent, Souad Mekhennet has had access to some of the world's most wanted men. Though she works as a reporter for *The Washington Post*, her background has made her more trusted than most Western journalists. In her memoir, she tells of firsthand reporting in Iraq and on the Turkish–Syrian border, interviewing members of ISIS and other terrorists.

Marina Nemat

Marina Nemat, *Prisoner of Tehran: One Woman's Story of Survival Inside an Iranian Prison*, 2007.

When Marina Nemat was sixteen, in 1979, her world was upended by the Iranian Revolution. She complained to her teachers about the Koran replacing the textbooks she had been using. For voicing her concerns, she was placed in a notorious prison, Evin, and she was interrogated, tortured, and sentenced to death. In this memoir, she tells how she survived and emigrated to Canada.

Pin Yathay

Pin Yathay, *Stay Alive, My Son*, 1987.

As an educated and successful engineer, Pin Yathay was happy when the Khmer Rouge first entered Phnom Penh in 1975. After the corrupt Lon Nol regime, he was hopeful that better things were ahead for Cambodia. But instead, for the next twenty-seven months, some of the most horrifying events of the twentieth century took place. Pin Yahay was there when it happened, and he chronicles his family's heartbreaking story and his decision to leave his son, Nawath, who was too ill to travel, to escape to Thailand.

Putsata Reang

Putsata Reang, *Ma and Me: A Memoir*, 2022.

In escaping Cambodia, Putsata Reang's mother saved Put's life when she defied the captain's orders to throw her daughter overboard from the naval vessel they were sailing on. The story of how her mother gave her to American military nurses and doctors instead literally saved her. So, as she was growing up, Put sought, above all, to be a perfect daughter to repay her debt. But her mother can never accept her for what she is: a lesbian who seeks, like we all do, to find love.

Edward W. Said

Edward W. Said, *Out of Place: A Memoir*, 1999.

Public intellectual and literary scholar Edward Said writes of his childhood in Palestine, Lebanon, and Egypt. He then describes his time in boarding schools and colleges in the United States. For his entire life as a Christian and a Palestinian, he felt like an outsider. Yet his memoir is a colorful and moving story of how he came to his unique perspective that bridges the Eastern and Western worlds, making works like *Orientalism* possible.

Zoya Phan

Zoya Phan, *Little Daughter: A Memoir of Survival in Burma and the West*, 2009.

Born into the Karen tribe in a remote Burmese jungle, Zoya Phan was only thirteen when the Burmese army attacked her home. She joined thousands of refugees hiding in the jungles for two years. She was nearly dead when she found herself in a Thai refugee camp. Making her way to the U.K., she became a spokesperson in the Burmese fight for freedom.

3

Black Experience

Ashley

Tiya Miles, *All That She Carried: The Journey of Ashley's Sack, a Black Family Keepsake*, 2021.

Historian Tiya Miles delves into the history of an artifact that can be found displayed in the Smithsonian's National Museum of African American History and Culture. The homemade cotton bag, Ashley's sack, was given to nine-year-old Ashley by her enslaved mother, Rose, in the 1850s. The two were separated when Ashley was sold from their South Carolina home. Years later, Ashley's granddaughter Ruth embroidered the family history on the bag. Miles uncovers what can be found about these women to create a moving portrait of their lives.

Brittany K. Barnett

Brittany K. Barnett, *A Knock at Midnight: A Story of Hope, Justice, and Freedom*, 2020.

When attorney and entrepreneur Brittany K. Barnett was still in law school, planning for a brilliant career in corporate law, she discovered a case that changed her life's trajectory. She found a single mother, business owner, and Black Southerner named Sharanda Jones, who was serving a life sentence without parole for a first-time drug offense. As Brittany investigated the case, she found parallels between Jones's life and her own, reinforcing her belief that the justice system was stacked against those of color. She went on to become a corporate lawyer by day. But at night, she donated her time to gaining justice for Jones and others. How much harm, she asks, are we doing to our society by silencing voices and denying gifted individuals the right to contribute?

Melba Pattillo Beals

Melba Pattillo Beals, *Warriors Don't Cry: A Searing Memoir of the Battle to Integrate Little Rock's Central High*, 1994.

After the 1954 Supreme Court ruling in *Brown v. Board of Education*, schools in Little Rock, Arkansas, were forced to integrate. Nine Black teenagers were chosen to be the first Black students enrolled in the previously all-White high school. Melba Pattillo was one of them. President Dwight D. Eisenhower had to send in the 101st Airborne Division to force the school to allow these students entrance. Now Beals expresses what it was like to be a terrified fifteen-year-old, running the gauntlet between screaming mobs to enter the school, and how every day in the school after that, she had to brace herself for the battle to come.

Ota Benga

Pamela Newkirk, *Spectacle: The Astonishing Life of Ota Benga*, 2015.

Journalist Pamela Newkirk tells of an almost unimaginably shameful episode in American history. In 1904, Ota Benga, a recent arrival from the Congo, was featured in an anthropology exhibit at the St. Louis World's Fair. At 4'11" in height and weighing 103 pounds, Benga was called a "pygmy," a person of small stature. Two years later, he was part of an exhibit in the New York Zoological Gardens, where he was kept in a cage with an orangutan. The exhibit became an international sensation. Newkirk explains how Benga was released from the zoo and wound up in Lynchburg, Virginia, where he died young.

Charles M. Blow

Charles M. Blow, *Fire Shut Up in My Bones: A Memoir*, 2014.

New York Times columnist Charles M. Blow tells of his upbringing in an African American town in Louisiana, where he was raised by a tough mother who worked in a poultry plant and where an older cousin secretly abused him. Believing that his entry to a state university and a Black fraternity will make all his wishes come true, he is shocked when he is forced to become an abuser himself.

Claude Brown

Claude Brown, *Manchild in the Promised Land*, 1965.

This classic autobiography was faintly fictionalized but still captures Claude Brown's childhood and young adult years as a hardened criminal in Harlem during the 1940s and 1950s. While Brown captured a place and a moment in time, his book still speaks to those raised in seemingly hopeless and desperate urban landscapes.

Stokely Carmichael

Peniel E. Joseph, *Stokely: A Life*, 2012.

Civil rights scholar Peniel E. Joseph traces the life of Stokely Carmichael, who began the Black Power movement in 1965. Early in the civil rights movement, Carmichael was among those activists who followed Martin Luther King Jr.'s calls for nonviolent opposition to injustice. But after becoming frustrated with the slow progress, he urged Black people to achieve equality by any means necessary. As a result, he helped organize the Black Panther Party, which he supported until, at age twenty-seven, he left the U.S. and adopted a pan-African ideology.

Eldridge Cleaver

Eldridge Cleaver, *Soul on Ice*, 1968.
Writer and political activist Eldridge Cleaver shocked the nation with this memoir detailing his career as a politically motivated serial rapist. After serving a prison sentence, Cleaver became a leader in the Black Panther movement and converted to Mormonism. His memoir is a classic of civil rights literature.

MacNolia Cox

A. Van Jordan, *M-A-C-N-O-L-I-A: Poems*, 2004.
A. Van Jordan uses a nonlinear narrative to tell the story of MacNolia Cox, the first African American to be a finalist in the National Spelling Bee competition. After her 1936 regional win in Akron, Ohio, the thirteen-year-old spelling prodigy headed to Washington, D.C., to participate in the national contest. Still, she wasn't allowed to stay in the same hotel or attend the same dinners as White contestants. As she neared winning the competition, the officials gave her a word to spell that wasn't on the official list, which ultimately kept Cox from her dreams of attending college in hopes of becoming a doctor. But that wasn't the end of her story.

Frederick Douglass

Frederick Douglass, *Narrative Life of Frederick Douglass: An American Slave: Written by Himself*, 1845.

Frederick Douglass, *My Bondage* and *My Freedom*, 1855.
Born enslaved in Maryland, Frederick Douglass escaped to the North in 1838 after teaching himself to read and write. Seven years later, he published *Narrative Life*, discussing the horrors of slavery, how he worked to educate himself, and his harrowing escape to freedom. After his emancipation, he wrote *My Bondage and My Freedom*, in which he eloquently details his activism for civil rights and liberty.

George Floyd

Robert Samuels and Toluse Olorunnipa, *His Name Is George Floyd: One Man's Life and the Struggle for Racial Justice*, 2022.
Washington Post reporters Samuels and Olorunnipa tell of George Floyd's

life until May 25, 2020, the day he lost his life in Minneapolis as White police officer Derek Chauvin was filmed holding him down while he struggled to breathe. His story is told in the larger context of what it is like to be a Black man in America. His tragic death set off a worldwide movement for justice and an end to police overreach.

Ashley C. Ford

Ashley C. Ford, *Somebody's Daughter: A Memoir*, 2021.

In this memoir, Ashley C. Ford recounts what it is like to grow up a poor Black girl who longs for an incarcerated father she barely knows. As a child, she used her idealized image of him to help her handle loneliness and worries. After being raped by a boyfriend, she learns why her father is in prison. Through it all, she ponders what family and love mean.

Marcus Garvey

Colin Grant, *Negro with a Hat: The Rise and Fall of Marcus Garvey and His Dream of Mother Africa*, 2008.

Historian Colin Grant recounts the story of Jamaican-born leader Marcus Garvey, a self-educated activist for Black causes who used propaganda to promote Black nationalism in the United States by evoking a lost African civilization. With his over-the-top style, Garvey proved to be a charismatic leader, but his insistence on racial purity led him into the crosshairs of American Black leadership of the time.

Fannie Lou Hamer

Keisha N. Blain, *Until I Am Free: Fannie Lou Hamer's Enduring Message to America*, 2021.

Fannie Lou Hamer was born in Mississippi in 1917. She was the youngest of twenty children and the granddaughter of enslaved grandparents. Historian Keisha N. Blain explains how her story serves as a template for others committed to social justice. Despite her impoverished background, Hamer's intellect and hard work changed the communities in which she lived and empowered the civil rights and women's rights movements.

Charlayne Hunter-Gault

Charlayne Hunter-Gault, *In My Place*, 1992.

At age nineteen, Charlayne Hunter-Gault became the first Black woman to attend the University of Georgia. But in doing so she exposed herself to a fierce court battle and violence. The award-winning correspondent for the MacNeil/Lehrer NewsHour relates the story in this powerful memoir.

Ona Judge

Erica Armstrong Dunbar, *Never Caught: The Washingtons' Relentless Pursuit of Their Runaway Slave, Ona Judge,* 2017.

George Washington took nine enslaved people to Philadelphia when he was elected America's first president. One of them was twenty-two-year-old Ona Judge. At the time, Pennsylvania law required any slave in the state to be set free after six months of service. Judge took advantage and escaped, making her way to freedom in New England on a spring day. Historian Erica Armstrong Dunbar researched the price Judge paid and the chase that followed at the Washington family's request.

Patrisse Khan-Cullors

Patrisse Khan-Cullors and Asha Bandele, *When They Call You a Terrorist: A Black Lives Matter Memoir,* 2018.

Artist, organizer, and freedom fighter Patrisse Khan-Cullors writes about her life as a Black person growing up with a single mother in L.A., where she witnessed the effects of police brutality firsthand. After coming out as queer at age sixteen, Cullors began working as an activist and at age twenty-two was the recipient of the Mario Savio Young Activist Award. In 2013, she founded the global movement Black Lives Matter after George Zimmerman was acquitted of the murder of Trayvon Martin. She tells her story in this memoir.

Martin Luther King Jr.

Taylor Branch, *Parting the Waters: America in the King Years 1954–63,* 1988.

American historian Taylor Branch wrote this first volume in a trilogy about the life of civil rights leader Martin Luther King Jr. He traces how King made a name for himself as a minister before he came out as the voice of the movement. In addition to the biography of King, Branch also tells the story of Jim Crow and the atmosphere of bigotry in the U.S. Events that precipitated the struggle beginning in the early 1960s, such as the Montgomery bus boycott, are also covered.

Carlotta Walls LaNier

Carlotta Walls LaNier, *A Mighty Long Way: My Journey to Justice at Little Rock Central High School,* 2009.

Like Melba Pattillo, Carlotta Walls, one of the Little Rock Nine, braved the angry White crowds to enter Little Rock Central High School in 1957. She was fourteen and spent her next three years attending the previously all-White high school. During those three years, her home was bombed and she was bullied. But she had been taught at home that education was the key to success, and she was determined to graduate.

Cudjo Lewis

Zora Neale Hurston, *Barracoon: The Story of the Last "Black Cargo,"* 2018.

In 1927, acclaimed writer Zora Neale Hurston traveled to Plateau, Alabama, as an anthropologist to interview eighty-six-year-old Cudjo Lewis. She recorded his account of being part of the last slave shipment bound for the U.S. when he was a young man. At the time, the slave trade had already been outlawed.

Malcolm X

Les Payne and Tamara Payne, *The Dead Are Arising: The Life of Malcolm X,* 2020.

Pulitzer Prize–winning author Les Payne spent thirty years interviewing anyone who knew Malcolm X. He collected hundreds of hours of tape, and the resulting biography is unlike any previous biography of Malcolm X. Using the history of the United States as a backdrop for the story, the Paynes present Malcolm X from his 1925 birth in Nebraska to his assassination in Harlem in 1965.

Anne Moody

Anne Moody, *Coming of Age in Mississippi,* 1968.

Essie Mae (later Anne) Moody, the daughter of tenant farmers near Centreville, Mississippi, came of age in 1940, a dangerous era of the pre-civil rights South. She learned of Emmet Till's lynching the week before she began high school and realized, for the first time, that her life could be in danger simply for being Black. Even though she was a straight-A student and went to college on a basketball scholarship, she was twenty before she joined the NAACP and began her time in the thick of the civil rights movement.

Gordon Parks

Gordon Parks, *A Choice of Weapons,* 1966.

Born in Kansas in 1912, Gordon Parks was only sixteen when he moved alone to St. Paul, Minnesota, after his mother died. He educated himself and managed to survive. This autobiography explains how he did it and what kept him going. Parks was the first African American to work for *Life* magazine and the first to write, direct, and score a Hollywood film. He was also an accomplished jazz pianist, novelist, and poet. This extraordinary man died of cancer at age ninety-three in 2006.

Ethel Payne

James McGrath Morris, *Eye on the Struggle: Ethel Payne, the First Lady of the Black Press*, 2015.

Ethel Lois Payne was a pioneering journalist and network news commentator who covered some of the most crucial civil rights events of her time. Because of her sex and race, she had to work doubly hard to cover events like the Montgomery bus boycott. However, in her efforts, she went beyond reporting to exhort President Eisenhower to support desegregation. She was later recognized by President Johnson, who presented her with a pen used to sign the Civil Rights Act.

Winfred Rembert

Winfred Rembert as told to Erin I. Kelly, *Chasing Me to My Grave: An Artist's Memoir of the Jim Crow South*, 2021.

Tufts professor Erin I. Kelly relates twentieth-century African American artist Winfred Rembert's story. Rembert was a field hand on a Georgia plantation. After spending seven years on a prison chain gang, Rembert used the leather tooling skills he had acquired in prison to etch and paint the world in which he was raised. Rembert talks about these works with prose renderings of the stories behind them. Despite his life of struggle, Rembert finds love and success.

Nate Shaw

Theodore Rosengarten, *All God's Dangers: The Life of Nate Shaw*, 1974.

When author Theodore Rosengarten was a Massachusetts graduate student in 1969, he was researching a 1930s organization called the Alabama Sharecropper Union. When he learned the group had one surviving member, he went to Alabama and found the eighty-four-year-old man, Nate Shaw. Rosengarten retells the story of how Shaw came to own substantial property in a culture of sharecroppers and the price he paid for standing up to White oppression.

Natasha Trethewey

Natasha Trethewey, *Memorial Drive: A Daughter's Memoir*, 2020.

American Poet Laureate Natasha Trethewey was the child of an illegal union in Gulfport, Mississippi, between a White father and a Black mother. Unfortunately, the marriage didn't last. At age nineteen, Trethewey watched as her former stepfather shot and killed her mother. Her despair and grief ran deep. Using these feelings as fuel, until her death, Trethewey researched her mother's history.

Harriet Tubman

Kate Clifford Larson, *Bound for the Promised Land: Harriet Tubman, Portrait of an American Hero*, 2003.

Critically acclaimed biographer Kate Clifford Larson chronicles the life of Harriet Tubman, a conductor on the Underground Railroad who led many enslaved individuals to freedom. Using new documents and genealogical research, Larson reveals a brilliant and complex woman who escaped slavery for a life of freedom as a young woman but who went on to risk all repeatedly to help others find their freedom too. Larson uncovers surprising facts about the people Tubman knew and the difficulties she suffered.

Nat Turner

Stephen B. Oates, *The Fires of Jubilee: Nat Turner's Fierce Rebellion*, 1975.

Historian Stephen B. Oates narrates the story of the nineteenth-century slave rebellion in Virginia led by Nat Turner. Oates finds Turner to be a gifted, driven, yet complex figure. First, he details the factors that led to the uprising and its brutal reprisals. Then he explains how the event set the stage for the American Civil War.

Booker T. Washington

Robert J. Norrell, *Up from History: The Life of Booker T. Washington*, 2009.

Before Martin Luther King Jr. led the nonviolent civil rights movement, Booker T. Washington worked within the Jim Crow system to help Black people rise from poverty by developing character and economic independence. This, he felt, would gain their full citizenship. Since then, his ideas have been denigrated as naïve and ineffective. But Robert J. Norrell uncovers the challenging climate in which Washington was working and shows that, in the context of the time, he provided Black people with much-needed hope.

D. Watkins

D. Watkins, *Black Boy Smile: A Memoir in Moments*, 2022.

What does manhood mean when you grow up in a tough neighborhood in a poverty-stricken and crime-ridden city like Baltimore at the end of the twentieth century? Writing professor and editor D. Watkins knows firsthand and lets us know in this memoir. He discusses his father and his relationships with the boys he grew up with. But rather than focus just on the hard times, he brings redemption out of bleakness. He wants to let other Black boys growing up in hard neighborhoods know that their life means something.

Gregory Howard Williams

Gregory Howard Williams, *Life on the Color Line: The True Story of a White Boy Who Discovered He Was Black,* **1995.**
Williams and his brother Mike were raised as the White sons of a White mother and a dark-skinned "Italian" father. But when their mother left and their father, "Tony," took his sons to his original home in Muncie, Indiana, they discovered their father was commonly known as "Buster," and he wasn't Italian, but Black. Even though their father neglected the boys, other community members helped the brothers, who took very different paths as adults. Gregory became a lawyer and writes of their experiences in White and Black communities, often a surprising mixture of agreeable and hard.

Damon Young

Damon Young, *What Doesn't Kill You Makes You Blacker: A Memoir in Essays,* **2019.**
Pittsburg native Damon Young is a professional Black person, making his living as the editor-in-chief of Very Smart Brothas (VSB). In this memoir, he uses humor to capture what it's like to be a Black man in America today. He also poignantly examines masculinity and the persistence cf White supremacy.

Indigenous Peoples

Ada Blackjack

Jennifer Niven, *Ada Blackjack: A True Story of Survival in the Arctic*, 2003.

In 1921, a twenty-five-year-old Inuit woman named Ada Blackjack traveled to the Arctic with four young men. The group aimed to colonize the extremely remote Wrangel Island for Great Britain. But two years later, Blackjack came back alone. All four of the men she traveled with had died. She refused to speak to anyone about her experiences until a newspaper declared she was responsible for her companions' demise. Only then did she tell the story recounted here.

Crazy Horse

Joseph M. Marshall III, *The Journey of Crazy Horse: A Lakota History*, 2004.

Lakota scholar Joseph M. Marshall tells the story of the Lakota hero and leader Crazy Horse, who defeated Custer at the Battle of Little Bighorn. Marshall brings this compelling man to life, providing details about his public and private life and celebrating Lakota culture. To read about the controversial death of Crazy Horse, see *The Killing of Crazy Horse* by Thomas Powers.

Davi Kopenawa

Davi Kopenawa and Bruce Albert, *The Falling Sky: Words of a Yanomami Shaman*, 2010.

Bruce Albert is a close friend of Brazilian Davi Kopenawa, a shaman and spokesperson for the Yanomami. Albert helps his friend tell the story of his childhood, his initiation as a shaman, and his experiences with cultural outsiders like government workers, missionaries, and cattle ranchers. The devastation his people have endured led him to become a global activist for them. In his pursuit of justice, he has traveled the globe to show people how industrialized society and its greed have been destroying the planet. Then, through his own culture and experience, he tries to show another way.

Opechancanough

James Horn, *A Brave and Cunning Prince: The Great Chief Opechancanough and the War for America*, 2021.

When the man known as Opechancanough was eleven years old, Spanish explorers kidnapped him from his home along the Chesapeake Bay sometime in the mid-sixteenth century. James Horn narrates how, after winding up in Mexico, Opechancanough converted to Catholicism and returned to his childhood home with a group of Jesuit missionaries. Not long after returning, he organized a war party that killed the Spanish. Then he spent forty years fighting the newly arrived English, nearly destroying the Virginia colony.

Red Cloud

Bob Drury and Tom Clavin, *The Heart of Everything That Is: The Untold Story of Red Cloud, an American Legend*, 2013.

Drury and Clavin use a recently discovered autobiography and additional thorough research to tell the story of the great Sioux warrior-statesman Red Cloud. The result is a revealing look at the man who led the only victory of a Native American force against the U.S. At one point, Red Cloud presided over a fifth of the landmass of the contiguous United States.

Tecumseh and Tenskwatawa

Peter Cozzens, *Tecumseh and the Prophet: The Heroic Struggle for America's Heartland*, 2020.

Award-winning historian Peter Cozzens tells the story of two brothers, Tecumseh and his younger sibling Tenskwatawa. While many are familiar with Tecumseh, whose diplomatic skills earned him respect from colonizers, it was Tenskwatawa who brought the tribes of the Old Northwest together. Cozzens demonstrates how these two Shawnee brothers, for a time, nearly brought the westward expansion to a halt.

Truganini

Cassandra Pybus, *Truganini: Journey Through the Apocalypse*, 2020.

In this haunting story, history professor Cassandra Pybus tells of a woman named Truganini, who belonged to one of the native clans, the Nuenonne, of Tasmania. She was a child in the 1820s when the British first arrived, and she survived the devastation of her people. Then she spent decades walking across southeast Tasmania with a missionary named George Augustus Robinson, helping find scattered survivors to send them to live on Flinders Island.

Jewish Experiences
and the Holocaust

Edith Hahn Beer

Edith Hahn Beer, *The Nazi Officer's Wife:*
***How One Jewish Woman Survived the Holocaust*, 1999.**

In this heart-wrenching memoir, Edith Hahn Beer tells how, as a Jewish woman studying law in Vienna, she was forced into a ghetto, then a labor camp, by the Nazis. After returning home, she went underground until a Christian woman supplied her with the identity papers Edith used to make her way to Munich. A Nazi party member who met her there fell in love with her and married her even though he knew she was Jewish. But after he was deported to Siberia, she and their daughter were forced to hide in a closet while Russian soldiers raped women in the streets. The Holocaust Museum in Washington, D.C., keeps her documents on exhibit.

Corrie Ten Boom

Corrie Ten Boom, *The Hiding Place:*
***The Triumphant True Story of Corrie Ten Boom*, 1971.**

Until she was in her fifties, Corrie Ten Boom was a contented unwed watch-maker who lived and worked with the family she loved. But when the Nazis invaded her beloved Amsterdam, she and her relatives became leaders in the Dutch underground, hiding Jewish people and helping them escape the Nazis. All of them except Corrie were killed in concentration camps for their efforts. Her story is ultimately one of faith.

Anne Frank

Anne Frank, *The Diary of a Young Girl*, 1947.

In 1942, at age thirteen, Anne Frank and her Jewish family fled their Amsterdam home and went into hiding from the invading Nazis. For two years, they and another family lived together in an old office building, unable to leave and often hungry. Then, after two years, they were betrayed and dis-covered. After the Nazis took the families, Anne's diary, recording the entire period, was found in the attic where she had hidden. Though Anne did not survive the war, her words did.

Viktor E. Frankl

Viktor E. Frankl, *Man's Search for Meaning*, 1946.

Holocaust survivor Viktor E. Frankl wrote one of the most famous memoirs ever published. After his rescue from the Nazi death camps, Frankl returned to his prewar career as a psychiatrist. But he also left the world this account of how he survived World War II's horrors. In his memoir, he describes how he developed his beneficial tool, logotherapy, to help us deal with suffering in life.

Eddie Jaku

Eddie Jaku, *The Happiest Man on Earth: The Biography of an Auschwitz Survivor*, 2020.

Born Abraham Jakubowicz in Germany in 1920, Eddie Jaku was proud to be German. But in November of 1938, that didn't matter because, as a Jew, he was beaten, arrested, and taken first to Buchenwald, then later to Auschwitz, and finally on a Nazi death march. But he vowed to smile every day. And he decided the best way to honor those who died was to tell his story, share his wisdom, and live the best life he could. So he tells his story here, as he turns one hundred years old. Despite his experiences, he sincerely considers himself the happiest man on earth.

Primo Levi

Ian Thomson, *Primo Levi: A Life*, 1999.

Italian Jewish chemist Primo Levi survived a year in Auschwitz. After being released, he wrote *Survival in Auschwitz* and *The Periodic Table*. His work after the war has made him one of the most important writers of Holocaust literature.

Lev Nussimbaum

Tom Reiss, *The Orientalist: In Search of a Man Caught Between East and West*, 2005.

Tom Reiss tells the incredible story of Lev Nussimbaum, a Jew born to a wealthy family at the edge of czarist Russia in 1905. Nussimbaum fled the Russian Revolution in a camel caravan and wound up in Germany. As Reiss tracks him across ten countries, he experiences events and meets people as dramatic as his subject. But in uncovering the truth about this Jewish man who spent time as a Muslim prince and then became a bestselling author in Nazi Germany, Reiss also finds forgotten worlds that existed in the underbelly of twentieth-century history.

Henrietta Szold

Dvora Hacohen, *To Repair a Broken World:*
***The Life of Henrietta Szold, Founder of Hadassah*, 2021.**

Israeli historian Dvora Hacohen traces the life of Henrietta Szold, who was born in Baltimore in 1860 and began a night school to teach English to the Russian Jews in her city. The school was open to anyone, regardless of their faith. In 1912, Szold began Hadassah, the Women's Zionist Organization of America. Her organization was devoted to humanitarian causes and community building from the beginning. A pacifist, she sought a peaceful solution for the Jewish–Arab conflicts in Palestine. This remarkable woman was also a champion of women's causes in Judaism. Hacohen reveals her private as well as public life.

6

Latino/a and Hispanic

Marie Arana

Marie Arana, *American Chica: Two Worlds, One Childhood*, 2001.

In this memoir, Marie Arana discloses what it was like to be raised by parents from two American continents—North and South. Her mother was a musician from Wyoming, and her father was an engineer from Peru. Until she was nine, Marie spent time on each continent. But when her family permanently moved to the United States, she had to come to terms with the influence of two completely different cultures on one person.

Cesar Chavez

Miriam Pawel, *The Crusades of Cesar Chavez: A Biography*, 2014.

Pulitzer Prize–winning journalist Miriam Pawel writes this comprehensive biography of Cesar Chavez, the founder of the United Farm Workers, a primarily Latino movement, in mid-twentieth-century California. Chavez was a self-educated man who admired Gandhi's principles of nonviolent protest. But he was also a flawed human being who allowed his union to become more about him than about the people it served. As a result, it lost a great deal of power.

Ernesto "Che" Guevara

Ernesto Che Guevara, *The Motorcycle Diaries: Notes on a Latin American Journey*, 1992.

Ernesto "Che" Guevara is known primarily today for overthrowing the Cuban government with Fidel Castro. Still, he was once a twenty-three-year-old man traveling around his native Latin America by motorcycle. His engaging account of this period was later made into a movie.

Luis J. Rodríguez

Luis J. Rodríguez, *Always Running: La Vida Loca: Gang Days in L.A.*, 1993.

While he was growing up in East L.A., gangs seemed an inevitable part of life to Luis Rodríguez. By age twelve, he was already a member and had witnessed shootings, beatings, and arrests. But he became increasingly fearful as he lost more of those closest to him to drugs and violence. Finally, through education, he made his way out, but he began to relive the nightmare when his son joined a gang.

7

LGBTQIA+

Brian Broome

Brian Broome, *Punch Me Up to the Gods: A Memoir*, 2021.
Poet and screenwriter Brian Broome uses Gwendolyn Brooks's iconic poem "We Real Cool" to frame his memoir of growing up Black and gay. In the process, he captures the pain and vulnerability of these young men to help us understand what they go through.

Garrard Conley

Garrard Conley, *Boy Erased: A Memoir of Identity, Faith, and Family*, 2016.
At age nineteen, Gerrard Conley was outed to his mother and his father, a Baptist pastor. They gave him the choice of attending a church-supported conversion therapy program to cure him of his homosexual impulses or to risk losing his family and the life he had known. Gamely trying the program, Garrard comes to the decision that he must ultimately be true to himself. This decision leads to a search for the truth about his family's past as well.

Alix Dobkin

Alix Dobkin, *My Red Blood: A Memoir of Growing Up Communist, Coming onto the Greenwich Village Folk Scene, and Coming Out in the Feminist Movement*, 2009.
Singer–songwriter and producer of women's music Alix Dobkin released the openly lesbian album *Lavender Jane* in 1973, the first album of its kind. Here she writes of growing up in a Communist family in the years after World War II. As a part of the Greenwich Village folk music scene of the 1950s and 1960s, she met many people, such as Bob Dylan and Flip Wilson, who would go on to become famous.

Glennon Doyle

Glennon Doyle, *Untamed*, 2020.
Are mothers supposed to give up their lives for their children? Not if they want to raise happy, independent adults, says activist and founder of Together Rising, Glennon Doyle. When Doyle divorced the father of her children, she discovered that family is not a matter of places and roles but a structure that

supports its members in becoming their whole true selves. Now raising her three children with her wife, Doyle urges us all to look at family in the same way, no matter our circumstances.

Lori Duron

Lori Duron, *Raising My Rainbow: Adventures in Raising a Fabulous, Gender Creative Son*, 2013.

Lori Duron describes her two beloved sons. The older, Chase, has always been a "typical" boy who played sports and built with Lego. But her younger son, C. J., always preferred to wear pink and play with Disney princess toys. Lori wants to help readers understand that gender is a spectrum, from ultra-masculine on one end to super-feminine on the other. We all have differing places on it. She urges us to accept our children where they are and to celebrate their uniqueness.

Lillian Faderman

Lillian Faderman, *Naked in the Promised Land: A Memoir*, 2003.

Internationally recognized scholar Lillian Faderman recalls growing up as the child of an uneducated, unmarried Jewish immigrant who came to America after losing her family in the Holocaust. Lilly's mother worked hard in a sweatshop to support them both while suffering periodic psychotic episodes. Lilly became Lil as she grew older and made her way to the University of California at Berkeley after discovering her attraction to women. She earned money for college as a burlesque stripper. After earning her Ph.D., she became Lillian, who pioneered gay and lesbian studies.

Susan Faludi

Susan Faludi, *In the Darkroom*, 2016.

After years of writing about social causes, journalist Susan Faludi decided to profile her absentee father. Angry at his neglect, Faludi tracks him down in Hungary where her seventy-six-year-old father had undergone a sex-change operation and was now living as a woman. Struggling to reconcile this person with the explosive father she had known, Faludi moves on to researching her father's history and uncovers many ways his life had been reinvented over the years. At the end of her long search, she's left wondering whether we can really choose our identity or whether it is something we can't outrun.

E. M. Forster

Wendy Moffat, *A Great Unrecorded History:*
***A New Life of E. M. Forster*, 2010.**

The British literary colossus E. M. Forster lived life as a gay man before it was legal in the U.K. Scholar Wendy Moffat studied a record he kept of his private life and determined that his homosexuality was the core of who he was. When his suppressed novel *Maurice* was released in 1970, the year he died, the world was finally ready to accept homosexuality.

Eddie Izzard

Eddie Izzard, *Believe Me:*
***A Memoir of Love, Death, and Jazz Chickens*, 2017.**

British comedian and actor Eddie Izzard describes how she began her career as a teenage street performer. Later, she became a standup comedian with a legendary act. Proclaiming herself an "executive transvestite," she has since become as famous for her LGBT activism as for her performances.

Maia Kobabe

Maia Kobabe, *Gender Queer: A Memoir*, 2019.

Author and illustrator Maia Kobabe writes honestly of what it is like to be a person of nonbinary gender. Using the pronouns e/em/eir to refer to eir, Kobabe reveals the experiences common to many adolescents as they strive to discover their own unique identity. Using a graphic arts format, Kobabe offers tips on coming out and making friends. Reading this book will help anyone discover what nonbinary individuals experience and how to relate to them.

Kiese Laymon

Kiese Laymon, *Heavy: An American Memoir*, 2018.

In *Heavy*, Kiese Laymon honestly and humorously explores what it's like to grow up Black, with a single mother in Jackson, Mississippi, suffering episodes of sexual abuse and violence. Now an author, Laymon writes about his formative years and missteps, his experimentation with gender bending, and his confrontations with the truth.

Carmen Maria Machado

Carmen Maria Machado, *In the Dream House:*
***A Memoir*, 2019.**

After years of dealing with the fallout of an abusive same-sex relationship, award-winning author Carmen Maria Machado uses horror themes to describe the dark events and psychic damage inflicted on her. Widely praised for this inventive memoir, Machado uses tropes to sharply depict her torment.

Thomas Page McBee

Thomas Page McBee, *Amateur: A Reckoning with Gender, Identity, and Masculinity*, 2018.

What is the relationship between masculinity and violence? To find out, author Thomas Page McBee, a trans man, decides to train to fight in a charity boxing match at Madison Square Garden. While being pummeled on and off the mat, McBee finds a way through. He is an expert on masculinity for *VICE* and writes columns on the topic for major publications.

Harvey Milk

Randy Shilts, *The Mayor of Castro Street: The Life and Times of Harvey Milk*, 1988.

In 1977, Harvey Milk became the first openly gay politician elected to office when he joined the San Francisco Board of Supervisors. Journalist Randy Shilts tells the story of Milk's life, how he rose to power, and his assassination in City Hall. Drawing parallels between the trajectory of his story and the gay community in America, Shilts presents Milk as a symbol of gay power and hope.

Janet Mock

Janet Mock, *Redefining Realness: My Path to Womanhood, Identity, Love & So Much More*, 2014.

In 2011, when Janet Mock was the editor of People.com, she was profiled in *Marie Claire* magazine. She chose that moment to step forward as a trans woman. Born a boy, Mock never felt like a boy, and her parents didn't have the resources to help her cope. In this memoir, she details her transition at the age of eighteen with the help of friends. After receiving a scholarship, she moved to New York City, earned a master's degree and began her career in media. Here she encourages other trans people to be themselves.

Billy Porter

Billy Porter, *Unprotected: A Memoir*, 2021.

The award-winning star of the television series *Pose* and Broadway's *Kinky Boots*, Billy Porter is also a playwright and director. In this memoir, he describes what life was like growing up in Pittsburgh as a Black and gay child. Misunderstood by the kids at school and the people in his church, and sexually abused by a stepfather, Porter had a childhood that was anything but easy.

But he describes how he overcame his trauma and emerged not just a successful entertainer but also a legend.

Jenn Shapland

**Jenn Shapland, *My Autobiography of Carson McCullers:
A Memoir*, 2021.**

  While working as an intern at the Harry Ransom Center, Jenn Shapland
  finds letters between Carson McCullers and a woman named Annemarie.
  Surprised by the tenor of their correspondence, Shapland seeks to find the
  real McCullers, because the one revealed in the letters reminds her so much
  of herself. She ultimately finds that in telling Carson's story, she must also tell
  her own.

Matthew Shepard

**Judy Shepard, *The Meaning of Matthew: My Son's Murder
in Laramie, and a World Transformed*, 2009.**

  Most of us have heard the tragic story of how gay American college student Matthew Shepard was beaten savagely by two men and left to die near
  Laramie, Wyoming, in 1998. Found alive and taken to the hospital, Matthew
  died later from his injuries. He has since become a symbol of gay rights in
  America. In this memoir, his mother tells what Matthew was like as a child,
  what it was like as a mother to face such a horrific ending for a child, and why
  she became a gay rights activist.

Samuel Steward

**Justin Spring, *Secret Historian:
The Life and Times of Samuel Steward, Professor,
Tattoo Artist, and Sexual Renegade*, 2010.**

  In a wildly unconventional life, novelist, poet, and university professor
  Samuel M. Steward left his friendships with Gertrude Stein and Alice B.
  Toklas in Paris to become Phil Sparrow, a tattoo artist on Chicago's South
  State Street. He later reinvented himself once again as Phil Andros, a writer
  of well-written homosexual pornography. Justin Spring accesses a previously
  lost archive of Steward's papers to write this insightful look at an unusual life.

Jim Stewart

**Jim Stewart, *Folsom Street Blues: A Memoir of the 1970s
SoMa and Leatherfolk in Gay San Francisco*, 2011.**

  This tell-all memoir brings back the 1970s sexual underground in San
  Francisco's South of Market (SoMa) through the eyes of one of its prominent

citizens, Jim Stewart. The artist and carpenter behind the leather bars and the Fey-Way Studio art gallery, Stewart shares intimate stories of his friendships and encounters with notables such as Chuck Arnett and Robert Mapplethorpe.

8

Women's Voices

Tarana Burke

Tarana Burke, *Unbound: My Story of Liberation and the Birth of the Me Too Movement*, 2021.

While growing up in the Bronx with her single mother, Tarana Burke was sexually assaulted. As a result, her psyche split in two to help her manage the pain. She had a good self to present to the world and a bad self she hid away. Later, as an adult working with abused young Black girls, she confronted her past and faced the truth. This reckoning led to her writing "me too," which became the rallying cry of a movement that has spanned the twentieth and twenty-first centuries and resonates with women worldwide.

Lacy Crawford

Lacy Crawford, *Notes on a Silencing: A Memoir*, 2020.

When she was a fifteen-year-old student at the elite, private K–12 St. Paul's School, Lacy Crawford was molested by two senior athletes. Faculty, doctors, and priests ignored her story at the time, and the boys who assaulted her were allowed to graduate with honors. But when she learned as an adult that the school was now under state investigation for sexual abuse, she contacted detectives. Once she had access to her student files, she saw that her story had been silenced before and attempts were still being made to keep it hidden. She reflects on what this says about class and gender in American society today.

Rachael Denhollander

Rachael Denhollander, *What Is a Girl Worth?: One Woman's Courageous Battle to Protect the Innocent and Stop a Predator—No Matter the Cost*, 2019.

As a young Olympic gymnastics team member, Rachael Denhollander was the first victim to publicly accuse former USA Gymnastics team doctor Larry Nassar of sexual abuse. In time, Nassar was found to have abused hundreds of young girls under cover of his job. Denhollander explains how she found the courage to confront the abuse and its impact on her and the other athletes. Denhollander is now an attorney who fights for justice.

Sharon Dukett

Sharon Dukett, *No Rules: A Memoir*, 2020.

At age sixteen, Sharon Dukett left her sheltered life, joining the hippies. It was the early 1970s, and she wanted her freedom. Unprepared for the adult world, she traveled across the U.S. and Canada however she could. As an award-winning author today, she reveals how she wound up in an off-grid commune. Now living with her husband in Connecticut, she reflects on her ten years as a hippie and how the era improved women's lives and their place in the world.

Zelda Fitzgerald

Nancy Milford, *Zelda: A Biography*, 1970.

Bestselling biographer Nancy Milford writes of Zelda Sayre Fitzgerald, wife of American author F. Scott Fitzgerald. Zelda was a beautiful young socialite from Mobile, Alabama. When she married Fitzgerald, the two were an international "it" couple who became symbols of the Jazz Age. After their marriage ended, Zelda lived in an Asheville, North Carolina, insane asylum until she died there in a tragic fire.

Roxanne Gay

Roxanne Gay, *Bad Feminist: Essays*, 2014.

Acclaimed writer Roxanne Gay writes about her life as a woman of color and how the current cultural climate has affected her. Musing about what women are expected to be like, she ponders what's acceptable and unacceptable for a feminist. In some ways, our expectations for ourselves and each other can be just as limiting as the expectations of men and traditional society. But, she challenges, what's wrong with enjoying *Vogue*?

Nell Gwyn

Charles Beauclerk, *Nell Gwyn: A Biography*, 2005.

Author Charles Beauclerk is a descendant of Nell Gwyn and King Charles II of England. He tells how after the Puritan rule of Oliver Cromwell, King Charles II, the newly restored monarch, caught sight of Nell Gwyn and thus began a seventeen-year affair that lifted her from her impoverished and abused childhood. Their romance survived the Great Fire of London, the Great Plague, and threats of political revolution. As the first "people's princess," Nell Gwyn lived a Cinderella story.

Emma Hamilton

Kate Williams, *England's Mistress: The Infamous Life of Emma Hamilton*, 2005.

Historian Kate Williams narrates the life of Emma Hamilton, who was born into poverty in a coal mining town and worked as a prostitute as a teenager. But her beauty helped her escape London's brothels. By age twenty-six, she was married to Sir William Hamilton, the aging British ambassador to Naples. Emma used her position as his wife to become a model and fashion icon. But when Lord Admiral Horatio Nelson met her after the Battle of the Nile, they began an affair that is one of the most famous in history.

Sue Hubbell

Sue Hubbell, *A Country Year: Living the Questions*, 1983.

After Sue Hubbell left a career at Brown University and moved to the Ozarks to raise bees, her husband left her to manage their small farm alone. For a year, she records her attempts at keeping mechanical equipment running, the bees happy, the honey selling, and herself alive. She was in her fifties at the time, and none of this came easy. But Hubbell found her way. Her story is both meditative and profound.

Anne Hutchinson

Eve LaPlante, *American Jezebel: The Uncommon Life of Anne Hutchinson, the Woman Who Defied the Puritans*, 2004.

Nathaniel Hawthorne used Anne Hutchinson as his model for Hester Prynne in *The Scarlet Letter*. Hutchinson's direct descendant Eve LaPlante begins this book with the forty-six-year-old Anne, pregnant with her sixteenth child, in a courtroom before forty men who were calling her the new Eve, a witch, and a Jezebel because the political power she had gained was reminiscent of "the most evil woman" in the Bible. In reality, Hutchinson's charismatic personality and unconventional ideas drew followers wanting social reform that secured their ire.

Hypatia of Alexandria

Maria Dzielska, *Hypatia of Alexandria*, 1993.

In 415 C.E., a beautiful woman was murdered by a mob of Christians in Alexandria. Her crime was being an intelligent woman—a mathematician and a Neoplatonist. Maria Dzielska seeks the real woman behind the symbol she has become. In doing so, she delves into the social and intellectual milieu of Hypatia's day and letters from her pupils. She also explores the known facts about her murder to shed further light on the era.

Chanel Miller

Chanel Miller, *Know My Name: A Memoir*, 2019.

Known as Emily Doe after her rapist, Brock Turner, was found assaulting her on Stanford's campus, Chanel Miller wrote a letter detailing his crime's impact on her. The letter was viewed by millions and ultimately caused changes in California law and the recall of the judge who sentenced Turner to six months in the county jail for his crime. In addition, she has helped turn the conversation to the devastation rape does to victims so that people will take it seriously.

Clarina Howard Nichols

Diane Eickhoff, *Revolutionary Heart: The Life of Clarina Nichols and the Pioneering Crusade for Women's Rights*, 2006.

Decades before women won the right to vote in 1920, there were pioneers in the struggle for women's rights. One of these, Clarina Howard Nichols, used her position as a Vermont newspaper publisher to make speeches for equality. Then, disillusioned with slow progress in the East, she headed for Bleeding, Kansas, where she made history.

Norma McCorvey ("Jane Roe")

Joshua Prager, *The Family Roe: An American Story*, 2021.

"Jane Roe" is the pseudonym for Norma McCorvey (1947–2017), who is the Roe in the Supreme Court case of *Roe v. Wade*. Journalist Joshua Prager met McCorvey and became close enough to be with her when she died. Using his access to her papers, he wrote the biography of this real woman at the center of the controversial Supreme Court decision that sparked the debate over the right to choose versus the right to life. In addition, Prager tells the stories of the activists and bystanders caught up in the case.

Vera Nabokov

Stacy Schiff, *Vera (Mrs. Vladimir Nabokov)*, 1999.

Vladimir Nabokov, the Russian-born American writer, was the author of such acclaimed works as *Lolita* and his memoir *Speak, Memory*. In this biography, Pulitzer Prize–winning author Stacy Schiff writes about the author's wife of fifty-two years, Vera. Nabokov once stated," Without my wife, I wouldn't have written a single novel." Schiff vividly portrays the woman who inspired one of the twentieth century's greatest writers.

Elizabeth Packard

Kate Moore, *The Woman They Could Not Silence: The Shocking Story of a Woman Who Dared to Fight Back*, 2021.

In the summer of 1860, a housewife and mother of six, Elizabeth Packard, was taken to the Illinois State Hospital in Jacksonville, Illinois. Her husband of twenty-one years, Theophilus, decided he needed to teach her a lesson. While there, Elizabeth discovered she was not the only woman assigned to this horrific fate. Many of the women in the asylum were perfectly sane. Elizabeth became convinced she had nothing to lose by fighting.

Diane K. Shah

Diane K. Shah, *A Farewell to Arms, Legs & Jockstraps: A Sportswriter's Memoir*, 2020.

Diane K. Shah was the first female sports columnist in America when she took a job working for the *Los Angeles Herald-Examiner*. She covered big names in pursuit of her stories. Here she provides behind-the-scenes looks at her experiences and the difficulties she faced.

Gloria Steinem

Gloria Steinem, *My Life on the Road*, 2015.

American feminist, journalist, and activist Gloria Steinem was a key spokesperson for the women's liberation movement in the 1960s and 1970s. She was a counterculture icon and a cofounder of *Ms.* magazine. In 2005 Steinem worked with Jane Fonda and Robin Morgan to cofound the Women's Media Center to give women a more prominent voice in the national conversation. She reflects here on her life as an activist.

Mary Wollstonecraft

Claire Tomalin, *The Life and Death of Mary Wollstonecraft*, 1974.

Biographer Claire Tomalin delves into the life of Mary Wollstonecraft, the eighteenth-century writer, promoter of women's rights, and author of *A Vindication of the Rights of Woman*. Her unconventional ideas and lifestyle, like her activities in the French Revolution, caused her to be shunned by society. After marrying William Godwin, she died in childbirth at age thirty-eight. One of her children was Mary Godwin Shelley, the author of *Frankenstein*.

Elissa Wall

Elissa Wall, *Stolen Innocence:*
My Story of Growing Up in a Polygamous Sect, Becoming
***a Teenage Bride, and Breaking Free of Warren Jeffs*, 2008.**
When the Church of Latter-Day Saints decided to end the practice of polygamy, the church split, with many members joining the Fundamentalist Church of Latter-Day Saints (FLDS), later solely led by Warren Jeffs. The testimony of Elissa Wall helped convict Jeffs of trafficking women and children and using them as favors to men in the congregation.

Malala Yousafzai

Malala Yousafzai, *I Am Malala: How One Girl Stood Up*
***for Education and Changed the World*, 2012.**
When the Taliban took over the Swat Valley in Pakistan, they denied girls the right to an education. Malala and her father decided to defy the ban, and Malala continued to go to school. But on October 9, 2012, she was shot in the head while riding the bus home. Despite the odds, she survived, and her family left Pakistan. Malala then began her campaign as an advocate for girls' education.

COLLECTIVE BIOGRAPHY

Hallie Rubenhold, *The Five: The Untold Lives*
***of the Women Killed by Jack the Ripper*, 2019.**
A biography of Jack the Ripper is out of the question because his identity has never been uncovered. But his victims, Polly, Annie, Elizabeth, Catherine, and Mary-Jane, are portrayed in this overdue look at their lives. Historian Hallie Rubenhold reveals that these women, contrary to the official narrative, were not prostitutes. They died, she says, because they were in the wrong place at the wrong time. And they died because they were women.

9

Monarchs, Caesars, and Ruling Classes

Augustus

Adrian Goldsworthy, *Augustus: First Emperor of Rome*, 2014.
At age nineteen, Augustus found himself the leader of the burgeoning Roman Empire when his great-uncle and adoptive father, Julius Caesar, was assassinated. Though young, Augustus proved himself a savvy leader, defeating rivals like Mark Anthony and Brutus. However, Adrian Goldsworthy reveals him to be a man of contradictory sides, both good and bad.

Anne Boleyn

Carolly Erickson, *Mistress Anne*, 1984.
The second wife of King Henry VIII and mother of Queen Elizabeth I, Anne Boleyn, was beheaded on charges of infidelity. Historian Carolly Erickson delves into the political and sexual machinations that resulted in her death.

Lucrezia Borgia

Sarah Bradford, *Lucrezia Borgia: Life, Love, and Death in Renaissance Italy*, 2004.
Historian Sarah Bradford researched Renaissance figure Lucrezia Borgia and finds that, contrary to popular perception, she was neither a monster nor a sexual puppet. Instead, she was a beautiful, intelligent woman who used her assets to influence the political theater of her day.

Catherine the Great

Henri Troyat, *Catherine the Great*, 1977.
French historian and biographer Henri Troyat narrates the story of Catherine, the German princess who became the sole ruler of the Russian empire. Catherine lived in a tough place and time, but she proved tougher. Troyat demonstrates how she used her lovers, the court, and the military to enlarge Russia's territory and burnish her reputation.

Charles I

Leanda de Lisle, *The White King: Charles I, Traitor, Murderer, Martyr*, 2017.

King Henry VIII and Queen Elizabeth I had declared England a Protestant nation, but with Catholics still loyal to the old religion, England became a divided, angry, bitter nation where family members and neighbors were all pitted against one another. Using Charles I's correspondence, Leanda de Lisle uncovers a man who fiercely believed in the monarchy but whose marriage to a French Catholic princess was seen by many as a betrayal. De Lisle reveals the shocking events that led to Charles I's execution, but how this, in turn, resulted in the ultimate continuance of the monarchy.

Edward I

Marc Morris, *A Great and Terrible King: Edward I and the Forging of Britain*, 2008.

Thanks to the movie *Braveheart*, many know him today as "Longshanks." Edward I of England was a medieval king motivated to unite all the British kingdoms under one banner, using the legend of King Arthur as his inspiration. His incredible life spanned continents, a crusade, and prolific castle-building. He produced fifteen children with his first wife and left monuments to her all over his kingdom. Yet he also notoriously expelled all the Jews.

Eleanor of Aquitaine

Alison Weir, *Eleanor of Aquitaine: A Life*, 1999.

British writer Alison Weir writes of a pivotal character of medieval Europe, Eleanor of Aquitaine. Celebrated as one of the most beautiful women of her day, she was married when she met King Henry II of England. With lands of her own, she left her husband for Henry and gave birth to Richard the Lionheart and other English monarchs. Not content to follow her husband's lead, she was determined to control fate herself, with sometimes disastrous consequences.

Elizabeth I

Alison Weir, *The Life of Elizabeth I*, 1998.

As the daughter of King Henry VIII and his second wife, Anne Boleyn, Elizabeth I of England was a cautious monarch who kept her private life private. Yet she was one of the most brilliant royals of any age, known to her subjects as "Good Queen Bess." She was a master of spectacle and public relations who roused her subjects to war when needed. Alison Weir peeks behind her veil to discover what Elizabeth was like as a person.

George III

Andrew Roberts, *The Last King of America: The Misunderstood Reign of George III*, 2021.

Historian Andrew Roberts asserts that King George III was a misunderstood monarch. Most Americans know him as the tyrant king who unfairly taxed the colonies. Roberts says much of our current perception of him was deliberately created by revolutionaries like Thomas Paine and Thomas Jefferson, who used propaganda against the king to further their agendas. But after examining the contemporary records George III left behind, Roberts uncovers a wise and humane leader derailed by mental illness and bad advice.

Henry VIII

Alison Weir, *Henry VIII: King and Court*, 2001.

Henry VIII stands out among British monarchs for his sheer force of will, which completely reshaped the nation. Famously married six times, he thrust England into the Protestant Reformation when he declared himself the head of the Church of England. In this way, he was free to divorce his first wife in defiance of the pope. Henry VIII had two of his wives executed, and Alison Weir reveals how it was as dangerous to be in his court as in his bed.

Julius Caesar

Adrian Goldsworthy, *Caesar: Life of a Colossus*, 2006.

Julius Caesar was one of the most fascinating characters in history. Adrian Goldsworthy portrays this triumphant Roman general, rising politician, seducer of women, husband, father, and high priest of a cult. He was a product of his times. Goldsworthy covers the story from his rise to power to his shocking assassination.

Marie Antoinette

Antonia Fraser, *Marie Antoinette: The Journey*, 2001.

Famed biographer Antonia Fraser examines the life of the last French queen, Marie Antoinette. Fraser specifically looks at accusations thrown at the queen and the rumors of sexual impropriety that swirled around her. She examines the queen's influence on her husband, Louis XVI, and her gruesome execution by guillotine in 1793.

Matilda

Tracy Borman, *Queen of the Conqueror: The Life of Matilda, Wife of William I*, 2011.

Matilda was the daughter of Baldwin V, the Count of Flanders. A few years before William, Duke of Normandy, conquered England at the Battle of Hastings, he offered to marry her. She declined, calling him a bastard. William then dragged her to the ground by her hair and publicly beat her. After her father came to her defense with arms, she declared she would marry William because "he must be a man of great courage and high daring" to beat her in the face of repercussions. Historian Tracy Borman tells of this diminutive woman (only 4'2" tall) who served as the first Queen of England. She bore William nine children and directed policy while sometimes flagrantly disobeying her husband's orders.

Catherine de Medici

Leonie Frieda, *Catherine de Medici: Renaissance Queen of France*, 2002.

Despite her dark reputation, in Leonie Frieda's critically acclaimed biography, Catherine de Medici is revealed to be an unfairly painted queen. Born in Florence and married to King Francis I of France, Catherine adjusted to French culture. But she was forced into a political battle to protect her and her son's status as royals. She succeeded, becoming one of the most influential queens in history.

Mithradates

Adrienne Mayor, *The Poison King: The Life and Legend of Mithradates, Rome's Deadliest Enemy*, 2009.

The ancestor of Alexander the Great and Darius of Persia, Mithradates, came to power in the first century B.C., at fourteen, when his mother poisoned his father. Wishing to begin an empire to the east to rival Rome to the west, he seized Greece and modern-day Turkey and finally threatened to invade Italy. Taking a cue from his mother, he was a master of poisons, helping him eliminate those opposed to him while avoiding the same fate.

Diana Mountbatten-Windsor (Princess Diana)

Andrew Morton, *Diana: Her True Story—in Her Own Words*, 1993.

Before Diana's tragic death, Andrew Morton had the cooperation of Diana's family and friends to create this biography, which served as a bestselling "tell-all" story of her life. The book was later turned into a television movie aired on NBC-TV in the U.S.

Nader Shah

Michael Axworthy, *The Sword of Persia: Nader Shah, from Tribal Warrior to Conquering Tyrant*, 2006.

From 1736 to 1747, Nader Shah ruled Persia. After defeating Moghul Delhi to claim much of India, the Ottoman Turks, and most of modern Iraq, he led the region's most important nation. He was also a despotic leader who tyrannized his people.

Robert the Bruce

Ronald McNair Scott, *Robert the Bruce, King of Scots*, 1982.

After examining accounts from the days of Robert the Bruce of Scotland, Ronald McNair Scott tells the story of one of the most remarkable medieval kings in Europe. Before Robert the Bruce was crowned King of the Scots in 1306, Scotland had largely been a vassal state to the England of King Edward I. His seizure of power is still seen as a symbol of Scottish independence.

Renée-Pélagie de Sade

Francine du Plessix Gray, *At Home with the Marquis de Sade: A Life*, 1998.

For over two hundred years, France's eighteenth-century Marquis de Sade has been infamous for his sexually deviant behavior. Literary critic Francine du Plessix Gray closely examines the two women who shared his home: his loving wife, Renée-Pélagie de Sade, and his formidable mother-in-law, Madame de Montreuil. Despite his hedonism, both women were devoted to protecting him from the law, helping him control himself. In the end, they confined him.

Victoria

Lytton Strachey, *Queen Victoria*, 1921.

British biographer Lytton Strachey is known today as the first modern biographer. He combined psychological insights into his subjects with sympathy and wit to make both entertaining and informative portraits. This classic biography portrays Queen Victoria, who until the reign of Elizabeth II, had been one of England's longest-reigning and most effective monarchs.

Bahadur Shah Zafar II

William Dalrymple, *The Last Mughal: The Fall of Dynasty: Delhi, 1857*, 2006.

When the East India Company took over much of India, the last Mughal Emperor, Bahadur Shah Zafar II was reduced to a shadow court, stripped of all political power. Nevertheless, Zafar, a mystic, poet, and calligrapher, presided over a court of creative brilliance that led to a cultural renaissance in India. In 1857, he gave the East India Company's Indian troops permission to mutiny against their British overlords. After the four-month Siege of Delhi was over, tens of thousands had perished, and Zafar was exiled to Burma (Myanmar), where he later died.

COLLECTIVE BIOGRAPHY

Robert K. Massie, *Nicholas and Alexandra*, 1967.

Pulitzer Prize–winning author Robert K. Massie recounts the lives and unimaginably luxurious world of Russia's last tsar and his wife, the Romanovs, Nicholas and Alexandra. He portrays Nicholas as politically naïve and describes Alexandra's obsession with Rasputin and their children's struggles. In the end, he discloses their horrific deaths at the hands of revolutionaries.

Suetonius, *The Twelve Caesars*, 121.

Roman historian Gaius Suetonius Tranquillus was a private secretary of Emperor Hadrian, which afforded him access to the imperial archives. He used these, and interviews with witnesses, to write portraits of the public and private lives of the Roman Empire's caesars from Julius Caesar and Augustus to Hadrian. The Robert Graves translation is recommended.

10

U.S. Presidents and First Ladies

Chester A. Arthur

Scott S. Greenberger, *The Unexpected President:*
***The Life and Times of Chester A. Arthur*, 2017.**

Chester A. Arthur never wanted to be president. Indeed, he was deemed unfit by just about everyone, including himself. But as vice president to James Garfield, he was forced into the top executive role when Garfield was assassinated. And somehow, he managed to rise to the occasion. He was honest and courageous, taking on corruption and championing civil rights for Black Americans and land rights for Native Americans. As Scott S. Greenberger shows, his story is fascinating and inspirational.

George H. W. Bush

Jon Meacham, *Destiny and Power:*
***The American Odyssey of George Herbert Walker Bush*, 2015.**

Using private interviews with Bush and his family and with access to Bush's diaries, Jon Meacham writes a full-length biography of America's forty-first president. From Bush's childhood in Connecticut to his heroic service in World War II and his Texas oil business. Meacham then covers his astounding political career from congressman to UN ambassador to CIA head to president.

George W. Bush

Peter Baker, *Days of Fire:*
***Bush and Cheney in the White House*, 2013.**

White House correspondent Peter Baker explores the eight years that George W. Bush and Dick Cheney were president and vice president, respectively. Bush was an untested figure on the national scene, but Cheney was a veteran. The two were tested by terror attacks, the Iraq War, Hurricane Katrina, and financial tragedy. Baker looks behind the scenes at the two men's evolving relationship, which went from dependency to conflict.

Jimmy Carter

Jimmy Carter, *An Hour Before Daylight:*
***Memories of a Rural Boyhood*, 2000.**

From 1977 to 1981, Jimmy Carter served as the thirty-ninth president of the

United States. In his memoir, he writes of his childhood growing up on a Georgia farm during the Great Depression. In his community, sharecropping was a way of life. Carter reveals that his father, a segregationist, treated Black workers respectfully. Following his father, his forceful, well-read mother and three Black people were the most important people in his life. He shares his life in the days before the civil rights movement and regrets his place in it.

Bill Clinton

David Maraniss, *First in His Class: A Biography of Bill Clinton*, 1995.

In referring to Bill Clinton as "first in his class," David Maraniss is speaking of his graduating class. Clinton had the latest birth date of any person to reach the Oval Office when he was elected in 1992. In the biography, Maraniss is candid about Clinton's many gifts and flaws in this outdated biography.

Hillary Rodham Clinton

Hillary Rodham Clinton, *What Happened*, 2017.

Hillary Clinton has been a magnet for criticism. But as a strong woman, unafraid to voice her opinions and fight for what she believes in, she is candid in this memoir of what it's like to be a woman in politics. As the first female to run for the U.S. presidency, Clinton was already breaking a barrier, but the experience of running against Donald J. Trump added an extra challenge. She's honest about her mistakes, foreign interference that influenced outcomes, and how we can protect our democracy in the future.

Calvin Coolidge

Amity Shlaes, *Coolidge*, 2013.

As one of America's most reserved presidents, Calvin Coolidge is also the least understood. He led America through the Roaring Twenties, from 1923 to 1929. Amity Shlaes reveals that the Massachusetts native believed in humble service to the nation. He was a steady hand during a bullish time, limiting government spending and refusing to fund new interest groups. At the same time, he supported the automobile and aviation industries. And he did it all amid personal tragedy.

Dwight Eisenhower

Stephen E. Ambrose, *Eisenhower: Soldier and President*, 1990.

American historian and biographer Stephen E. Ambrose used interviews with Eisenhower and other primary sources to give an objective yet complete life story of the general who became president. While he details Eisenhower's brilliant career as Allied Supreme Commander in World War II, he also tells of his relationships with those closest to him, such as his wife, Mamie, and the world leaders he interacted with, such as Winston Churchill, Charles de Gaulle, and Richard M. Nixon.

James A. Garfield

Candice Millard, *Destiny of the Republic: A Tale of Madness, Medicine, and the Murder of a President*, 2011.

Acclaimed biographer Candice Millard tells of the life and death of James A. Garfield, a man born into poverty who became a highly respected scholar, Civil War hero, and progressive congressman. Never wanting the presidency, he was nevertheless nominated and won it. Shortly after his inauguration, a mentally ill man shot him in the back. Garfield's body and health became a battleground for power behind the scenes. The results were a death that was avoidable and tragic.

Ulysses S. Grant

Ulysses S. Grant and Elizabeth D. Samet, *The Annotated Memoirs of Ulysses S. Grant*, 2018.

General Ulysses S. Grant, son of a tanner, served as general-in-chief for the Union Army during the American Civil War from 1864 to 1869. He became the eighteenth president of the United States in 1869. Mark Twain published the first edition of Grant's memoirs. In this annotated edition, Elizabeth Samet notes the history and cultural backdrop for his writing. For a third-person look at Grant's life, see *Grant* by Jean Edward Smith.

Rutherford B. Hayes

Ari Hoogenboom, *Rutherford B. Hayes: Warrior and President*, 1996.

Rutherford B. Hayes served as president directly after Ulysses S. Grant. Although Hayes was previously regarded as a Southern sympathizer, Ari Hoogenboom finds him to have been a champion of civil rights and other progressive causes. Hayes grew up in the Ohio frontier and was wounded five times in the Civil War. His many detractors have blamed him for the failure of Reconstruction and criticized him for sticking with the gold standard. Hoogenboom says the criticisms of Hayes fail to consider the realities of the time and the president's limited options for dealing with them.

Herbert Hoover

Kenneth Whyte, *Hoover: An Extraordinary Life in Extraordinary Times*, 2017.

Many forget that Herbert Hoover, the reviled president in office at the beginning of the Great Depression, was elected to the office in a landslide vote. Kenneth Whyte outlines Hoover's life from his childhood as an orphan in Iowa to his accumulation of a fortune, his heroism in World War I, and his devastating defeat by Franklin D. Roosevelt. Whyte also tells of his final years of service after World War II, beginning with the Truman administration, under which he helped European refugees. His story is a uniquely American tale that deserves to be known.

Andrew Jackson

Jon Meacham, *American Lion: Andrew Jackson in the White House*, 2008.

Pulitzer Prize–winning author Jon Meacham chronicles the life of "Old Hickory," President Andrew Jackson, who began as an impoverished orphan, yet reached the height of power. He was loved and hated in equal measure, but he ultimately put democratic control in the hands of ordinary Americans instead of the elite. Jackson was a forceful personality who could be a vicious opponent. This contradictory man, the founder of the Democratic Party, has influenced presidents who followed him.

Thomas Jefferson

Kevin J. Hayes, *The Road to Monticello: The Life and Mind of Thomas Jefferson*, 2008.

Using Thomas Jefferson's letters, journals, and commonplace books, Kevin J. Hayes provides a literary and spiritual biography of America's most literary president. He traces the books Jefferson read and what he thought about them, from *The History of Tom Thumb*, which he enjoyed as a child, to the verses of Ossian, a third-century Gaelic warrior-poet. Hayes provides a little-known portrait of America's third president. For a full treatment of Jefferson's political career, see *Thomas Jefferson: The Art of Power* by Jon Meacham.

Lyndon B. Johnson

Doris Kearns Goodwin, *Lyndon Johnson and the American Dream*, 1976.

In the spring of 1967, a young Doris Kearns Goodwin met President Johnson at a White House dance. She was fascinated by him. As a member of his White House staff, she became his confidante. He told her things he revealed to no one else. Knowing Johnson as she did, Goodwin provides a unique biography of the president who led the nation after the assassination of Kennedy through the Vietnam War and his attempts to create the Great Society.

John F. Kennedy

Robert Dallek, *An Unfinished Life: John F. Kennedy, 1917–1963*, 2011.

Using previously unopened archives, Robert Dallek presents John Fitzgerald Kennedy in all his brilliance and bravery while exploring his faults and weaknesses. Of course, plenty of examples of both made this president relatable and inspirational. Dallek also speculates on what JFK's choices would have been in problems like Vietnam if he hadn't been assassinated.

Abraham Lincoln

David Herbert Donald, *Lincoln*, 1995.

Pulitzer Prize–winning author David Herbert Donald traces the humble Kentucky childhood of Abraham Lincoln through his political ascension in Illinois. Donald focuses on Lincoln's developing character to explain how a man of his background could have risen to such great moral heights and managed to keep the nation together during its greatest threat.

James Madison

Kevin R. C. Gutzman, *James Madison and the Making of America*, 2012.

Historian Kevin Gutzman seeks to reveal the human being behind the founding myths. Best known for his work on *The Federalist Papers*, the Bill of Rights, and the Constitution, James Madison's actual stance on issues is often misunderstood. He wasn't happy with the Constitution and thought the Bill of Rights was unnecessary. His opinions and actions were often contradictory. And his record as president, in some ways, led to the conflicts we face today.

William McKinley

Scott Miller, *The President and the Assassin: McKinley, Terror, and Empire at the Dawn of the American Century*, 2011.

At the time of the Pan-American Exposition of 1901, the United States was transforming itself from an agrarian society to an industrial powerhouse. As a result, America was splitting in two: there were the rich, who seemed to have a system set up to make them richer; and there were the poor, working away most of their lives with little to show for it. The two sides collided when Polish immigrant and anarchist Leon Czolgosz assassinated President William

McKinley. Journalist Scott Miller talks about an America divided against itself in a time much like ours.

James Monroe

Harlow Giles Unger, *The Last Founding Father: James Monroe and a Nation's Call to Greatness*, 2009.

Journalist and historian Harlow Giles Unger tells of America's fifth president and founding father, James Monroe. Monroe fought in four Revolutionary War battles and nearly died after a wound received at the Battle of Trenton, leading to a decoration by George Washington. He later served as a congressman, senator, minister to France and Britain, governor of Virginia, secretary of state, and secretary of war before becoming president. He dreamed of making America an empire.

Richard M. Nixon

Rick Perlstein, *Nixonland: The Rise of a President and the Fracturing of America*, 2008.

American historian and journalist Rick Perlstein details how Richard Nixon resurrected his political career to become president of the United States. In Perlstein's view, the years between 1965 and 1972 constituted a second civil war. In 1968, the nation was shocked from its liberal trajectory by the Watts riots and student Vietnam protests. With the Democratic Party fracturing, Nixon promised national unity but led the criminal Watergate conspiracy, resulting in his 1974 resignation.

Barack Obama

Barack Obama, *Dreams from My Father: A Story of Race and Inheritance*, 1995.

The first Black American and forty-fourth president of the United States, Barack Obama, shares memories of growing up in New York, where he first discovered that his father, whom he didn't know personally, had died in a car accident. The event brought back memories, and Obama traces them, beginning with his mother's journey from Kansas to Hawaii and then to Kenya, where Obama meets his father's family and discovers unpleasant truths about his heritage. The former president then picks up the story in his next memoir, *A Promised Land*, published in 2020. For a third-party perspective, see *The Bridge: The Life and Rise of Barack Obama* by David Remnick.

Michelle Obama

Michelle Obama, *Becoming*, 2018.

As the wife of Barack Obama, Michelle Obama served as America's First Lady from 2009 to 2017. She was the first African American woman to do so. In her memoir, Obama takes us through her childhood on Chicago's South Side, her career as an executive before the family took up residence in the White House, and her time spent at 1600 Pennsylvania Avenue in Washington, D.C. She reveals her mistakes and disappointments—and the wisdom she has gained from each—in addition to her proudest moments.

Jacqueline Bouvier Kennedy Onassis

Clint Hill, *Mrs. Kennedy and Me*, 2012.

Clint Hill served as Jackie Kennedy's personal Secret Service agent while and after President John F. Kennedy was in office. He was there at the birth of John Jr., and he was right beside her in Dallas when President Kennedy was fatally shot. He credits Jackie for her dignity in the days after the tragedy, which he feels helped hold the country together.

Franklin Pierce

Peter A. Wallner, *Franklin Pierce: Martyr for the Union*, 2007.

America's fourteenth president was New Hampshire native Franklin Pierce, who served in the White House from 1853 to 1857. In this second volume of his Franklin Pierce biography, Peter A. Wallner tells of the obstacles that confronted Pierce, including corruption, ineptitude, reformers, fraud, and speculation in a nation increasingly divided over the question of slavery.

James Polk

Robert W. Merry, *A Country of Vast Designs: James K. Polk, the Mexican War, and the Conquest of the American Continent*, 2008.

American journalist and commentator Robert W. Merry writes about James K. Polk, who was elected president in 1844. During his one term in office, Polk expanded U.S. territory by a third, adding Washington, Oregon, Idaho, Texas, California, Nevada, Utah, Arizona, New Mexico, and part of Colorado. Merry tells of Polk's relationships with historical figures of note like Andrew Jackson, Henry Clay, James Buchanan, and Daniel Webster. With the anti-slavery forces building, it was a crucial time in U.S. history.

Ronald Reagan

H. W. Brands, *Reagan: The Life*, 2015.

Comparing Ronald Reagan's influence with that of Franklin Delano Roosevelt, H. W. Brands places Reagan in the category of the greatest presidents of the twentieth century. Crediting Reagan's dedication to conservative principles, Brands finds him essential in ending communism in the Soviet Union. To understand Reagan, one must know where he came from—a small town in Illinois. And from there, he became a movie star. His role as the voice for corporate America while working on television's *The General Electric Theater* led to his political career. Brands shows how Reagan was misunderstood as he transformed the nation and the world.

Eleanor Roosevelt

Blanche Wiesen Cook, *Eleanor Roosevelt: 1884–1933* (Volume 1), 1992.

History professor Blanche Wiesen Cook writes of the childhood of one of America's most memorable first ladies, Eleanor Roosevelt, wife of President Franklin D. Roosevelt. She covers how Franklin and Eleanor's marital woes began but how Eleanor nevertheless had a tremendous influence on his policies. Cook's series has two more biographies: *Volume 2, The Defining Years, 1933–1938,* and *Volume 3, The War Years and After, 1939–1962.*

Franklin D. Roosevelt

H. W. Brands, *Traitor to His Class: The Privileged Life and Radical Presidency of Franklin Delano Roosevelt*, 2008.

History and government scholar H. W. Brands proclaims FDR the greatest president of the twentieth century. In this biography, he chronicles Roosevelt's privileged early life and shows how his concern for the poor and downtrodden helped him save democracy during the Great Depression. This success, in turn, gave him the stature to lead the world through World War II's threats. Brands also profiles Eleanor and the invaluable contributions she made to her husband's presidency. Finally, he stresses that Roosevelt had a rare genius for leadership that made him liked by both liberals and conservatives.

Theodore Roosevelt

David McCullough, *Mornings on Horseback: The Story of an Extraordinary Family, a Vanished Way of Life, and the Unique Child Who Became Theodore Roosevelt*, 1981.

Acclaimed biographer David McCullough tells of Teddy Roosevelt's childhood, when he was handicapped by severe asthma but managed to make himself an energetic and high-achieving individual despite his issues. His extraordinary success is due in no small part to his incredible family. Covering the first seventeen years of his life, this book is about love, loyalty, and what made Roosevelt the captivating figure he was.

Harry S. Truman

Harry S. Truman, *1945: Year of Decision: Memoirs* (Volume 1), 1955.

Harry Truman records his first year as president, which was a job he never wanted but was forced into with the death of President Franklin D. Roosevelt near the end of World War II. He tells what it was like when he unexpectedly became president and explains his decision to drop the atomic bomb on Japan to end the war in the Pacific. Truman also tells of growing up in Missouri and becoming involved in politics. Finally, he evaluates fellow world leaders like Winston Churchill, Charles de Gaulle, and Joseph Stalin. For another view of Truman, see *Harry S. Truman*, written by his daughter Margaret Truman.

Donald J. Trump

David Cay Johnston, *The Making of Donald Trump*, 2016.

After thirty years of reporting on Donald Trump, investigative journalist David Cay Johnston looks at Donald Trump's celebrity and political entry. He covers Trump's boyhood in Queens, N.Y., his development of media savvy, as well as his legal issues and the controversy surrounding him. This well-researched biography is as objective and fair as possible, though it was published before Trump's presidential term began.

George Washington

Ron Chernow, *Washington: A Life*, 2010.

Renowned historian Ron Chernow writes a sweeping view of the life of America's first president, George Washington, beginning with Washington's difficult childhood. Washington's early successes in the French and Indian War led to his role in the American Revolution. Chernow analyzes Washington's precedent-setting performance as the first to hold the top executive office. Rather than the staid figure many have come to associate with Washington, Chernow presents a dashing man with uncommon self-control who surrounded himself with brilliant companions who helped him steer the young nation toward an established government. For another view of Washington's private life, look at *You Never Forget Your First: A Biography of George Washington* by Alexis Coe.

Woodrow Wilson

John Milton Cooper Jr., *Woodrow Wilson: A Biography*, 2009.

Woodrow Wilson scholar John Milton Cooper Jr. chronicles the life of America's twenty-eighth president, who managed to recapture the executive office for the Democratic Party after sixteen years of Republican leadership. Wilson created the Federal Reserve, led the nation through World War I, and joined the League of Nations, paving the way for the United Nations to come. But despite his progressive agenda, he was no champion of civil rights. Instead, he was an intellectual (and president of Princeton) who used reason to win over Americans.

COLLECTIVE BIOGRAPHY

J. B. West, *Upstairs at the White House: My Life with the First Ladies*, 1973.

J. B. West worked for twenty-eight years as assistant to or as chief usher of the White House. The job entailed directing the operations and maintenance of the president's mansion, including state functions, parties, weddings, funerals, gardens, playgrounds, and renovations. In his time, he served under six presidents and first ladies. Here, he tells what it was like to work with the Roosevelts, Trumans, Eisenhowers, Kennedys, Johnsons, and Nixons.

11

Politicians and Leaders

Winston Churchill

Martin Gilbert, *Churchill: A Life*, 1991.

British prime minister Winston Churchill is considered one of the greatest statesmen in history. This official biography by Martin Gilbert, a single-volume abridgment of an eight-volume work, summarizes Churchill's life from beginning to end. There is a lot to tell. His courage and leadership of Britain against Nazi invaders in World War II saw the nation through to victory.

Cicero

Anthony Everitt, *Cicero: The Life and Times of Rome's Greatest Politician*, 2001.

Cicero lived during the days of Julius Caesar and Mark Anthony, at the height of Rome's power. In the centuries since his death, he has proven to be the most influential, and perhaps the greatest, politician in Western history. Historian Anthony Everitt provides this biography detailing Cicero's dedication to freedom, which later inspired the American and French Revolutions. The times in which Cicero lived were, in many ways, much like our own.

Henry Clay

David S. Heidler and Jeanne T. Heidler, *Henry Clay: The Essential American*, 2010.

Henry Clay shaped American history from its earliest years until just before the Civil War. During his long career, he served as speaker of the house, a senator, and the secretary of state. He served under ten presidents and ran for president himself five times, although he never won. The Heidlers present him as a brilliant politician who influenced everything from banking to slavery.

Davey Crockett

Buddy Levy, *American Legend: The Real-Life Adventures of David Crockett*, 2005.

Most Americans of a certain age are familiar with the name Davey Crockett, "the king of the wild frontier." But is their image correct? Not entirely, according to author Buddy Levy. Crockett was a self-promotion pioneer. In 1834, he published a memoir that created a media frenzy and made him an exceptionally popular author. He served three terms in Congress and was nominated for president. Crockett later lost his life while fighting at the Alamo in Texas. Levy tells the real story and how it fits into the myth.

Jefferson Davis

William J. Cooper Jr., *Jefferson Davis, American*, 2000.

As a West Point graduate, U.S. senator from Mississippi, and secretary of war under President Franklin Pierce, Jefferson Davis had a brilliant career in the United States. He owned a productive plantation and decided that keeping slavery, even if it meant dividing the United States, was worth it. After becoming the president of the Confederacy, Davis became increasingly autocratic. Imprisoned after the war, Davis professed faith in the union in the end. William J. Cooper also discusses the perennial tension between states' rights and the need for centralized leadership.

John Foster Dulles and Allen Dulles

Stephen Kinzer, *The Brothers: John Foster Dulles, Allen Dulles, and Their Secret World War*, 2013.

During the Cold War years of the 1950s, two powerful and influential brothers made U.S. foreign policies and made other decisions that still shape the world. John Foster Dulles was secretary of state. His brother, Allen Dulles, was the director of the CIA. Author Stephen Kinzer demonstrates how the brothers led the country to sow the seeds for hostility and repercussions that have endangered the U.S. ever since.

Benjamin Franklin

Walter Isaacson, *Benjamin Franklin: An American Life*, 2003.

Celebrated biographer and historian Walter Isaacson covers the life of American founding father Benjamin Franklin. In his eighty-four years, Franklin rose from working-class beginnings, making a fortune as an entrepreneur, scientist, inventor, publisher, writer, and statesman. American culture would likely be different without Franklin, as it was Franklin's sense of humor, values, and pragmatism that shaped the popular ethos; he was, at heart, a champion of the working class. In addition to Isaacson's biography, read *The Autobiography of Benjamin Franklin* for a firsthand look at Franklin's perspective and personality.

Charles de Gaulle

Julian Jackson, *A Certain Idea of France: A Life of Charles de Gaulle*, 2018.

Julian Jackson shows that France would be a different nation today if Charles de Gaulle hadn't made his way to England after Germany invaded in 1940. The contradictory French general stayed in London, directing British policy toward France and urging the French people from a distance. Due to his efforts, France emerged from World War II as a victorious power. De Gaulle became president of France's current government, the Fifth Republic.

Rudy Giuliani

Andrew Kirtzman, *Giuliani: The Rise and Tragic Fall of America's Mayor*, 2022.

In the years immediately following the 9/11 attacks, the mayor of New York City, Rudy Giuliani, had more admirers than the pope. Andrew Kirtzman was with Giuliani at the World Trade Center and has followed him ever since. He reveals how Giuliani rose to such great heights and how a combination of self-destructive behavior and regrettable choices led to his lost reputation and possible financial ruin.

John Hay

John Taliaferro, *All the Great Prizes: The Life of John Hay, From Lincoln to Roosevelt*, 2013.

For over fifty years, John Hay was a significant player in the United States government. He began his career on the national stage as personal secretary to Abraham Lincoln, attending his address at Gettysburg and being present at his death. He went on to work for James Garfield, Rutherford B. Hayes, William McKinley, and Theodore Roosevelt, on whom he had great influence. But his public service is only part of his story. Hay was also a public man-about-town who knew most of the major celebrities of his day.

Patrick Henry

John Kukla, *Patrick Henry: Champion of Liberty*, 2017.

Remembered primarily for his "Give me liberty, or give me death" proclamation, Patrick Henry was an attorney and planter who served as Virginia's first governor after the Revolutionary War. He opposed the Constitution because he felt it gave too much power to the federal government. Contradictorily, he opposed slavery but owned slaves. His influence was huge but is nearly forgotten today. John Kukla brings him back to life in this thoroughly researched biography.

Adolf Hitler

John Toland, *Adolf Hitler*, 1976.

Calling Adolf Hitler "a hybrid of Prometheus and Lucifer," Pulitzer Prize–winning historian John Toland treated the man deemed one of the evilest men of the twentieth century as a distant historical figure to be as objective as possible. He interviewed people who knew the führer firsthand. Covering Hitler's life from start to finish, Toland created a detailed yet readable account of his life.

Richard Holbrooke

George Packer, *Our Man: Richard Holbrooke and the End of the American Century*, 2019.

George Packer used American diplomat Richard Holbrooke's diaries and papers to draw this portrait of the man and the recent history he so profoundly influenced. From the Vietnam War era through the war in Afghanistan, Holbrooke's personality reflected America's role in the post–World War II world. He sought to lead on the global stage, but his self-absorption and appetites tempered his greatness.

Barbara Jordan

Mary Beth Rogers, *Barbara Jordan: American Hero*, 1998.

Barbara Jordan entered politics at the beginning of the civil rights movement. She was the first African American to serve in the Texas Senate after Reconstruction. And she was the first Black woman to be elected to Congress from the South. Yet, while her influence was significant, most knew little about her private life. Mary Beth Rogers uncovers a passionate patriot who lived with an illness for two decades before it took her life at age fifty-nine.

Edward M. Kennedy

Edward M. Kennedy, *True Compass: A Memoir*, 2009.

The youngest son of the Kennedy dynasty, Edward, called "Ted," served nine terms in the U.S. Senate beginning in 1962. He recollects growing up in the large Kennedy family with parents who expected much of their children. He fondly remembers working with his brother JFK on his presidential campaign. He gives his perspective on the assassinations of his brothers, John and Robert, and the major news stories of the day, like Vietnam and Watergate. He also highlights his personal life, the triumphs and tragedies, through the lens of his deep Catholic faith.

Joseph P. Kennedy

David Nasaw, *The Patriarch: The Remarkable Life and Turbulent Times of Joseph P. Kennedy*, 2012.

Written by history scholar and eminent biographer David Nasaw, this work traces the career trajectory of the founder of one of the twentieth century's most influential and important American political dynasties. Joseph P.

Kennedy was an East Boston outsider, an Irish Catholic who began his career as a banker, moved on to become a shipyard manager in World War I and then became a Hollywood studio head, a Wall Street broker, a New Deal advisor to the president, and finally, the first chairman of the Securities and Exchange Commission. His offspring became a political enterprise: Senator Edward Kennedy, U.S. Attorney General Robert F. Kennedy, and President of the United States John F. Kennedy. Nasaw sheds light on many previously unanswered questions about the senior Kennedy.

Robert F. Kennedy

Thurston Clarke, *The Last Campaign: Robert F. Kennedy and 82 Days That Inspired America*, 2008.
As the younger brother of John F. Kennedy, Robert Kennedy served as JFK's attorney general. After his brother's assassination, Bobby, disheartened by problems that continued to beset the nation, announced his run for the presidency. But he was to share his brother's fate as he was assassinated on the campaign trail in 1968. Thurston Clarke narrates the life of Bobby Kennedy and his fight for a better, more equitable America.

Kim Jon Un

Anna Fifield, *The Great Successor: The Divinely Perfect Destiny of Brilliant Comrade Kim Jong Un*, 2019.
North Korea is a notoriously difficult place to live. Anna Fifield explains how generations of the ruling Kim dynasty have kept it in poverty, hardship, and deep suppression. Kim Jong Un was expected to have a brief leadership since he was young and unhealthy when his father died. But through ruthlessness and luck, he has managed to hold on to his regime, which wields outsized influence. It is a nation of poverty with nuclear weapons, and Kim Jong Un threatens to use them.

Nikita Khrushchev

William Taubman, *Khrushchev: The Man and His Era*, 2003.
Nikita Khrushchev served as leader of the Soviet Union for a decade after Joseph Stalin's death. William Taubman says while Khrushchev was party to Stalin's crimes, he condemned them after Stalin died and tried to reform the nation in ways that ultimately caused its fall.

Henry Kissinger

Henry Kissinger, *White House Years*, 1979.
In this first of his memoirs, Henry Kissinger writes about his first four years in the White House as President Nixon's assistant on national security and

foreign policy. He describes his first meeting with Nixon and offers insights into the overthrow of Cambodia's Prince Sihanouk. In addition, he details U.S. policy in the Middle East. This book is more than just a memoir; it is considered a significant contribution to United States history. For a broader perspective on Kissinger's life, see *Kissinger: A Biography*, by Walter Isaacson, published in 1992, and *Kissinger: 1923–1968: The Idealist*, by Niall Ferguson.

John Lewis

John Lewis, *Walking with the Wind: A Memoir of the Movement*, 1998.

United States Representative John Lewis was the son of an Alabama sharecropper. In the 1950s and 1960s, he was at the front of the nation's fight for civil rights. He was arrested over forty times and sometimes beaten for participation in activities sponsored by the Student Nonviolent Coordinating Committee (SNCC), of which he was chairman. His account of events, such as the march on the Edmund Pettus Bridge in Selma, Alabama, provides a unique look at major historical episodes.

Huey Long

T. Harry Williams, *Huey Long: A Biography*, 1969.

Historian T. Harry Williams wrote this award-winning biography of one of the most colorful and contradictory politicians in American history, Huey Long. When Long became governor of Louisiana in 1928, he championed "poor White" causes. Long earned many enemies by railing against big businesses, including Standard Oil. But he was also an autocratic leader who made free and fair elections nearly impossible in his state. Even after becoming a senator, he insisted on managing Louisiana politics from afar. He was assassinated in 1935 at age forty-two.

John McCain

John McCain, *Faith of My Fathers: A Family Memoir*, 1999.

In this memoir, United States Senator John McCain writes about the code of honor he inherited from his father and grandfather, who were four-star U.S. Navy admirals. It is these two men that McCain admires most. After outlining their distinguished careers, McCain III tells how he, as a naval aviator, was shot down over Hanoi during the Vietnam War in 1967. McCain refused the Vietnamese offer of early release that was meant to embarrass the U.S. Consequently, he was tortured, held in solitary confinement, and imprisoned for over five years. McCain later served as a U.S. senator from Arizona from 1987 to his death in 2018.

Angela Merkel

Kati Marton, *The Chancellor:*
***The Remarkable Odyssey of Angela Merkel*, 2021.**
Journalist Kati Marton interviewed the people who know German chancellor
Angela Merkel best and examined recently available documents to understand
this wildly successful but private world leader. Merkel's father was a pastor
in Communist East Germany. She began her career as a chemist and entered
politics after the Berlin Wall fell.

Pol Pot

Philip Short, *Pol Pot: Anatomy of a Nightmare*, 2000.
The killing fields of Cambodia. The very name sends chills up the spine. Philip
Short met Pol Pot in 1975, when the dictator was on his only official visit to
China. He found the leader charming and charismatic, but this was before
his reign of terror began. By the time it was over, more than a million of his
people, one in five Cambodians, had died. Short traveled to Cambodia after
the collapse of the Khmer Rouge to figure out what happened and why.

Maximilien Robespierre

Colin Jones, *The Fall of Robespierre:*
***24 Hours in Revolutionary Paris*, 2021.**
During the French Revolution, Robespierre was a leader of the Committee of
Public Safety, which directed the Reign of Terror that resulted in the deaths
of individuals deemed enemies of the new republic. They aimed to keep
various groups of revolutionaries united to one cause. But by July 28, 1794,
Robespierre was on the run as an outlaw. Colin Jones narrates the final days
of his life in which he tried to kill himself before succumbing to the guillotine.

Benjamin Rush

Stephen Fried, *Rush: Revolution, Madness, and the Visionary*
***Doctor Who Became a Founding Father*, 2018.**
Award-winning journalist Stephen Fried tells of one of the most underappreciated founding fathers, Dr. Benjamin Rush, who was the youngest signer of
the Declaration of Independence at age thirty. Rush was also known as the
"American Hippocrates" for his efforts to upgrade national healthcare and
improve the treatment of addiction and mental illness. He was a progressive
who opposed slavery, capital punishment, and special treatment for race, religion, or gender. His influence on the young nation has been largely overlooked
until now.

Shabtai Shavit

Shabtai Shavit, *Head of the Mossad: In Pursuit of a Safe and Secure Israel*, 2020.

Shabtai Shavit recalls his seven years as director of Mossad, Israel's equivalent of the CIA, from 1989 to 1996. From his singular vantage point, he had a unique perspective on events such as the collapse of the Soviet Union and the assassination of Yitzhak Rabin. In this memoir, he discloses his philosophy about the operations of Mossad.

Robert Smalls

Cate Lineberry, *Be Free or Die: The Amazing Story of Robert Smalls' Escape from Slavery to Union Hero*, 2017.

Robert Smalls was born enslaved in the United States. In 1862, at age twenty-three, he seized a Confederate steamer, stowed his wife and two children aboard, and ran a gauntlet of fortifications in Charleston Harbor to deliver the steamer to the Union forces. He was immediately emancipated, becoming a Union hero. Cate Lineberry tells how he went on to serve on the Union side. After the war, he became a member of the United States Congress.

Joseph Stalin

Oleg V. Khlevniuk, *Stalin: New Biography of a Dictator*, 2015.

Ukrainian and Russian historian Oleg V. Khlevniuk writes about Soviet dictator Joseph Stalin, who led the Soviet Union from 1929 through 1953. Khlevniuk looks at the factors that caused Stalin to make the decisions he did, including his execution of estimated millions of his citizens. Using letters, memos, reports, and diaries, he sheds light on Stalin's childhood and his role in the Russian Revolution, World War II, and the postwar years.

Elizabeth Warren

Elizabeth Warren, *A Fighting Chance*, 2014.

Growing up in a small Oklahoma town, Elizabeth Warren wanted to be an elementary school teacher. But despite her modest means, she became a law professor. Then, while working with bankruptcy cases, she was asked to go to Washington and advise Congress on rewriting bankruptcy laws. In this memoir, she reveals how her efforts to improve the system were opposed. As a result, she became a target for big banks that would lose revenue from her ideas. Finally, after years of this, at age sixty-two, she ran for a U.S. Senate seat and won.

12

Invaders, Warriors, and Spies

Aetius

Ian Hughes, *Aetius: Attila's Nemesis*, 2012.

In 435 C.E., Attila the Hun was plowing a path through Gaul (modern-day France) to add territory to his empire. Had he succeeded, his kingdom would have stretched from the Atlantic Ocean through the Eurasian steppes. Ian Hughes explains how he was defeated by Aetius, who quickly assembled an army to fight the Huns. Yet little has been known about this early leader until now.

Alexander the Great

Robin Lane Fox, *Alexander the Great*, 1973.

By his death at age thirty-two, Alexander the Great had amassed an empire that stretched from Greece to India. Moreover, his victories spread Greek culture over much of the East. Robin Lane Fox, a scholar of the ancient world, used historical sources and psychological insight to bring this incredible man to life.

Attila the Hun

Christopher Kelly, *Attila the Hun: Barbarian Terror and the Fall of the Roman Empire*, 2008.

As the most famous chief of the Huns during the fall of the Roman Empire, Attila has always had a reputation as a fierce and destructive leader. Historian of ancient Rome Christopher Kelly seeks to set the record straight. The Huns, he says, were no more brutal than the Romans. In using archaeological discoveries, he asserts that Attila was a savvy leader who was intent on building an empire of his own.

Josephine Baker

Damien Lewis, *Agent Josephine: American Beauty, French Hero, British Spy*, 2022.

Not many today know about Josephine Baker. Bestselling author Damien Lewis says she was the highest-paid female performer in Europe before World War II, famous for her singing and dancing. When the Nazis invaded France, she was banned from the Paris stage, along with "negroes and Jews." The move caused Baker to become a Resistance spy who performed top-notch work for the United States, France, and Britain.

Eddie Chapman

Ben Macintyre, *Agent Zigzag: A True Story of Nazi Espionage, Love, and Betrayal*, 2007.

Ben Macintyre follows the career of British double agent Eddie Chapman, a dual character, inside and out. After being trained as a German spy, he was parachuted into Britain in 1941 with orders to explode an airplane factory. But instead of following orders, he contacted MI5 and joined the British Secret Service. For four years, he managed to keep the confidence of both countries while also seducing beautiful women. And both countries considered him a hero when the war was over.

George Armstrong Custer

Evan S. Connell, *Son of the Morning Star: Custer and the Little Bighorn*, 1984.

When thousands of Lakota Sioux, Cheyenne, and Arapaho Indians and 262 American cavalries clashed in Montana on that June day in 1876, not one American soldier remained to talk about it. The story of the Battle of Little Bighorn, aka "Custer's Last Stand," is told by novelist Evan S. Connell, who used impeccable research to provide the facts.

Francis Drake

John Sugden, *Sir Francis Drake*, 1990.

Sir Francis Drake was an Elizabethan Age admiral who helped England become a world power. As a pirate, he bedeviled the Spanish in the New World. His trip around the globe aboard the *Golden Hind* brought untold wealth in seized Spanish treasure to the queen.

Nathanael Greene

Terry Golway, *Washington's General: Nathanael Greene and the Triumph of the American Revolution*, 2004.

When the American Revolutionary War broke out, Nathanael Greene renounced his Quaker faith and left his family to become a soldier. He educated himself in military tactics after joining the Rhode Island militia in 1774. As George Washington's right-hand man, he led the Southern campaign and pioneered guerilla fighting techniques that the British found difficult to defend against. Terry Golway asserts that had Greene not been appointed commander of the Southern Department of the Continental Army, the British would have most likely won the war.

Virginia Hall

Sonia Purnell, *A Woman of No Importance: The Untold Story of the American Spy Who Helped Win World War II*, 2019.
She was known as the "Madonna of the Resistance." Yet the story of World War II American spy Virginia Hall has been neglected. Even though she had been rejected from American foreign service because she was female and because she had a prosthetic leg, Hall traveled to Britain and became a spy for Churchill, who sent her into occupied France. Once her cover was blown, this woman, called "The most dangerous of Allied spies" by the Gestapo, had to hike across the Pyrenees to Spain to escape certain death. Yet, even then, she was not done.

William Halsey

Thomas Alexander Hughes, *Admiral Bill Halsey: A Naval Life*, 2016.
Known as the "Patton of the Pacific," William Halsey was World War II's most famous naval officer. Thomas Hughes traces his life from childhood with an alcoholic naval officer for a father to become a practical and inspiring commander. While he led American carrier raids against Japan and at Guadalcanal, his major contribution was his mediation work between General Douglas MacArthur and Admiral Chester Nimitz. His efforts were crucial to Allied success in the Pacific.

Hannibal

Harold Lamb, *Hannibal*, 1958.
American historian and novelist Harold Lamb narrates the story of the brilliant general who almost brought Rome to its knees. The Carthaginian leader eluded Roman legions when Rome invaded Spain, and he led a small army over the Alps and into the Po Valley. He spent the next eighteen years patrolling the Italian peninsula, harassing Rome wherever he could. Hannibal has been seen as one of the most brilliant military leaders in history.

Mildred Harnack

Rebecca Donner, *All the Frequent Troubles of Our Days: The True Story of the American Woman at the Heart of the German Resistance to Hitler*, 2021.
Rebecca Donner details the astonishing story of her great-great-aunt Mildred Harnack, who was born and raised in Milwaukee but became a Ph.D. student in Germany at age twenty-six. Appalled by what she witnessed during the Nazi rise to power, she began holding secret meetings with a small group of political activists in her apartment in 1932. By the time of her execution

in 1943, Harnack had started a resistance movement, plotted sabotage, and called for a revolution against Hitler. She was also a spy who provided top-secret information to the Allies.

Thomas "Stonewall" Jackson

S. C. Gwynne, *Rebel Yell: The Violence, Passion, and Redemption of Stonewall Jackson*, 2014.

Stonewall Jackson served as general for the Confederacy until his own troops accidentally shot him. Author S. C. Gwynne provides plenty of history and personality conflicts between historical figures. While covering Jackson's notoriously regimented personal habits, Gwynne also explains why he was one of the greatest military geniuses in American history, changing much about how wars are fought.

Joan of Arc

Larissa Juliet Taylor, *The Virgin Warrior: The Life and Death of Joan of Arc*, 2009.

During the Hundred Years' War between France and England, a teenage French peasant girl began hearing voices urging her to lead France to victory over the English invaders. Amazingly enough, the king agreed to let her try. Larissa Juliet Taylor examines her story in the context of culture at a time when visions and witchcraft were both taken seriously. Joan managed to rally the French troops and populace while terrifying the English. Examining the stories surrounding her after her violent death, Taylor seeks to uncover the real person behind the legends.

John Paul Jones

Samuel Eliot Morison, *John Paul Jones: A Sailor's Biography*, 1959.

Historian Samuel Eliot Morison narrates the dramatic story of John Paul Jones, an early naval hero. Jones trained in the British West Indies merchant trade, served in the newly formed United States navy, then became an admiral in the Russian navy, where he served in the Black Sea. He managed spectacular victories at sea despite the odds against him.

Ron Kovic

Ron Kovic, *Born on the Fourth of July*, 1976.

After two tours of duty in Vietnam as a patriotic marine, Ron Kovic returned to America as a disabled antiwar activist. He wrote this book about his war experiences and his efforts to end the war. The book was later made into a motion picture directed by Oliver Stone and starring Tom Cruise.

Marquis de Lafayette

Mike Duncan, *Hero of Two Worlds:*
The Marquis de Lafayette in the Age of Revolution, 2021.

Popular history podcaster Mike Duncan provides this look at the fifty-year history of the Marquis de Lafayette, who ran away from France as a teenager to serve illustriously in the American Revolution. Inspired by his experiences in America, he helped start the French Revolution and spent five years in dungeons for his efforts. Upon release, Lafayette bedeviled Napoleon. However, in the years since his death, he has become a symbol of liberty and human rights.

T. E. Lawrence (Lawrence of Arabia)

Michael Korda, *Hero:*
The Life and Legend of Lawrence of Arabia, 2010.

Novelist and editor Michael Korda tells of the early-twentieth-century exploits of Thomas Edward Lawrence, a colorful British adventurer who helped sponsor the Arab Revolt of World War II. This biography is 784 pages of exciting accounts of his exploits. For those interested in a firsthand account, Lawrence wrote *The Seven Pillars of Wisdom* to tell the story from his perspective.

Robert E. Lee

Jonathan Horn, *The Man Who Would Not Be Washington:*
Robert E. Lee's Civil War and His Decision
That Changed American History, 2015.

Former presidential speechwriter Jonathan Horn narrates the life of Robert E. Lee, the general who was sought for leadership by the armies of both the Union and Confederacy. Lee was the son-in-law of George Washington's adopted child and the son of his most famous eulogist, Henry "Light Horse Harry" Lee. Yet he chose to fight for what Washington had fought to preserve, the United States as a united whole. In addition, Horn dives into the role of slavery, a legacy Robert E. Lee inherited from Washington.

Jacques Lusseyran

Jacques Lusseyran, *And There Was Light:*
The Extraordinary Memoir of a Blind Hero
of the French Resistance in World War II, 1963.

When he was eight years old, Jacques Lusseyran of Paris was blinded in an accident. But this didn't prevent him from finishing school. When he was seventeen, the Nazis invaded France, and Lusseryan recruited fifty-two boys to help him in his resistance group. Later, he was rounded up with two thousand resistance fighters and sent to Buchenwald. Only thirty-one of these survived, and Lusseyran was one of them. His descriptions of surviving and thriving while blind are astounding and inspirational.

Douglas MacArthur

William Manchester, *American Caesar: Douglas MacArthur, 1880–1964,* 1978.

As commander of the U.S. Pacific Theater in World War II, General Douglas MacArthur proved to be a war hero for generations of Americans. Yet biographer William Manchester reveals a private man who defies the expectations of those who revered and criticized him.

William Marshal

Thomas Asbridge, *The Greatest Knight: The Remarkable Life of William Marshal, the Power Behind Five English Thrones,* 2014.

Condemned to die at the gallows at age five by his father, William Marshal survived to become the power behind five English monarchs beginning with King Henry II and his wife, Eleanor of Aquitaine. Marshal's life in the early Middle Ages sheds light on the age of knights in Britain. Thomas Asbridge details the training, weapons, and battle tactics of knights and the role of chivalry and courtliness in their conduct.

Chester Nez

Chester Nez, *Code Talker,* 2011.

American World War II veteran Chester Nez was the last original Navajo code talker to serve the U.S. Marine Corps and the first and only one to write a published memoir. In this book, written when he was eighty-nine years old, Nez talks about growing up on the Checkerboard area of the Navajo Reservation and how those experiences left him well suited for the Marine Corps. He became one of twenty-nine code talkers. All of them were forbidden to speak of their covert mission until 1968. Their code has proven to be the only one still unbroken.

George Smith Patton

Carlo D'Este, *Patton: A Genius for War,* 1995.

Retired U.S. Army lieutenant colonel Carlo D'Este was provided full and exclusive access to the personal and public papers of General George S. Patton by his family. And these, along with interviews with those who knew the general, are used by D'Este to explore the controversial and charismatic World War II general, who was respected and feared, even by the Nazis.

Witold Pilecki

Jack Fairweather, *The Volunteer: The True Story of the Resistance Hero Who Infiltrated Auschwitz*, 2019.

Journalist Jack Fairweather tells the story of a forgotten hero of World War II. Witold Pilecki was an underground operative who volunteered to be one of the people rounded up on Poland's streets to be taken to Auschwitz. No one was sure what was happening at the camp, so Pilecki went in to find out. While there for two and a half years, he smuggled out reports of the hellscape he was a part of. He also worked to raise a secret army that would be ready to revolt against the Nazis when the opportunity presented itself. His efforts shaped the Allied response to the Holocaust.

Colin Powell

Colin Powell, *My American Journey*, 1995.

U.S. Army five-star general and former secretary of state Colin Powell writes of his childhood in Harlem as the son of Jamaican immigrants. His school career was unremarkable, but he began to excel after joining the army, and he performed distinguished service in Vietnam, at the Pentagon, and on Operation Desert Storm. He shares his views on the greatness of America.

Manfred "The Red Baron" von Richthofen

Peter Kilduff, *The Illustrated Red Baron: The Life and Times of Manfred von Richthofen*, 1999.

As the top-scoring ace fighter pilot of World War I, Manfred von Richthofen, a member of German nobility, is still a legend. Peter Kilduff explains how this handsome and gallant man brought down eighty airplanes before he died after his plane was shot down over France.

Robert Rogers

John F. Ross, *War on the Run: The Epic Story of Robert Rogers and the Conquest of America's First Frontier*, 2009.

In the early days of the American colonies, a group of handpicked soldiers, chosen for their wilderness survival skills, courage, and endurance, were led by a young man named Robert Rogers. Known as Roger's Rangers, they worked for the British government, using guerilla war tactics against their French and Indian adversaries, attacking and gathering intelligence. Rogers is considered the father of today's elite special forces.

Ethel Rosenberg

Anne Sebba, *Ethel Rosenberg: An American Tragedy*, 2021.
In June of 1953, during the Cold War, husband and wife Julius and Ethel Rosenberg were executed for espionage in electric chairs only moments apart. The evidence against Ethel was slight and primarily based on her brother's witness, even though he perjured himself in his testimony. As uncovered in this tragic biography, Ethel's crime was likely her overabundance of love and loyalty for her husband. The couple's deaths left their children orphaned and the world horrified.

Saladin

John Man, *Saladin: The Sultan Who Vanquished the Crusaders and Built an Islamic Empire*, 2015.
British historian John Man narrates the life of twelfth-century military leader Saladin, who saved Islam from the Christian crusaders by uniting the Arabs. In addition to his military prowess, Saladin was a theologian and builder whose legacy endures across the Arab world.

Scipio Africanus

Richard A. Gabriel, *Scipio Africanus: Rome's Greatest General*, 2008.
Military scholar Richard A. Gabriel maintains that the Roman general Scipio Africanus is the greatest general of the ancient era. Though Hannibal still gets more attention, Gabriel points out that Scipio defeated him. Without the victories of Scipio Aricanus, Rome would have been unlikely to ever form an empire.

William Tecumseh Sherman

Robert L. O'Connell, *Fierce Patriot: The Tangled Lives of William Tecumseh Sherman*, 2014.
Historian Robert L. O'Connell traces the life of William Tecumseh Sherman, the Union Civil War general known for the swath he burned across the South, which brought the Civil War to an end. There were many contradictions in his life, and O'Connell goes on to explore Sherman's stormy family relationships and his work on the transcontinental railroad.

Edward Snowden

Luke Harding, *The Snowden Files: The Inside Story of the World's Most Wanted Man*, 2014.
British journalist Luke Harding writes of Edward Snowden, who, at age

twenty-nine, stole information from the United States National Security Agency and turned it over to the news media to reveal the U.S. government's use of technology to spy on its citizens and others. For his efforts, Snowden spent years seeking asylum. His story reads like a spy thriller.

Agent Sonya

**Ben Macintyre, *Agent Sonya:*
Moscow's Most Daring Wartime Spy, 2020.**
"Sonya" was the code name for a high-ranking intelligence officer who ran a spy ring across Europe, collecting information that would ultimately allow the U.S.S.R. to build an atomic bomb. To her neighbors in the English Cotswolds, she was Ursula Burton, a friendly mother of three who was married to a machine worker. But as Macintyre reveals, her husband was also a spy. Sonya was hunted by the Chinese, Japanese, British Secret Service, and the FBI during her career, and she managed to evade them all.

Pat Tillman

**Jon Krakauer, *Where Men Win Glory:*
The Odyssey of Pat Tillman, 2009.**
After 9/11, NFL player Pat Tillman followed his conscience, leading him to drop a $3.6 million football contract to enlist in the U.S. Army to fight al-Qaeda and the Taliban. When he died two years later of gunshot wounds, the facts surrounding his death, mainly that his own platoon had killed him, were kept from his family and the American public. To tell the story, Jon Krakauer used Tillman's journals, letters, interviews, and research to tell Tillman's complicated story.

Arthur Wellesley (the Duke of Wellington)

Richard Holmes, *Wellington: The Iron Duke*, 2002.
Queen Victoria called Arthur Wellesley, the Duke of Wellington, the greatest man the nineteenth century produced. Military scholar Richard Holmes describes a brilliant, often idealistic man who was no fan of warfare. And yet, he led his men to victory over Napoleon at Waterloo. Despite these successes, Holmes reveals, Wellington was a lady's man who often didn't even like the soldiers he commanded.

Yasuke

**Thomas Lockley and Geoffrey Girard, *African Samurai:*
The True Story of Yasuke, a Legendary Black Warrior
in Feudal Japan, 2019.**
As a child in Africa, Yasuke was kidnapped. After traveling around much of

the known world, he became a servant and bodyguard to the head of the Asian Jesuits. In the late sixteenth century, when he arrived in Kyoto, he caused a riot because most people there had never seen a person with dark skin. They saw him as an embodiment of the local, black-skinned Buddha. The head of Japan's most powerful clan, Lord Nounaga, made Yasuke a samurai in his court. And thus, he began his ascent to the highest levels of feudal Japanese society.

Sir Francis Younghusband

Patrick French, *Younghusband: The Last Great Imperial Adventurer*, 1994.

British historian Patrick French delves into the life of one of Great Britain's last adventurers, Sir Francis Younghusband. Serving as a spy for the empire, Younghusband invaded Tibet alone and wiped out its army. After this feat, he became a mystic. But he managed other exploits in Central Asia. His athletic accomplishments and adventures garnered the admiration of such luminaries as H. G. Wells and Bertrand Russell.

Emiliano Zapata

John Womack Jr., *Zapata and the Mexican Revolution*, 1968.

During the Mexican Revolution, from 1910 to 1920, Emiliano Zapata was a guerilla leader who aided the peasants and indigenous people who rose against the Spanish ruling class seeking land reforms. Zapata had been a peasant leader who quickly became a hero to his people.

13

Witnesses to History

Vera Brittain

Vera Brittain, *Testament of Youth*, 1933.

In 1915, Vera Brittain left her studies at Oxford to become a nurse for the armed services. Her work took her from London to Malta, to the Western Front. By the end of the war, almost everyone she loved was gone. She later became a pacifist. This book captures a time and place that few lived to talk about.

Landon Carter

Rhys Isaac, *Landon Carter's Uneasy Kingdom: Revolution and Rebellion on a Virginia Plantation*, 2004.

Historian Rhys Isaac studied the diaries of eighteenth-century Virginia plantation owner Landon Carter and wrote this fascinating biography based on his findings. Carter supported the American Revolution and liberty (apart from the enslaved). But he was profoundly uneasy at the rupture with tradition that it would bring. Carter also had troubles with his children and the people he enslaved. So while he feared for the country, his private world was crumbling.

Robert Graves

Robert Graves, *Goodbye to All That: An Autobiography*, 1929.

After an unhappy experience in Britain's Charterhouse School, Robert Graves signed up to become an officer in World War I. The experience haunted him for the rest of his life. He wrote this autobiography as he was leaving England "forever." He talks about his experiences growing up, his attraction to men, the famous writers he met, and his unhappy marriage to his wife, Nancy Nicholson. His autobiography was an instant classic because it captured the changes that World War I had wrought on English society.

Michael Herr

Michael Herr, *Dispatches*, 1977.

Novelist and war correspondent Michael Herr wrote this classic memoir from his time reporting on the Vietnam War for *Esquire* in the 1960s. His honest, no-holds-barred approach is by turns terrifying and surreal.

Marta Hillers

Anonymous, *A Woman in Berlin: Eight Weeks in the Conquered City: A Diary*, 1953.

Marta Hillers, a German journalist, was in Berlin when the city fell to the Russian army in 1945. She kept a diary for eight weeks detailing who among the Berliners around her rose or sunk to the occasion. The Russian forces also came under her sharp observation because the conquerors held both the key to survival and the means of humiliation for the defeated. The author herself was forced to make difficult decisions to survive. The book was published anonymously until after her death in 2001.

Samuel Pepys

Claire Tomalin, *Samuel Pepys: The Unequalled Self*, 2002.

While he served as a naval administrator and an advisor to King Charles II, Samuel Pepys is known today mainly for his diary that chronicled much of seventeenth-century English history. He wrote honestly about his experiences during the shocking execution of Charles I, the Civil War, episodes of plague, and the Great Fire of London. Claire Tomalin, in turn, tells us about his life.

Megan K. Stack

Megan K. Stack, *Every Man in this Village Is a Liar: An Education in War*, 2010.

War correspondent Megan K. Stack was only twenty-five when the planes crashed into the World Trade Center in 2001. She was initially sent to cover the war in Afghanistan, then spent years in the Middle East covering Iraq, Lebanon, Israel, Egypt, Libya, and Yemen in combat zones and amid upheavals everywhere. Initially, she was excited to be in the thick of things. But slowly, she became disillusioned by the violence, and she began to wonder whether Western ideals of democracy and freedom were worth the price.

14

Activists and Advocates

Grace Lee Boggs

Grace Lee Boggs, *Living for Change: An Autobiography*, 1998.
Chinese American Grace Lee Boggs always believed in a better, more just society. Raised in New York City, she attended Barnard and Bryn Mawr. After leaving school, she chose Black causes for her activism. After moving to Detroit, she married James Boggs, a Black autoworker who joined her in her quest for justice. Together, they worked with some of the most influential names in the Black rights movement, including Malcolm X, Ruby Dee, and Stokely Carmichael. She tells her story in this autobiography.

John Brown

Richard O. Boyer, *The Legend of John Brown: A Biography and a History*, 1973.
In addition to retelling abolitionist John Brown's life, Richard O. Boyer provides a sweeping vista of slavery in the United States. He highlights the differences between the representatives opposed to it and those in its favor, both the unknown and the famous. Boyer adds depth to the story by explaining how and why John Brown did what he did. For a Black perspective written closer to his own time, see *John Brown* by African American intellectual W. E. B. Du Bois, published in 1909.

Mohandas Karamchand Gandhi

Mohandas K. Gandhi, *An Autobiography: The Story of My Experiments with Truth*, 1927.
The leader of Indian nationalism whose method of nonviolent civil disobedience ended British rule and established India's independence, Mohandas Gandhi, writes here of his "experiments" with the truth. He writes not so much of all he accomplished in his life as about his efforts to purify himself to be worthy of knowing God.

Emma Goldman

Candace Falk, *Love, Anarchy, and Emma Goldman*, 1983.
Emma Goldman shocked people in late-nineteenth and early-twentieth-century America with her radical insistence on the complete upheaval of

societal norms. She was a feminist, an advocate of free love and free speech, a promoter of birth control, a labor reformer, and an anarchist. Candace Falk draws on intimate letters between Goldman and her decade-long lover, Ben Reitman, an equally colorful character. Falk's efforts lift the curtain on Goldman's private and inner life.

Chico Mendes

Andrew Revkin, *The Burning Season: The Murder of Chico Mendes and the Fight for the Amazon Rain Forest*, 1990.

In the late twentieth century, over five hundred people were killed violently in the Amazon rainforest for speaking out against ranchers who had stolen their land and were burning large tracts of the forest. On December 2, 1988, Chico Mendes joined them. Unlike the other victims, Mendes created alliances with the global environmental movement. So, when Mendes was murdered, the Brazilian government was pressured to capture and try those responsible. Science reporter Andrew Revkin uses the Mendes story as a model for global environmental activists to follow.

Pauli Murray

Rosalind Rosenberg, *Jane Crow: The Life of Pauli Murray*, 2017.

Twentieth-century activist Pauli Murray was a mixed-race woman who left North Carolina in the 1930s to attend college and become a labor activist. She was first in her class as a law student at Howard Law School. She helped Thurgood Marshall in the *Brown v. Board of Education* case and fought against gender discrimination while on the President's Commission on the Status of Women. After obtaining her J.S.D. from Yale Law School, she convinced Betty Friedan to become the founder of NOW, meant to serve as an advocacy group for women. Later, she became an ordained priest in the Episcopal Church. In addition, she was convinced from childhood that her identity was male, and she argued publicly that identities are not fixed. History professor Rosalind Rosenberg recounts the story of this remarkable individual.

Helen Prejean

Helen Prejean, *Dead Man Walking: An Eyewitness Account of the Death Penalty in the United States*, 1993.

Roman Catholic nun Helen Prejean began a spiritual correspondence in 1982 with Louisiana death row inmate Elmo Patrick Sonnier, who had been convicted of murdering two teenagers. As their letters continued, Sister Helen realized she was communicating with a terrified man. She met the victims' families and talked with the men paid to perform executions. Through it all, she kept the Christian imperative to love in mind. After Sonnier was executed, she founded Survive, an organization devoted to helping the families of victims of violence, and she began to speak out against capital punishment.

Megan Rapinoe

Megan Rapinoe, *One Life*, 2020.

Soccer giant Megan Rapinoe garnered fame for her athletic talent. But she is equally as dedicated to social justice causes. Her outspoken messages for equal pay and LGBTQ rights have made her a hero to many globally. In this memoir, she shares how she was raised in a conservative small town and how her parents urged her to volunteer at homeless shelters and food banks. Reliving the backlash she endured as the first White athlete to take a knee in solidarity with NFL player Colin Kaepernick, she reflects on the support she also received and decides it was well worth it.

Harriet Beecher Stowe

Joan D. Hedrick, *Harriet Beecher Stowe: A Life*, 1994.

In her influential novel *Uncle Tom's Cabin*, nineteenth-century writer Harriet Beecher Stowe made a case for abolition. Though the novel has always been criticized for the ways it portrayed African Americans, it was influential enough that Abraham Lincoln said on meeting her, "So you are the little woman who wrote the book that created this great war!" Joan D. Hedrick explains the complex society in which Stowe lived and the difficult burdens placed upon women at the time. Stowe was the mother of seven children, the wife, daughter, and sister of prominent ministers, and a voice for the oppressed.

Sojourner Truth

Nell Irvin Painter, *Sojourner Truth: A Life, A Symbol*, 1996.

Historian Nell Irvin Painter recounts the life of Sojourner Truth, who was born into slavery and lived a life of physical and sexual abuse until her release. After gaining freedom, she championed the rights of Blacks in the South and women in the North. She ultimately became a symbol for both movements.

15

Environmentalists

Edward Abbey

**Charles Bowden, *The Red Caddy:*
Into the Unknown with Edward Abbey, 2018.**
> Charles Bowden, like Edward Abbey, has spent a fair amount of time in the deserts of the American Southwest. In this literary biography, he examines Abbey's work and his legacy. While Abbey wanted to protect and preserve the desert wilderness, his attention to it attracted scores of people who would have otherwise left it alone.

Andrew Blackwell

**Andrew Blackwell, *Visit Sunny Chernobyl: And Other*
Adventures in the World's Most Polluted Places, 2012.**
> Journalist Andrew Blackwell travels the world to visit the most environmentally devastated and polluted places on the planet. But rather than lament the state of these locales, Blackwell finds surprising reasons for us to accept our world as it is.

Jessica Ernst

**Andrew Nikiforuk, *Slick Water: Fracking and One Insider's*
Stand Against the World's Most Powerful Industry, 2014.**
> When Canadian biologist and oil patch consultant Jessica Ernst noticed her well water had become undrinkable and, worse, flammable, she discovered that the energy provider Encana had been fracking gas wells around her home. In the process, they had pierced her community's aquifer. Investigative journalist Andrew Nikiforuk tells how Ernst waged a legal battle against Encana, Alberta Environment, and the Energy Resources Conservation Board while explaining the science of fracking and the devastation it leaves in its wake.

Kristen Iversen

**Kristen Iversen, *Full Body Burden: Growing Up*
in the Nuclear Shadow of Rocky Flats, 2012.**
> While growing up in a town near Rocky Flats, a secret nuclear weapons plant, author Kristen Iversen often wondered why the children in her neighborhood had unusual cancers. There were other unsettling signs that things were off.

As she got older, she began investigating events like potentially catastrophic fires. But somehow, all the accidents are recorded as "incidents." Iverson eventually uncovers the government's cover-up of the damage the plant was inflicting on the environment and the people who worked there.

J. Drew Lanham

J. Drew Lanham, *The Home Place: Memoirs of a Colored Man's Love Affair with Nature*, 2016.

Naturalist, ornithologist, and professor J. Drew Lanham writes of Edgefield County, South Carolina, where he grew up. In the 1970s, he became enthralled with the natural world and wrote of it in haunting prose, earning him the Reed Award from the Southern Environmental Law Center and the Southern Book Prize.

Barry Lopez

Barry Lopez, *Embrace Fearlessly the Burning World: Essays*, 2022.

The author of *Arctic Dreams* and *Of Wolves and Men*, Barry Lopez, wrote this collection of essays in the months before he died in 2020. In it, he records his childhood memories and the expeditions he took as an adult to study life in remarkable landscapes. He also writes about a wildfire the summer before his passing, which destroyed his home place and the surrounding community. Finally, reflecting on the dangers our planet faces, he urges us to be truly present in our miraculous world.

Gerald May

Gerald G. May, *The Wisdom of Wilderness: Experiencing the Healing Power of Nature*, 2006.

Psychiatrist and author Gerald May conveys the benefits he experienced from his time in nature while hiking, camping, canoeing, fishing, or sitting. He says we don't have to drive to parks to experience wildness. Instead, we can get in touch with the wilderness no matter where we happen to be. And through rediscovering our connection to wildness, we can, in turn, begin to heal our planet.

John Muir

Linnie Marsh Wolfe, *Son of the Wilderness: The Life of John Muir*, 1978.

First published in 1945, this book about American conservationist John Muir traces his life from Scotland to the Wisconsin wilderness and finally to California. Wolfe based her book on interviews with people who knew Muir and on his papers. Muir founded the National Park System, which proved invaluable in preserving the nation's natural treasures. For his personal account of his adventures, read *My First Summer in the Sierra,* published in 1911.

Bren Smith

Bren Smith, *Eat Like a Fish: My Adventures as a Fisherman Turned Restorative Ocean Farmer,* 2019.
Former fisherman Bren Smith writes this memoir of his life on the seas, working the commercial fishing trawlers to become an ocean farmer. He wishes to renew the oceans, feed the world, and create new jobs through his vision.

16

Explorers

Neil A. Armstrong

James R. Hansen, *First Man: The Life of Neil A. Armstrong*, 2005.

History professor James R. Hansen traces the life of Neil A. Armstrong, the first human to walk on the moon. He demonstrates how Armstrong's famous quote that begins "One small step..." was misunderstood and has been cemented incorrectly in countless memories. Hansen looks at Armstrong's life against America's propensity for hero worship.

Richard E. Byrd

Richard E. Byrd, *Alone: The Classic Polar Adventure*, 1937.

When this book about Admiral Richard E. Byrd's second Antarctic expedition was published, it was an instant bestseller. And for a good reason. The famous explorer had already set records for being the first to fly over both the North Pole and South Pole. Here, he tells of his six-month solo expedition through an Antarctic winter. After he became both mentally and physically ill, he discovered a defective stovepipe was causing carbon monoxide poisoning that almost took his life.

Apsley Cherry-Garrard

Sara Wheeler, *Cherry: A Life of Apsley Cherry-Garrard*, 2001.

British explorer Apsley Cherry-Garrard had no experience or training in Antarctic exploration when he was chosen to accompany Robert Scott on his 1910–13 expedition to reach the South Pole. However, Sara Wheeler reveals, he survived the mission because he was left out of the small group chosen to travel with Scott to the actual pole. As a result, he was able to help recover the ill-fated group's bodies. Then he moved on to other adventures, including collecting emperor penguin eggs.

Michael Collins

Michael Collins, *Carrying the Fire: An Astronaut's Journeys*, 1974.

Before he became a NASA astronaut, Michael Collins was an experimental test pilot. In his accounts of the early days of the space race, he focuses on the excitement, emotions, and personalities involved in the early space explorations, in addition to his journey to the moon.

Christopher Columbus

Samuel Eliot Morison, *Admiral of the Ocean Sea: A Life of Christopher Columbus*, 1942.

To write this biography of the life of Christopher Columbus, historian Samuel Eliot Morison organized and commanded the Columbus Expedition, which sailed the same routes that Columbus followed, traveling from Spain to the U.S. and back again in 1939–40. The book contains fifty drawings, maps, and charts. Historians have revisited Columbus many times since this book was published. It may be interesting contrast this one with a more recent work like *Columbus in the Americas* by William Least Heat-Moon.

James Cook

Richard Hough, *Captain James Cook: A Biography*, 1994.

Eighteenth-century British navigator and explorer Captain James Cook became famous for his daring voyages in the Royal Navy. Cook took crews around North America, the Arctic, and the Antarctic as well as the South Pacific. His maps were astoundingly accurate. British naval historian Richard Alexander Hough tells his story.

William Dampier

Diana & Michael Preston, *A Pirate of Exquisite Mind: Explorer, Naturalist, and Buccaneer: The Life of William Dampier*, 2004.

William Dampier, dubbed the "man of exquisite mind" by Samuel Taylor Coleridge, has been overlooked by history. The Prestons tell how after beginning his career as a buccaneer in the Caribbean, Dampier circumnavigated the world three times, writing bestselling books about his adventures. He was the first to discover that ocean currents were driven by wind, and he made the finest wind maps of the time. His concept of "subspecies" influenced Darwin's work, and his description of breadfruit was the impetus behind Captain Bligh's voyage on the *Bounty*. He even beat James Cook to Australia by eighty years.

Colin Fletcher

Colin Fletcher, *The Man Who Walked Through Time*, 1967.

In 1963, Colin Fletcher hiked the length of the Grand Canyon, making him the first person ever to complete the hike in one trip and the second person ever to hike its entirety. His feat was completed before the Grand Canyon became the massive tourist destination it is today. His descriptions of the landscape, the wildlife, and the indigenous cultures he encountered are the only records of a place that no longer exists.

Sven Hedin

Sven Hedin, *My Life as an Explorer*, 1925.
Sven Hedin lived a life of adventure as a Swedish geographer, topographer, explorer, photographer, travel writer, and illustrator. In this bestselling autobiography, he shares how he discovered the sources of several rivers, including the Indus, during his four expeditions along the Silk Road in Central Asia. From the late nineteenth through the early twentieth century, he lived a life that Indiana Jones would envy.

Thor Heyerdahl

Thor Heyerdahl, *Kon-Tiki: Across the Pacific in a Raft*, 1948.
After studying Polynesian folklore, Norwegian biologist and ethnologist Thor Heyerdahl became convinced that the South Sea Islands were first populated by an ancient race from South America, led by a mythical figure named Kon-Tiki. In 1947, he set sail with a crew from Peru on a balsa raft. After three months on the open Pacific, they came to the Polynesian island of Puka Puka. Here's the firsthand account.

Scott Kelly

Scott Kelly, *Endurance: A Year in Space, A Lifetime of Discovery*, 2017.
Retired astronaut and U.S. Navy captain Scott Kelly can tell us things most people have never imagined. Here he details his full year aboard the International Space Station, where, in 2015, he and Mikhail Kornienko, a Russian cosmonaut, set the record for the most consecutive days spent in space. He details what life on board a space station is really like, the effects on the body, the fear of collision, and the agony of being separated from loved ones.

Charles A. Lindbergh

Charles A. Lindbergh, *The Spirit of St. Louis*, 1950.
This Pulitzer Prize winner recounts Charles A. Lindbergh's first nonstop flight from New York to Paris in 1927. At the time, Lindbergh was just twenty-five years old, and this flight in his single-engine monoplane, *The Spirit of St. Louis*, catapulted him to international fame. As he grew older, he wrote more award-winning books and became an environmentalist and inventor.

Fridtjof Nansen

Fridtjof Nansen, *Farthest North*, 1897.

Norwegian explorer, scientist, diplomat, and humanitarian Fridtjof Nansen tells of his incredible voyage to the North Pole in 1893 aboard the *Fram*, a ship designed to withstand the pressures of ice in the polar regions. Since the ship's technology was untried, many predicted a tragic end for the voyage. Yet the future Nobel Laureate detailed his trip and his fifteen-month sled ride to the North Pole.

Marco Polo

Marco Polo, *The Travels of Marco Polo*, 1298.

In the thirteenth century, young Marco Polo traveled to China along the Silk Road. He later retold his adventures that are recorded in this work. While the original copies of this book have been lost, his story has been copied and recopied since it was first written. His descriptions of sights, such as the court of Kublai Khan, offer a peek at a world long gone.

John Wesley Powell

Donald Worster, *A River Running West: The Life of John Wesley Powell*, 2000.

The story of John Wesley Powell, the nineteenth-century explorer and scientist who led the first expedition to the Colorado River in 1869, is told by Donald Worster, historian of the American West. Powell introduced the Grand Canyon to the world. While experiencing dangers and accidents, he made important rock and fossil discoveries. Though he became a conservationist and advocate for the land, he was silenced by a powerful group of politicians bent on the region's economic development.

Ernest Shackleton

Alfred Lansing, *Endurance: Shackleton's Incredible Voyage*, 1959.

American journalist Alfred Lansing tells the story of Ernest Shackleton's 1914 effort to make it to the South Pole, only to be locked in by ice with his twenty-seven-man crew. After their ship was crushed, they attempted to cross 850 miles of monstrous seas to get to the closest human settlement.

Chuck Yeager

Chuck Yeager, *Yeager: An Autobiography*, 1985.

General Chuck Yeager, an American hero, talks about his incredible career, first as a fighter pilot in World War II who escaped the Nazis after being shot down over France, then as a test pilot after the war. Yeager was the first person to break the sound barrier.

17

Travelers

Gertrude Bell

Georgina Howell, *Gertrude Bell: Queen of the Desert, Shaper of Nations*, 2006.

Born to a wealthy British family in 1868, Gertrude Bell was a maverick who was once the most powerful woman in the British Empire. Her amazing life included careers as an archaeologist, spy, linguist, author, photographer, and mountaineer. Bell was so determined to succeed that when her skirt got in her way, she took it off to climb the Alps in her underwear. She traveled the Middle East with only her servants and guns, and she had a hand in shaping Iraq's boundaries.

Robert Byron

Robert Byron, *The Road to Oxiana*, 1937.

Early-twentieth-century British traveler Robert Byron set off for the Middle East, making his way to Oxiana through Beirut, Jerusalem, Baghdad, and Teheran. Oxiana was the ancient name for the region along the Amu Darya River between Afghanistan and Russia at the time of the Soviet Union. The area is now inaccessible to most Westerners, making Byron's descriptions informative and entertaining. He includes all sorts of artifacts from his travels in the book, like newspaper clippings, signs, and comic dialogues.

Bruce Chatwin

Nicholas Shakespeare, *Bruce Chatwin: A Biography*, 1993.

Award-winning British novelist Nicholas Shakespeare writes about the perplexing travel writer Bruce Chatwin. As a largely self-educated man, Chatwin traveled the world gathering accolades for his first book, *In Patagonia*. Yet, while he collected art and served as a director of Sotheby's, he lived a nomadic life and looked down on material possessions. And while he was married for twenty-three years, Chatwin had a string of male lovers from all over the globe. Shakespeare exposes the personal myth that followed him to his death.

Richard Henry Dana Jr.

Richard Henry Dana Jr., *Two Years Before the Mast*, 1840.

In 1834, Harvard student Richard Henry Dana Jr. decided to take a few years off to explore, as was typical for Harvard students at the time. But as his family wasn't wealthy, he enlisted as a common sailor aboard the *Pilgrim* and set sail around Cape Horn. He kept a diary, and upon returning to Massachusetts, he used it to write this classic travelogue.

William Dalrymple

William Dalrymple, *In Xanadu: A Quest*, 1989.
Internationally recognized Scottish history writer William Dalrymple wrote this bestselling book when he was twenty-two. After finishing his undergraduate work, he decided to take a trip. Instead of heading to the South of France or Italy, like many of his classmates, he retraced the steps of Marco Polo from Jerusalem to Xanadu, where the palace of Kublai Khan was located, north of Peking. His account of this trip is entertaining and informative.

Alexandra David-Néel

Alexandra David-Néel, *My Journey to Lhasa: The Classic Story of the Only Western Woman Who Succeeded in Entering the Forbidden City*, 1927.
French explorer, scholar, anarchist, and Buddhist writer Alexandra David-Néel, though a Parisian of genteel background, had to disguise herself with yak hair extensions to pass as a beggar so she could get into Tibet and reach Lhasa, the forbidden city. The journey, which she undertook in 1923, was her fifth journey to Asia. She was the first Western woman to be received by the Dalai Lama.

Martin Fletcher

Martin Fletcher, *Walking Israel: A Personal Search for the Soul of a Nation*, 2010.
News correspondent Martin Fletcher spent a year walking the 100-mile coast of Israel, from Lebanon to Gaza, searching for the region's history and seeking to understand its current state.

Richard Halliburton

Richard Halliburton, *The Royal Road to Romance*, 1925.
When writer Richard Halliburton graduated from Princeton, he decided to travel the world. Visiting all sorts of exotic places, he used every situation to experience all the adventure he could. He climbed the Matterhorn, and he was jailed in Gibraltar. Halliburton died young after drowning while attempting to sail a Chinese junk as a publicity stunt in 1939.

Signe Pike

Signe Pike, *Faery Tale: One Woman's Search for Enchantment in a Modern World*, 2010.

Like many of us today, former editor Signe Pike realized she had lost her zest for life in everyday routines of overwork. So to regain her "lost sense of wonder and the joy of surprise," she decided to embark on an international search for faeries. She records her experiences from Mexico to Scotland and helps readers understand that it's possible to regain enchantment in seeking.

George Frederick Ruxton

George Frederick Ruxton, *Life in the Far West*, 1848.

In the 1840s, British explorer and travel writer George F. Ruxton, a former lieutenant in the British Army, traveled around Africa, Canada, the United States, and Mexico. In this book, he discusses his time with the trappers and traders of America's West, also known as the Mountain Men. He introduces readers to companions he met on prairies and in forests, like Killbuck and Old Bill Williams, sharing what they eat and the stories they tell around campfires. Ruxton later died in St. Louis at age twenty-seven.

Freya Stark

Freya Stark, *The Valleys of the Assassins: And Other Persian Travels*, 1934.

Born in Paris, early-twentieth-century traveler Freya Stark traveled to Luristan, between Iraq and present-day Iran. Without a lot of money and usually with a single guide, she met the nomadic peoples who lived in the region. Gaining their trust, she was welcomed into their world. She retells their ancient stories, including the ones about the Assassins, a group of hashish-eating terrorists from the Elburz Mountains.

Paul Theroux

Paul Theroux, *The Old Patagonia Express: By Train Through the Americas*, 1979.

Travel writer and novelist Paul Theroux began this journey in Boston on a commuter train. From train to train, he makes his way from New England to South America's southernmost tip. He recounts his experiences and the (sometimes famous) people he meets along the way.

18

Immigrant Accounts

Elizabeth Miki Brina

Elizabeth Miki Brina, *Speak, Okinawa: A Memoir,* **2021.**
Elizabeth Miki Brina reveals the sense of unease she felt growing up in her youth in upstate New York as the daughter of a former U.S. soldier stationed in Okinawa and a former nightclub hostess he met there. As she comes to terms with her mother's estrangement and her sense of inferiority due to her own experiences, Brina grapples with her identity and what it means to be American.

Francisco Cantú

Francisco Cantú, *The Line Becomes a River: Dispatches from the Border,* **2018.**
After being raised by a mother who was a former park ranger and daughter of a Mexican immigrant in the American Southwest, Francisco Cantú joined the U.S. Border Patrol. However, he resigned after tracking smugglers across their routes days and nights; finding the dead and rescuing the living became too much. Here he writes a personal account of the issues and impacts surrounding the U.S. and Mexican border.

Marcelo Hernandez Castillo

Marcelo Hernandez Castillo, *Children of the Land: A Memoir,* **2020.**
Marcelo Hernandez Castillo came to America with his undocumented parents when he was only five years old. He learned early that survival in his new country meant staying invisible. Honing his ability to speak English for survival, he fit in seamlessly. But he always feared his family would one day be ripped apart. Then his worst fears were realized. Now an award-winning poet, essayist, and translator, Castillo traces his journey to immigration advocacy.

Deogratias

Tracy Kidder, *Strength in What Remains,* **2000.**
After escaping from Burundi, Deo, a Rwandan Tutsi, arrives in America with no contacts. He has only two hundred dollars in his pocket and doesn't speak English. But, after sleeping in Central Park and eking out a living delivering

groceries, he meets people willing to help. He makes his way through medical school and devotes himself to healing. Acclaimed writer Tracy Kidder helps him tell his story of hope and heroism.

Enrique

Sonia Nazario, *Enrique's Journey: The Story of a Boy's Dangerous Odyssey to Reunite with His Mother*, 2005.

At age five, Enrique watched his mother pack to leave him and his siblings in Honduras so she could go to the United States to find work. Eleven years passed without his mother's return. Finally, at age sixteen, Enrique leaves Honduras to find her. Journalist Sonia Nazario traces his dangerous journey through Mexico with other migrants, many children, playing a deadly game of hide-and-seek with gangsters, bandits, corrupt police, and immigration authorities. Enrique is one of the thousands of children who risk the desperate path to find their parents.

Aida Hernandez

Aaron Bobrow-Strain, *The Death and Life of Aida Hernandez: A Border Story*, 2019.

When she was eight, Aida Hernandez and her siblings crossed the Mexican border with their mother to live in Arizona. Aida learned to speak English and fit in with her peers by watching TV shows like *Friends*. Then, at sixteen, she gave birth to a son. But, as Aaron Bobrow-Strain relates, a misstep led to her deportation to Mexico, a country that now felt foreign. Separated from her son, she fought to make her way back to the U.S.

Lia Lee

Anne Fadiman, *The Spirit Catches You and You Fall Down: A Hmong Child, Her American Doctors, and the Collision of Two Cultures*, 1997.

Born to a family of recently arrived Hmong immigrants, Lia Lee developed signs of epilepsy early on. By 1988, when she was just six years old, she lived with her family at home but had become brain-dead due to repeated misunderstandings between the doctors and the family. Anne Fadiman writes the account objectively and refuses to blame either side. But the outcome of failure to communicate was a tragedy that perhaps could have been avoided.

Domingo Martinez

Domingo Martinez, *The Boy Kings of Texas: A Memoir*, 2012.

Writer Domingo Martinez relates what it was like to grow up in the border town of Brownsville, Texas, beside the Rio Grande, in the 1980s. He writes poetically about the important people in his life, like his brother Daniel and "the Mimis," two of his older sisters who managed to convince people they were upper-class White girls. The world he reveals is by turns brutal and charming.

Wayétu Moore

Wayétu Moore, *The Dragons, the Giant, the Women: A Memoir*, 2020.

The First Liberian Civil War broke out when Wayétu Moore was five years old. She, her father, and her grandmother fled their home in Monrovia, Liberia, and set off on foot, traveling for three weeks. After making it to the village of Lai, a rebel soldier smuggled them into Sierra Leone. From there, they made it to the United States. Moore writes about this experience and what life was like for her as an African immigrant growing up in Texas. In the end, she returns to Liberia and deals with the memories.

Phuc Tran

Phuc Tran, *Sigh, Gone: A Misfit's Memoir of Great Books, Punk Rock, and the Fight to Fit In*, 2020.

When Phuc Tran immigrated with his family to the United States during the 1975 fall of Saigon, he had difficulty fitting in with his schoolmates in Carlisle, Pennsylvania. In this memoir, he captures what it was like to be a self-conscious teen who doesn't fit in and seeks solace in classic literature and punk rock music.

Erika L. Sánchez

Erika L. Sánchez, *Crying in the Bathroom: A Memoir*, 2022.

Poet, novelist, and essayist Erika L. Sánchez grew up in Chicago in the 1990s as the daughter of Mexican immigrants. Often in trouble for her irrepressible sense of humor, foul language, and gothic sense of style, she nevertheless overcame the forces against her with great success. Her memoir comes across as a confessional with a best friend who leaves you exhilarated and emotionally spent.

Michelle Zauner

Michelle Zauner, *Crying in H Mart: A Memoir*, 2021.

Michelle Zauner, singer, songwriter, and guitarist for the band Japanese Breakfast, reflects on what it was like to grow up as one of a handful of Asian American kids in Eugene, Oregon. Her high school years were painful, but she fondly remembers visiting her grandmother in Seoul. After moving to the East Coast to attend college, she begins to lose her grip on her sense of being Korean. After discovering her mother has terminal cancer, Zauner reconnects with her heritage and realizes all she inherited from her mother.

19

The Courts and Justice

Clarence Darrow

John A. Farrell, *Clarence Darrow: Attorney for the Damned*, 2011.

Progressive lawyer Clarence Darrow left a lucrative career representing railroads to take up the causes of poor workers, Black individuals, and other social and political outcasts. He is perhaps most famous for arguing the Scopes "Monkey Trial" as portrayed in *Inherit the Wind*. John A. Farrell used unpublished correspondence and memoirs to reveal a man who, while brilliant, was also terrible with finances and with his relationships with women and with his law partner, the famous poet Edgar Lee Masters. The book contains shocking disclosures about the legendary lawyer.

Wyatt Earp

Casey Tefertiller, *Wyatt Earp: The Life behind the Legend*, 1997.

Most are familiar with Wyatt Earp as the lawman who killed several rogue cowboys at the shootout at the O.K. Corral. But there was much more to Earp than an upright lawman in the lawless West. Casey Tefertiller supplies the facts surrounding Earp and his brothers, who sometimes played surprising roles in crime and politics. In addition, Tefertiller reveals the origins of the myths.

Ruth Bader Ginsberg

Irin Carmon and Shana Knizhnik, *Notorious RBG: The Life and Times of Ruth Bader Ginsberg*, 2015.

In this biography of Supreme Court justice Ruth Bader Ginsberg, Carmon and Knizhnik tell how Ginsberg worked as an advocate for women and gender rights. "RGB," as her supporters called her, was the second woman to serve on the Supreme Court. The authors seek to show the human being behind the icon. The book was published before Ginsberg's death in 2020.

John Marshall Harlan

Peter S. Canellos, *The Great Dissenter: The Story of John Marshall Harlan, America's Judicial Hero*, 2021.
When John Marshall Harlan first took his place on the U.S. Supreme Court in 1877, he was reluctant to stand against his fellow justices. But as he witnessed northern White people moving to take away Black people's rights to appease the South, he decided to break with his colleagues. In his dissents, like *Plessy v. Ferguson*, he provided a path to end segregation. Without his opinions, the New Deal and the civil rights movement may not have been successful.

Paul Holes

Paul Holes, *Unmasked: My Life Solving America's Cold Cases*, 2022.
The Golden State Killer, Laci Peterson, Jaycee Dugard—what they all have in common is that detective Paul Holes doggedly stayed on the trail to bring justice to each victim involved. Now he writes a memoir about the impacts his work on these cases over twenty years have had on his life. He admits he has paid a tremendous personal price in fighting evil.

Oliver Wendell Holmes

Thomas Healy, *The Great Dissent: How Oliver Wendell Holmes Changed His Mind— and Changed the History of Free Speech in America*, 2013.
The First Amendment to the U.S. Constitution clarifies that the government can make no law curtailing Americans' right to free speech. But until the first few decades of the twentieth century, Americans were often imprisoned for speaking out against the government. Supreme Court justice Oliver Wendell Holmes was a lifelong conservative who took a dim view of individual rights. Yet, in 1919, he wrote the court opinion that set the standard for free speech as we know it today.

Thurgood Marshall

Gilbert King, *Devil in the Grove: Thurgood Marshall, the Groveland Boys, and the Dawn of a New America*, 2012.
In 1949, Thurgood Marshall was preparing to argue the *Brown v. Board of Education* suit before the U.S. Supreme Court. But before it went to trial, he became involved in a case in the Florida citrus groves that began when a White girl claimed to have been raped by four Black men. By that day's end, the Ku Klux Klan had burned Blacks' homes to the ground and chased hundreds of people into the swamps to find "the Groveland Boys"—four young

men who stood accused. Gilbert King tells us how Thurgood Marshall risked his career and life to bring justice to the people of Groveland.

Sonia Sotomayor

Sonia Sotomayor, *My Beloved World*, 2013.

Sitting justice Sonia Sotomayor is the first Latinx and the third woman ever appointed to the U.S. Supreme Court. Growing up in a Brooklyn housing project, the child of Puerto Rican parents, she decided as a young girl that she would become a lawyer one day. She became her class valedictorian, graduated with honors from Princeton, and went to Yale Law School. In this memoir, she tells of her mentors, her created family, and her vision for America.

20

Law and the Prison System

John Wilkes Booth

Michael W. Kauffman, *American Brutus:*
***John Wilkes Booth and the Lincoln Conspiracies*, 2004.**

Lincoln assassination expert Michael W. Kauffman conducted exhaustive research into archives and recent scholarship to understand why famed actor John Wilkes Booth shot and killed President Abraham Lincoln. He even recreated some of the events himself and spent time in Booth's house to understand what happened. As a result, he determines that Booth truly believed that Lincoln was set to become "an American Caesar" who would end American liberty.

Lizzie Borden

Cara Robertson, *The Trial of Lizzie Borden:*
***A True Story*, 2019.**

In August 1892, a couple named Andrew and Abby Borden were hacked to death in their home in Fall River, Massachusetts. When their daughter Lizzie was arrested for the murders, an international media circus erupted. The hype and fascination with the case lasted for over a century. Attorney Cara Robertson revisited the case, diving into the lawyers' journals, legal proceedings, and a previously unknown letter written by Lizzie to come to her conclusion about the case.

Anders Behring Breivik

Åsne Seierstad, *One of Us: The Story of Anders Breivik*
***and the Massacre in Norway*, 2013.**

July 22, 2011, was a dark day in Norwegian history. A gifted young man named Anders Breivik first set off a bomb outside government buildings in the capital, Oslo, then made his way to a youth camp on the island of Utova, where he killed sixty-nine teens, most of whom belonged to Norway's Labor Party. Åsne Seierstad explores how Breivik became a right-wing activist who wanted to save Norway from the threats of Islam and multiculturalism.

Cyntoia Brown-Long

Cyntoia Brown-Long, *Free Cyntoia: My Search for Redemption in the American Prison System*, 2019.

Cyntoia Brown had been behind bars for almost half her life when she gained freedom at age thirty-one. At age sixteen, Cyntoia committed a murder and was sentenced to prison for life. While serving time, she wrote this memoir to explain how she wound up where she did. As a child of an alcoholic, sex-trafficked teenager, Cyntoia had nowhere to turn growing up. As a result, she became the victim of a predator. Once in prison, she decided to make her life worth living, even if she spent the rest of her life incarcerated. When her story became public, calls for her release led to clemency.

James "Whitey" Bulger

Kevin Cullen and Shelley Murphy, *Whitey Bulger: America's Most Wanted Gangster and the Manhunt That Brought Him to Justice*, 2013.

Boston Globe reporters Kevin Cullen and Shelley Murphy tell how one of the most wanted men of his generation was arrested and tried for his prolific criminal career that included everything from bank robberies to murders. After serving time in prison, Bulger reunited with his brother Billy and the FBI agent, John Connolly, who helped him become a powerful Massachusetts politician. With Connolly's help, Whitey became an almost untouchable crime boss. This sordid story only ended with Bulger's capture in Santa Monica in June 2011.

Ted Bundy

Ann Rule, *The Stranger Beside Me*, 1980.

Crime reporter Ann Rule was in a chilling position when she discovered her co-worker on a crisis hotline and close friend was, in fact, a serial killer. What makes the situation doubly disturbing is that when Rule began researching the case, the murders were still unsolved. Rule goes into harrowing detail about the horrors she endured as she slowly realized she had a personal relationship with the killer of at least thirty-six women.

Al Capone

Jonathan Eig, *Get Capone: The Secret Plot That Captured America's Most Wanted Gangster*, 2010.

Jonathan Eig narrates the rise and fall of America's most notorious crime boss. Arriving in Chicago in 1920, Capone took advantage of Prohibition to begin a bootlegging business that set off a wave of terror that eventually corrupted the Chicago police department and court system. Eig uses newly uncovered information to shed light on the St. Valentine's Day massacre and Capone's capture.

Henri Charrière

Henri Charrière, *Papillon*, 1969.

In 1931, Henri Charrière, called Papillon because of a butterfly tattoo on his chest, was convicted of committing a murder of which he was innocent. After his imprisonment in French Guiana, he became determined to escape. Over the years, he tried many times and failed. Finally, he was sent to Devil's Island. From here, he made his final escape. In 1973, a major motion picture starring Steve McQueen and Dustin Hoffman told his story.

David Crow

David Crow, *The Pale-Faced Lie: A True Story*, 2019.

David Crow grew up with his siblings on a Navajo reservation. As children, they thought their dad, Thurston Crow, was the greatest man alive. A self-taught Cherokee, he thrilled them with his World War II stories. But as David grew older, he discovered his dad was also a criminal who compelled his son to help with his crimes, threatening him with violence if he refused. David's mentally ill mother was no help. Amazingly, David got into college and began a successful career. But when he refused to continue helping his father with his lawless enterprises, his dad set out to get revenge.

Alfonso "Little Al" D'Arco

Jerry Capeci and Tom Robbins, *Mob Boss: The Life of Little Al D'Arco, the Man Who Brought Down the Mafia*, 2013.

Growing up in Brooklyn and working in Manhattan's Little Italy, "Little Al" D'Arco learned the lessons of the mafia early on. But when he found he had been marked for death, he turned on the Lucchese crime family and became a government witness who helped bring down the boss John Gotti. After spending hours conversing with D'Arco, Capeci and Robbins relate incredible stories of New York City's organized underbelly.

Al Dunlap

John A. Byrne, *Chainsaw: The Notorious Career of Al Dunlap in the Era of Profit-at-Any-Price*, 1999.

They called him "Chainsaw Al," and Al Dunlap earned the moniker through his ruthless downsizing of corporations for short-term shareholder profit. Unfortunately, his actions paved the way for the downfalls of Enron, WorldCom, and Tyco, where the use of the illusion of gain and outright lies misled investors, resulting in illegal profits. *Business Week* writer John A.

Byrne tells how Dunlap came to power and of the massive damage he did when he got there.

Adolf Eichmann

David Cesarani, *Becoming Eichmann: Rethinking the Life, Crimes, and Trial of a "Desk Murderer,"* 2004.

Adolf Eichmann held an essential role in Nazi concentration camps. He was the bureaucrat in charge of the massive logistics involved in deporting and executing two million Jews. In this first biography of Eichmann since the years immediately following his execution in Jerusalem, historian David Cesarani uses previously unavailable documents to present a picture previously hidden.

Pablo Escobar

Gabriel García Márquez, *News of a Kidnapping*, 1996.

In 1990, Medellin drug boss Pablo Escobar abducted ten men and women, primarily journalists, to extort the Colombian government for guarantees that he and other traffickers would not be extradited to the U.S. Acclaimed novelist Gabriel García Márquez uses his sizable journalistic skills to tell this fantastic story of a nation where corruption is rampant, but so is hope.

Chris George

John Temple, *American Pain: How a Young Felon and His Ring of Doctors Unleashed America's Deadliest Drug Epidemic*, 2015.

Investigative journalist John Temple traces the incredible story of Chris George, the founder of American Pain, a clinic in Florida that employed doctors to distribute oxycodone to customers, most of whom were traffickers and addicts. George grew up in South Florida, the son of a home builder. He and his twin brother spent their younger years involved in all sorts of shady dealings when, at age twenty-seven, George discovered the market for painkillers. At the time, in Florida, no one was tracking the patients. After just two years in the business, George had made over $40 million. Most of the pills were sold on the streets in the rest of the country, ruining countless lives.

Gary Gilmore

Mikal Gilmore, *Shot in the Heart*, 1994.

In 1977, Gary Gilmore was executed, as he had requested. Norman Mailer recorded the event in *The Executioner's Song*. In this biography and memoir, Gilmore's brother Mikal tells how Gilmore became a murderer. It's a story of a family racked by generations of child abuse, alcoholism, crime, adultery, and murder.

Willie J. Grimes

Benjamin Rachlin, *Ghost of the Innocent Man: A True Story of Trial and Redemption*, 2017.

In 1988, a North Carolina man with no record of violence named Willie J. Grimes was wrongly convicted of first-degree rape and sentenced to life in prison. Benjamin Rachlin tells how the efforts of Christine Mumma, a cofounder of the state's Innocence Inquiry Commission, helped clear his name. While he was eventually acquitted, Grimes's story is far from unique. Rachlin sheds light on the inadequacies of our criminal justice system and makes suggestions to improve it.

Patty Hearst

Jeffrey Toobin, *American Heiress: The Wild Saga of the Kidnapping, Crimes and Trial of Patty Hearst*, 2016.

As an heir to the William Randolph Hearst fortune, college sophomore Patty Hearst seemed to have it all. But on February 4, 1974, she was kidnapped by an odd assortment of people calling themselves the Symbionese Liberation Army. Her desperate family tried to get her back, but then she was captured on bank security cameras holding a machine gun during a bank robbery. The bizarre story, including her trial, was a media circus. Her experience was seen as an example of Stockholm syndrome.

Jesse James

T. J. Stiles, *Jesse James: Last Rebel of the Civil War*, 2002.

While the popular image of Jesse James has often been as an apolitical hero who robbed from the rich to give to the poor, the real Jesse James uncovered by T. J. Stiles is quite different. James, born in Missouri to a pro-slavery home, became a Confederate guerrilla soldier, called a bushwhacker, who terrorized border states. When the war was over, James continued to perpetrate often savage acts of terror to bring the Confederate cause back to life.

Jim Jones

Jeff Guinn, *The Road to Jonestown: Jim Jones and Peoples Temple*, 2017.

Journalist Jeff Guinn delves into the history of twentieth-century minister, civil rights leader, and cult leader Jim Jones. He traces Jones's early days of preaching a blend of Christianity and Marxism. After moving his racially mixed congregation, Peoples Temple, to Northern California, Jones became involved in politics. Guinn covers the unsavory aspects of Jones's life, from drug use to fraudulent faith healings. His life ended in Guyana, South America, when he led a murder–suicide in which he ordered nine hundred of his followers, including infants and children, to consume a cyanide-laced drink.

Ted Kaczynski

Jamie Gehring, *Madman in the Woods: Life Next Door to the Unabomber*, 2022.

For sixteen years, Jamie Gehring's family shared a backyard with a man who lived alone and only occasionally interacted with her family. They noted his unusual behavior but assumed he was "just the odd hermit" and, in hindsight, overlooked clues that could have indicated his propensity for violence. After finding that he had spent seventeen years sending explosives to strangers, Gehring began investigating Kaczynski's past and discovered that she and her family were future targets.

Charles Manson

Jeff Guinn, *Manson: The Life and Times of Charles Manson*, 2013.

In the late 1960s, the world was shocked by a series of brutal murders in California, including the stabbing of pregnant actress Sharon Tate. The story got even more bizarre when the crimes were traced to Charles Manson and his commune of followers, mostly young women. Jeff Guinn gained access to relatives that had never been willing to do interviews. They talk about Manson's life of crime from a young age. Guinn discusses how and why Manson had such influence over his followers and what led him to such horrific actions.

Lee Harvey Oswald

Gerald Posner, *Case Closed: Lee Harvey Oswald and the Assassination of JFK*, 1993.

Since 1963, conspiracy theories and sincere questioning have led many to doubt whether Lee Harvey Oswald acted alone when he shot and killed President John F. Kennedy in Dallas. Attorney and award-winning journalist Gerald Posner examined all the available evidence to conclude reasonably and finally that Oswald was solely responsible and that he acted alone.

Sister Ping

Patrick Radden Keefe, *The Snakehead: An Epic Tale of the Chinatown Underworld and the American Dream*, 2009.

In the 1980s, the United States began to receive Chinese immigrants from the Fujian province, many of whom settled in New York's Chinatown. Once here, they formed a shadow economy that was run by criminal gangs. Sister Ping, a middle-aged grandmother, became the head of this business empire. She ran an underground bank for illegal Chinese immigrants from the back of a noodle store on Hester Street. But that was just a cover for her real business: smuggling people globally. No one knew about the activities until 1993 when a ship with three hundred undocumented immigrants ran aground off a beach in Queens.

Edwin Rist

Kirk Wallace Johnson, *The Feather Thief: Beauty, Obsession, and the Natural History Heist of the Century*, 2018.

Author and fly fisherman Kirk Wallace Johnson became intrigued with the story of American flute player Edwin Rist when he heard about him from a fly fishing guide in New Mexico. He learned that after performing in a concert at London's Royal Academy of Music, Rist took a train to the British Museum of Natural History. From there he stole hundreds of bird skins, some from birds 150 years old, to feed his salmon fly fishing obsession. Johnson soon became obsessed with Rist and spent years investigating the story of the crime and what became of the skins.

Aleksandr Solzhenitsyn

Aleksandr I. Solzhenitsyn, *The Gulag Archipelago, 1918–1956: An Experiment in Literary Investigation*, 1973.

In this first volume of his memoir detailing his time in a Soviet gulag, Russian novelist and historian Aleksandr Solzhenitsyn narrates how he was arrested and interrogated before being sent to a forced labor camp. His writing shed light on the secret police and their web of spies who existed to keep citizens in line.

Albert Speer

Gitta Sereny, *Albert Speer: His Battle with Truth*, 1995.

Austrian-born journalist and historian Gitta Sereny examines the life and motivations of Albert Speer, Hitler's armaments minister and close friend. Sereny became intimately acquainted with Speer in the years before he died. She recounts his insider story of the Third Reich while trying to understand the capacity of ordinary people to commit acts of evil.

Adnan Syed

Rabia Chaudry, *Adnan's Story: The Search for Truth and Justice After* Serial, 2016.

Attorney Rabia Chaudry was a friend of Adnan Syed, who was convicted and sentenced to life in prison plus thirty years for the murder of Hae Min Lee, a high school senior in Baltimore, Maryland. Syed, who was Lee's ex-boyfriend, had always claimed to be innocent, and Chaudry believed his story. In 2013, she contacted Sarah Koenig, a producer of *This American Life,* who turned the story into the podcast *Serial.* Chaudry, however, says *Serial* didn't reveal everything. She sets forth her arguments for his innocence here.

Lori Vallow and Chad Daybell

Leah Sottile, *When the Moon Turns to Blood: Lori Vallow, Chad Daybell, and a Story of Murder, Wild Faith, and End Times*, 2022.

Investigative reporter Leah Sottile explores what can happen when extreme religious beliefs combine with end-of-world prophecies through the story of former beauty queen Lori Vallow and her husband, doomsday novelist Chad Daybell. Dead bodies, including those of their children, seemed to accumulate around the couple.

Alia Volz

Alia Volz, *Home Baked: My Mom, Marijuana, and the Stoning of San Francisco*, 2020.

Alia Volz writes fondly of her mother, an early entrepreneur in marijuana sales. Running Sticky Fingers Brownies in the 1970s, when marijuana was completely illegal and in the same category as heroin, was a risky venture. Her mom made a lot of money delivering brownies all over San Francisco, sometimes hidden in Alia's stroller. After her parents divorced, Alia and her mom returned to San Francisco in the 1980s to use the Sticky Fingers distribution channels to provide medical marijuana.

Abdulrahman and Kathy Zeitoun

Dave Eggers, *Zeitoun*, 2009.

In August 2005, Hurricane Katrina hit New Orleans. Kathy Zeitoun left the city days ahead of landfall, leaving her husband, Abdulrahman, to watch over their house-painting business. In the aftermath, Zeitoun makes his way around the city in a canoe, helping the stranded and the elderly. But on September 6, he was arrested by police officers bearing M-16s and accused of terrorism.

Butch Cassidy and the Sundance Kid

Thom Hatch, *The Last Outlaws: The Lives and Legends of Butch Cassidy and the Sundance Kid*, 2013.

In the late 1890s, the Wild Bunch, a group of criminals led by Butch Cassidy and the Sundance Kid, conducted bank and train robberies across the American West. Robbing only from the wealthy, they evaded capture until the early twentieth century. Then, knowing that their robbing methods would no longer work, they left with a woman named Etta Place to go to South America, where their careers finally ended. Thom Hatch uses new material to shed light on this pair of outlaws.

21

Moneymakers and Industrialists

Benjamin Graham

Benjamin Graham, *Benjamin Graham: The Memoirs of the Dean of Wall Street*, 1996.

American economist and professional investor Benjamin Graham was an early practitioner of value-based fundamental analysis. He later took his ideas to Columbia Business School, where he began teaching in 1928. Among his acolytes were Walter J. Schloss and Warren Buffett.

Milton S. Hershey

Michael D'Antonio, *Hershey: Milton S. Hershey's Extraordinary Life of Wealth, Empire, and Utopian Dreams*, 2006.

Most Americans have enjoyed at least one Hershey's chocolate bar, but few know the story of the company's founder. Pulitzer Prize–winning author Michael D'Antonio writes his rags-to-riches story. After being raised by a single mother who was left by Hershey's father when he was still a boy, Hershey began his career with two unsuccessful candy shops. Then, he went on to start the Lancaster Caramel Company. Selling this profitable company allowed him to begin his successful chocolate company. But Hershey was also a progressive thinker who believed in treating his employees well. And in the end, he left his fortune to a boys' school and an orphanage.

Howard Hughes

Donald L. Barlett and James B. Steele, *Empire: The Life, Legend, and Madness of Howard Hughes*, 1979.

During his heyday, Howard Hughes was one of the wealthiest men in the world. He made his money through a combination of his father's business, Hollywood movies, and aviation. He was an international celebrity during his younger years, and his name was synonymous with great wealth. But later, Hughes became a recluse and a notorious germaphobe. In this book, Donald Barlett and James Steele seek to crack the façade to reveal the man.

Phil Knight

Phil Knight, *Shoe Dog: A Memoir by the Creator of Nike*, 2016.

In many ways, Phil Knight, founder and CEO of Nike, is a self-made man. After finishing business school in 1962, he forged his own path. Knight borrowed fifty dollars from his father and invested it in inexpensive athletic shoes from Japan. He sold them from his car's trunk, earning $8,000 his first year. By 2016, his company was earning more than $30 billion a year. He writes here of the obstacles he overcame and the friendships he cultivated along the way.

Charles and David Koch

Christopher Leonard, *Kochland: The Secret History of Koch Industries and Corporate Power in America*, 2019.

Koch industries has affected your life even if you're unaware of it. Christopher Leonard reveals how CEO Charles Koch has taken the enterprise he and his brother David inherited and expanded it to become one of the biggest private corporations on the planet. They are responsible for the fertilizers used on our food and produce the synthetics that make our diapers and fabrics. They have a hand in other businesses as well. Before David died in 2019, the brothers made more money than Goldman Sachs, Facebook, and U.S. Steel combined. They also influenced the loss of unions, the growth of the income divide, and the lack of progress on climate change. Read this book to understand why.

J. P. Morgan

Jean Strouse, *Morgan: American Financier*, 1999.

Using previously unavailable material, biographer Jean Strouse wrote an entirely updated biography of J. Pierpont Morgan. In it, she reveals a human being who rose to great heights, earning the nickname "the Napoleon of Wall Street," by creating trusts. He even made a one-man bank that served as the U.S. Federal Reserve System before the institution was created in 1913. His private life, filled with art, family, and mistresses, was as colorful as his career.

Elon Musk

Ashlee Vance, *Elon Musk: Tesla, SpaceX, and the Quest for a Fantastic Future*, 2015.

Award-winning writer Ashlee Vance's biography of Elon Musk takes readers from his turbulent childhood in South Africa to his innovations and financial success through companies like SpaceX and Tesla. Through his wealth and future-driven vision, Musk has become a celebrity with quirks and choices that make him as compelling and controversial as Howard Hughes. In the years since this book's publication, Musk has stayed in the spotlight, continuing to confound and amaze.

Peter Thiel

Max Chafkin, *The Contrarian:*
Peter Thiel and Silicon Valley's Power of Pursuit, 2021.

Billionaire Peter Thiel enormously influenced the development of Silicon Valley, Wall Street, and Washington. Yet he is a very private man who, unlike Elon Musk and Mark Zuckerberg, spends little time in the mainstream media spotlight. Yet Thiel has directly influenced the technology we use, how we handle our finances, and even the candidates we choose to vote for. Moreover, he has used his substantial wealth to back far-right candidates. Max Chafkin details Thiel's background from childhood with his immigrant parents to his education at Stanford and his massive influence on today's world.

Cornelius Vanderbilt

T. J. Stiles, *The First Tycoon:*
The Epic Life of Cornelius Vanderbilt, 2009.

America's first industry magnate was Cornelius "Commodore" Vanderbilt. T. J. Stiles describes how Vanderbilt rose from humble beginnings on Staten Island, where he was born while George Washington was president. From there, he became the head of a railroad empire that launched the transportation revolution. But Vanderbilt did more than amass wealth. Stiles demonstrates how Vanderbilt helped create the world we live in today. He shows Vanderbilt's contradictory but very human private life by providing behind-the-scenes looks.

Madame C. J. Walker

A'Lelia Bundles, *All About Madam C. J. Walker*, 2018.

Madame C. J. Walker was the first Black female multi-millionaire in America. A'Lelia Perry Bundles writes of how Walker, her great-great-grandmother, went from her childhood as the daughter of enslaved persons to her place as one of the wealthiest women in the nation. After divorcing her husband at age twenty, Walker spent twenty years earning a living as a scrubwoman. Then, as she told it, she had a dream that gave her the formula for a revolutionary hair-care product for Black women. In her later years, Walker devoted much of her time and resources to philanthropy.

22

Journalists

Nellie Bly

**Deborah Noyes, *Ten Days a Madwoman:
The Daring Life and Turbulent Times
of the Original "Girl" Reporter, Nellie Bly*, 2016.**
Nellie Bly was a household name in the late nineteenth century. Her impressive career began with a stunt: while pretending to be insane, she spent time on Blackwell Island, which was home to a notorious asylum. The result was a startling series of articles detailing the abuses of the patients there. Deborah Noyes writes of Bly's inspiring life and unforgettable experiences.

Tina Brown

Tina Brown, *The Vanity Fair Diaries: 1983–1992*, 2017.
For eight years, Tina Brown was the editor-in-chief of *Vanity Fair* magazine. When the young British journalist takes the helm of the high-profile Condé Nast offering, she keeps a diary of her daily struggles and successes in the face of politics and interference. In the process, she reveals behind-the-scenes stories of the day's rich, famous, and infamous.

Marie Colvin

**Lindsey Hilsum, *In Extremis: The Life and Death
of the War Correspondent Marie Colvin*, 2018.**
Foreign correspondent Lindsey Hilsum writes of her glamourous and daring fellow war reporter Marie Colvin. During a few highlights of her career, Colvin had to fight off the attentions of Muammar Gaddafi, was hit by a grenade in Sri Lanka, and lost her left eye. Then, in 2012, she was killed by a rocket in Syria. Hilsum digs deep into unpublished diaries and notebooks and conducts interviews to honor the life of her unconventional peer.

Walter Cronkite

Douglas Brinkley, *Cronkite*, 2012.
From 1962 until 1981, news anchor Walter Cronkite was "the most trusted man in America," bringing the nation the news every weeknight on the CBS television network. Yet, despite his familiar face, Cronkite was a private man.

Douglas Brinkley follows his life from the Great Depression through his coverage of the Iran hostage crisis.

John Howard Griffin

John Howard Griffin, *Black Like Me*, 1961.

White American journalist John Howard Griffin recounts his experiences traveling the American South in 1959 after darkening his skin with medication so he could pose as a Black man. Unfortunately, the harsh treatment he received compelled him to cut his experiment short. His account is disturbing and, unfortunately, still relevant today.

Gilbert M. Grosvenor

Gilbert M. Grosvenor, *A Man of the World: My Life at National Geographic*, 2022.

For over sixty years, Gilbert Grosvenor was head of National Geographic. The National Geographic Society, founded in 1888, was led by four generations of Grosvenor's family before he took the helm. Even his childhood home was regularly visited by explorers and scientists, from Robert Peary to Jane Goodall. Grosvenor discloses how he successfully navigated the massive changes in the media landscape to help the organization thrive today.

Suzy Hansen

Suzy Hansen, *Notes on a Foreign Country: An American Abroad in a Post-American World*, 2017.

After the September 11 attacks on the United States and the resulting War on Terror, journalist Suzy Hansen moved to Istanbul to discover the truth of the Muslim world. In the following years, she traveled to Greece, Egypt, Afghanistan, and Iran. The experience left her feeling there were two Americas. One consisted of its people and the other of its global power.

Amanda Lindhout

Amanda Lindhout and Sara Corbett, *A House in the Sky: A Memoir*, 2013.

Canadian reporter Amanda Lindhout achieved her childhood dreams of traveling around the world when she began a career as a television reporter in the Middle East. But four days after traveling to Somalia in August of 2008, she was captured by a group of men and held hostage with other women for 460 days while she plotted her escape. When things are harrowing, she escapes in her mind to a house in the sky.

Walter Lippmann

Ronald Steel, *Walter Lippmann and the American Century*, 1980.

Walter Lippmann enjoyed a sixty-year career in journalism that spanned most of the twentieth century. As an insider with direct access to many presidents, Lippmann had the opportunity to report on policy and help shape it. His biography provides a comprehensive history of the rise of the U.S. to a world-dominating power.

Henry Luce

Alan Brinkley, *The Publisher: Henry Luce and His American Century*, 2010.

Twentieth-century publisher Henry Luce founded *Time*, *Fortune*, and *Life* magazines. In doing so, he changed how Americans got their news while strongly influencing public opinion. Yet despite his successful career, his personal life, including his marriage to playwright, politician, and diplomat Clare Boothe Luce, left him isolated and embittered.

Robert Maxwell

John Preston, *Fall: The Mysterious Life and Death of Robert Maxwell, Britain's Most Notorious Media Baron*, 2021.

John Preston relates the dramatic account of Robert Maxwell, who mysteriously drowned while out on his yacht, named the *Lady Ghislaine* after his daughter, Ghislaine Maxwell. Preston traces Maxwell's story and tells how he reached the heights of business success and his ignoble end.

Keith Murdoch

Tom D. C. Roberts, *Before Rupert: Keith Murdoch and the Birth of a Dynasty*, 2015.

Rupert Murdoch's father, Keith Murdoch, is the subject of Tom D. C. Roberts's biography. Roberts traces the Australian's career, beginning with his days as a journalist and war correspondent, through his rise to media magnate. In telling the story, he reveals a great deal about the Murdochs' corporate culture and how they have come to have such an outsized influence on the perceptions of world events.

Anna Politkovskaya

Anna Politkovskaya, *Is Journalism Worth Dying For?: Final Dispatches*, 2001.

In 2006, journalist Anna Politkovskaya was shot and killed in the elevator of her Moscow apartment. She was one of twenty-two reporters murdered between 2000 and 2006. This book contains essays and investigative reports that landed her in trouble. Her book also includes bits of her writings on world leaders she encountered, from George W. Bush to Vladimir Bukovsky.

Ernie Pyle

James Tobin, *Ernie Pyle's War: America's Eyewitness to World War II*, 1997.

Ernie Pyle kept Americans up to date on World War II through his talented reporting as a war correspondent. But most of his readers had no idea how miserable his private life was. They mourned him as a hero when he was killed by machine-gun fire. James Tobin mimics Pyle's style in his account of the life of the man who brought Americans firsthand dispatches from D-Day to Okinawa.

James Thurber

James Thurber, *My Life and Hard Times*, 1933.

As one of the most famous humorists of the twentieth century, James Thurber, in his inimitable style, looks back on his life growing up in Columbus, Ohio, as the son of an underemployed dreamer for a father and a natural comedian for a mother. His stories hilariously detail youthful escapades, canine friends and acquaintances, and the odd and irritating bits of life familiar to us all.

Katy Tur

Katy Tur, *Rough Draft: A Memoir*, 2022.

MSNBC anchor Katy Tur tells how she became enamored of journalism at her parents' knees while they covered the big stories of their day from a helicopter in Los Angeles. Today, many know her as "Little Katy" from her time following the Trump campaign in 2016. But, while Tur sees television journalism from backstage, she also weighs in on issues surrounding it.

Elaine Welteroth

Elaine Welteroth, *More Than Enough: Claiming Space for Who You Are (No Matter What They Say)*, 2019.

Elaine Welteroth made her name as the editor-in-chief of *Teen Vogue*. A Black woman, she changed the magazine from a pure fashion focus to one of social consciousness. In this memoir, she discusses how she found her way and how her readers can successfully follow their paths as well.

T. H. White

Theodore H. White, *In Search of History: A Personal Adventure*, 1978.

American political journalist, historian, and novelist (the author of *The Once and Future King*), T. H. White, writes of his career as a global reporter while sharing his encounters with personalities like Douglas MacArthur and leaders like Mao Tse-Tung. White did more than report on the day's stories. His style has influenced journalism to this day.

Anna Wintour

Amy Odell, *Anna: The Biography*, 2022.

Journalist Amy Odell tells the story of Anna Wintour, a fashionista who came of age in 1960s London. Her father, a newspaper editor, believed she would make an excellent editor-in-chief for *Vogue*. She succeeded after a tempestuous takeover of the magazine and later came out on top of the Condé Nast empire. Odell tells the story, interweaving Wintour's intimate stories throughout.

23

Photographers

Lynsey Addario

Lynsey Addario, *It's What I Do: A Photographer's Life of Love and War*, 2015.

On September 11, 2001, Lynsey Addario began her career as a photojournalist. Choosing to cover the American invasion of Afghanistan that followed, she took pictures of the civilians she encountered there. From there, she exposed the violence against women in the Congo and was a kidnapping victim in the Libyan civil war. In this memoir, she talks of photographing heartbreaking scenes while fighting to be taken seriously as a woman in a male-dominated field.

Diane Arbus

Patricia Bosworth, *Diane Arbus: A Biography*, 1984.

Before this biography came out, twentieth-century photographer of the unusual Diane Arbus was largely a mystery. Beginning her career as a fashion photographer with her husband, Allan Arbus, in the 1950s, her photographs turned dark after the marriage ended. Nevertheless, her haunting images capture dwarves, trans individuals, and other people outside mainstream society. Biographer Patricia Bosworth uncovers the life of this artist, who died by suicide in 1971.

Peter Beard

Graham Boynton, *Wild: The Life of Peter Beard: Photographer, Adventurer, Lover*, 2022.

In some ways larger than life, twentieth-century international playboy and superstar photographer Peter Beard disappeared mysteriously from his home in Montauk, New York, in 2020. His friend Graham Boynton narrates the life of this aristocratic heir, who spent his fortune partying, chasing women, and photographing elephants in Africa. Beard's relationships with the rich and famous add to his interest.

Arthur Fellig ("Weegee")

Christopher Bonanos, *Flash:*
The Making of Weegee the Famous, **2018.**
> In mid-twentieth century America, Arthur Fellig was a photojournalist well
> known for his ability to show up at crime scenes exactly when the police did.
> To explain this talent, he renamed himself, Weegee, after the popular Ouija
> boards. Growing up as an immigrant, he taught himself his photographic
> skills, from which he earned a living on the streets of New York. He later
> pioneered a form of experimental photography that captured the art world's
> attention.

Osa Johnson

Osa Johnson, *I Married Adventure:*
The Lives of Martin and Osa Johnson, **1940.**
> When she was a teenager, Osa Leighty married Martin Johnson, who was back
> in the States after serving as a photographer on a global cruise with writer
> Jack London. Osa traveled the world with Martin, often holding a rifle, so if
> the game he captured on film decided to attack, she could defend her hus-
> band. The book includes photographs of the Johnsons and the subjects they
> recorded in still and motion photography. Their pictures of big game animals
> in Africa are still prized, because they captured a world long gone.

Dorothea Lange

Linda Gordon, *Dorothea Lange: A Life Beyond Limits,* **2009.**
> Historian Linda Gordon traces the life of Dorothea Lange, the twentieth-
> century photographer who produced such masterpieces as the "Migrant
> Mother." Moving from her childhood, which was spent contending with
> polio, through her marriage and her years as a portrait photographer in San
> Francisco, Gordon shows how her images of the Great Depression and World
> War II captured the social history of her era.

Sally Mann

Sally Mann, *Hold Still: A Memoir with Photographs,* **2015.**
> Sally Mann, an award-winning American photographer of black-and-white
> portraits from the American South, presents a memoir using old family
> records and photographs. During her search, she finds evidence of disturbing
> chapters in her family history, from secret affairs to a possible murder.

24

Artists, Architects, and Designers

John James Audubon

Nancy Plain, *This Strange Wilderness:*
The Life and Art of John James Audubon, **2015.**
John James Audubon did much more than create his noted bird paintings. Spending much of his life in the American wilderness of the early nineteenth century, Audubon was an explorer, hunter, and writer. Observing that the American wilderness was disappearing due to increasing populations and technology like railroads, he set out to capture all he could, particularly birds, in paint. In all, he captured almost five hundred species in life-sized and full-color detail.

Lynda Barry

Lynda Barry, *One Hundred Demons,* **2002.**
American author and cartoonist Lynda Barry uses watercolor images to illustrate stories about the irritating people she's encountered. Calling this book a "autofictionalography," she presents a cast of characters from hell.

Romare Bearden

Mary Schmidt Campbell, *An American Odyssey:*
The Life and Work of Romare Bearden, **2018.**
Art scholar Mary Schmidt Campbell tells the story of underappreciated twentieth-century artist Romare Bearden. An African American who had previously been a cartoonist, Bearden became a painter of note during the final years of the Harlem Renaissance. He later became an artist supported by the WPA. Campbell traces Bearden's life from his years in Paris to his return to New York, where his work focused on America's Black community during the 1950s and 1960s, when the civil rights movement was gaining momentum. His medium, which he called "projection," provides an excellent look at mid-twentieth century America, particularly the African American cultural milieu.

Edward Burne-Jones

Fiona MacCarthy, *The Last Pre-Raphaelite:*
Edward Burne-Jones and the Victorian Imagination, **2011.**
While you may not recognize the name of Edward Burne-Jones, you've likely

seen his influence in pictures of angels and stained glass in churches. In the 1880s, Burne-Jones created the "Burne-Jones look." His work connected Victorian to modern art and influenced later artists like Picasso. Biographer Fiona MacCarthy explores his private life, how his romantic attraction to female beauty ruined his marriage, and how his later views on politics and art created a wedge between him and his close friend William Morris.

Caravaggio

Peter Robb, *M: The Man Who Became Caravaggio*, 1998.
The end of the sixteenth century bore witness to the Counter-Reformation and the Inquisition. In this tempestuous period, an artist who captured its drama and tensions was known variously as Marisi, Moriggia, Merigi, and sometimes only as M. Today, he is known as Caravaggio. Of him, art critic Robert Hughes once said, "There was art before him, and art after him, and they were not the same." Peter Robb tells the story of this mysterious and unconventional artist.

Benvenuto Cellini

Benvenuto Cellini, *My Life*, 1558.
Florentine Renaissance sculptor Benvenuto Cellini produced exquisite statues and ornamental goods. His life was every bit as colorful as his masterpieces. His grandiose opinion of himself may have led to his involvement in physical battles, murder, theft, and sodomy. Yet his work was sought out by royalty, popes, and the Medici family. His biography looks at life during sixteenth century Italy and France.

Leonardo da Vinci

Walter Isaacson, *Leonardo da Vinci*, 2017.
Italian Renaissance polymath Leonardo da Vinci was a scientist, inventor, and above all, an artist. Historian and acclaimed biographer Walter Isaacson pored over thousands of pages of da Vinci's notebooks and combined what he found there with recent discoveries about Leonardo's life to provide this portrait of one of the most brilliant and creative minds in history.

M. C. Escher

Bruno Ernst, *The Magic Mirror of M. C. Escher*, 1976.
Dutch graphic artist Maurits Cornelis Escher was famous for his three-dimensional prints. To write his biography, mathematician Bruno Ernst spent a year visiting Escher once a week, going through his life's work with him. They became friends, giving Ernst an insider look at the artist. Escher's

pictures have amazed and confounded countless admirers. Ernst examines why and how Escher created the images.

Francisco Goya

Janis A. Tomlinson, *Goya: A Portrait of the Artist*, 2020.

Goya expert Janis A. Tomlinson writes a surprising biography of the artist who lived during one of the most turbulent periods in Spain's history. Unlike common perception, Goya was not a dark, isolated figure with a bleak outlook on life. Using his letters, court papers, and sketchbook, Tomlinson reveals Goya to have been a sociable young man with many successful friends at court. Using his prints, paintings, and frescoes, she shows him to be a man of his time who developed his genius through his art.

Walter Gropius

Fiona MacCarthy, *Gropius: The Man Who Built the Bauhaus*, 2019.

Historian Fiona MacCarthy narrates the life of an influential architect and instructor, Walter Gropius, whose students included I. M. Pei, Anni Albers, and Philip Johnson. Professionally and personally, Gropius held court in European modernist and avant-garde circles from 1910 to 1930. During the Nazi era, he lived in the U.K. The buildings he designed include the Fagus Factory, Bauhaus Dessau, and Pan Am.

Frida Kahlo

Hayden Herrera, *Frida: A Biography of Frida Kahlo*, 1983.

Twentieth-century Mexican painter Frida Kahlo was a charismatic genius who grew up during the Mexican Revolution. Art historian Hayden Herrera covers her marriage to muralist Diego Rivera and her numerous affairs with famous and infamous men. She also discusses Kahlo's involvement in the Communist Party. Kahlo's art is renowned for its vibrant and colorful images that reflect Mexican folklore and culture.

Shunmyo Masuno

Mira Locher, *Zen Gardens: The Complete Works of Shunmyo Masuno, Japan's Leading Garden Designer*, 2012.

World-class garden designer Shunmyo Masuno is also an eighteenth-generation Zen Buddhist priest. Mira Locher provides a biography of this celebrated landscape architect, providing over four hundred drawings and photographs of his work. His Zen background inspired Masuno to make each garden "a special spiritual place where the mind dwells."

Michelangelo

Ross King, *Michelangelo and the Pope's Ceiling*, 2003.

Famed art biographer Ross King details the four years that Renaissance artist Michelangelo Buonarroti spent painting the Vatican's Sistine Chapel ceiling for Pope Julius II. Previously acclaimed for his sculpture, such as *David*, Michelangelo had little experience as a painter and didn't want to accept the commission. Yet, despite the many obstacles and problems surrounding his efforts, the artist produced one of the most famous and celebrated works of art in history. King also details other historical developments as a backdrop for Michelangelo's achievement.

Edvard Munch

Sue Prideaux, *Edvard Munch: Behind the Scream*, 2005.

British biographer Sue Prideaux's godmother was once painted by Norwegian artist Edvard Munch. His twentieth-century painting *The Scream* is one of the most iconic images worldwide. Using her research skills as a scholar, Prideaux narrates his tumultuous life. The secret to understanding Munch, she says, is that he strived to capture his emotional reactions to events, his personal experience of them rather than what he saw. And his life had its share of pain.

George Nakashima

Mira Nakashima, *Nature Form & Spirit: The Life and Legacy of George Nakashima*, 2003.

Architect and furniture designer George Nakashima was known for his furniture's wood grains and natural lines. This book discusses the philosophical underpinnings of his work and how he integrated them into his life. His daughter, colleague, and fellow designer Mira Nakashima highlights her father's influence on modern design and traces the progression of his art.

Isamu Noguchi

Hayden Herrera, *Listening to Stone: The Art and Life of Isamu Noguchi*, 2015.

Born and raised in Japan, twentieth-century sculptor Isamu Noguchi was the son of an unwed American mother and a famous but reclusive Japanese father. His parents' disparate backgrounds led to a lifelong search for identity, which Noguchi found primarily in nature. Traveling the world, he had many famous friends and many lovers. He later designed furniture in addition to his sculpture. Art historian Hayden Herrera captures the life of this influential artist.

Nell Painter

**Nell Painter, *Old in Art School:*
A Memoir of Starting Over, 2018.**

After respected historian Nell Painter retired from Princeton in her sixties, she was ready to begin something completely different. So she entered the Rhode Island School of Design to earn a BFA and then an MFA in painting. While sharing her journey, she contemplates the meaning of art, how one becomes an artist, and the criteria by which women and artists are judged. Her experience should inspire others who, like her, would like to start over.

Pablo Picasso

John Richardson, *A Life of Picasso, Vol. 1: 1881–1906*, 1991.

After living near him in Provence for ten years, British art historian John Richardson knew Picasso personally. After Picasso died, his widow allowed Richardson access to her husband's studios and storerooms. He seeks to explain the paradoxes and contradictions for which the artist was famous. In this first of a four-volume set, he takes us from Picasso's birth to age twenty-five and his early successes in Barcelona and Paris.

Jackson Pollock

**Steven Naifeh and Gregory White Smith, *Jackson Pollock:*
An American Saga, 1988.**

In this Pulitzer Prize–winning biography, Naifeh and Smith combed through letters and family documents to present the life of twentieth-century painter Jackson Pollock. They also interviewed Pollock's widow, Lee Krasner, and a psychologist and psychoanalyst who worked with the artist. Finally, they clarify what happened when Pollock died in 1956.

Norman Rockwell

**Norman Rockwell and Thomas S. Buechner,
Norman Rockwell, Artist and Illustrator, 1970.**

Norman Rockwell was known for his early- to mid-twentieth-century covers for the *Saturday Evening Post*. Brooklyn Museum director Thomas S. Buechner showcases the artist who captured ordinary Americans amid great societal upheaval.

Cy Twombly

**Joshua Rivkin, *Chalk:*
The Art and Erasure of Cy Twombly, 2018.**

Joshua Rivkin received a Fulbright grant to study the life of twentieth-century American painter Cy Twombly. For years, Twombly's life has been a mystery because of his efforts to manage his image. He purposely kept his personal life out of the limelight, granting few interviews. Rivkin's scholarship brings Twombly's fascinating life into focus.

Vincent van Gogh

Steven Naifeh and Gregory White Smith, *Van Gogh: The Life*, 2011.

Seeking to provide a comprehensive and serious look at painter Vincent van Gogh's life and art, Naifeh and Smith used their full access to previously unused materials about him at the Van Gogh Museum in Amsterdam. Using these sources, they explore Van Gogh's relationship with his brother Theo, his love life, and his mental illnesses. They look at his incredible works of art dating from his time in Provence and try to clarify precisely what caused his death at age thirty-seven.

25

Musicians and Composers

Gregg Allman

Gregg Allman, *My Cross to Bear*, 2012.

As a founding member of The Allman Brothers Band, Gregg Allman was rock royalty from the late 1960s onward. Here, he chronicles his youth, the band's early years, the devastating death of his brother Duane, and his marriages, including the very brief one to Cher. While his brother Duane was a virtuoso rock guitarist, Gregg was the band's vocalist and played keyboards and guitar. He is also famed for his songwriting.

Louis Armstrong

Thomas Brothers,
***Louis Armstrong, Master of Modernism*, 2014.**

During his career in the twentieth century, famed artist Louis Armstrong created two entirely new styles of jazz music. In his second biography of the pop culture icon, Thomas Brothers picks up in the 1920s and 1930s, following Armstrong through his apex of fame. Against a backdrop of racist social practices and laws, Brothers explains how Armstrong managed to thrive.

Johann Sebastian Bach

Christoph Wolff, *Johann Sebastian Bach:*
***The Learned Musician*, 2000.**

Musicologist Christoph Wolff presents a readable biography of the German eighteenth-century Baroque composer J. S. Bach. Seeking to present Bach not as a larger-than-life figure but as a very human man, Wolff uses the most recent scholarship on his life to present his career as a composer, musician, scholar, and teacher.

Ludwig van Beethoven

Lewis Lockwood, *Beethoven: The Music and the Life*, 2002.

Music scholar Lewis Lockwood takes Beethoven's musical and personal stories and weaves them together to create a complete look at the great composer's life within its historical context. Beethoven serves as a bridge from the Classical to the Romantic period and is considered the greatest Western composer who ever lived, a fact even more miraculous considering some of his greatest pieces were written after he completely lost his hearing.

Harry Belafonte

Harry Belafonte, *My Song: A Memoir*, 2011.

While Harry Belafonte's career as an entertainer is well known, he focuses on his activism in this memoir. Raised in Harlem and Jamaica, Belafonte did not have an easy youth. After his release from the U.S. Navy after World War II, Belafonte moved to Harlem and took on odd jobs until he discovered and fell in love with the theater. His involvement soon got him noticed for his musical talent, and his career as a brilliant singer soon began. During the civil rights movement, Belafonte served as a go-between for Martin Luther King Jr. and the Kennedys. He speaks with candor about his life and the many famous figures he knew.

Johannes Brahms

Jan Swafford, *Johannes Brahms: A Biography*, 1997.

Romantic composer Johannes Brahms was a musical superstar by the age of twenty. But according to composer Jan Swafford, his personal life was largely hidden until now. Brahms grew up in Hamburg, Germany, where he played piano in beer halls. His love life was unhappy, and he burned his papers, scores, and notebooks late in life to hide his failings from biographers. But Swafford digs out all the available material to provide a balanced portrait of the great composer.

James Brown

James McBride, *Kill 'Em and Leave:*
Searching for James Brown and the American Soul, 2016.

Journalist James McBride received a tip that began his journey to discover the real story of James Brown, from his sharecropping childhood in South Carolina to the tragic fight over his estate, which deprived the poor children Brown hoped to help of millions of dollars and left his body in a casket in his daughter's yard in South Carolina. Despite his fame, American culture left scars on Brown's life.

Carrie Brownstein

Carrie Brownstein, *Hunger Makes Me a Modern Girl:*
A Memoir, 2015.

In 2006, Carrie Brownstein was voted one of *Rolling Stone* magazine's "25 Most Underrated Guitarists of All Time." As a member of the feminist punk band Sleater-Kinney, she was a leading musician in the riot-grrrl era. The band made waves with their defiant lyrics against war and traditional expectations for women. Later, Brownstein co-developed and starred in the television show *Portlandia*. Here, she reveals what it was like to be a woman in the sexist world of rock music.

Mariah Carey

Mariah Carey, *The Meaning of Mariah Carey*, 2020.

Known for her beautiful voice with a five-octave range, Mariah Carey gained fame in 1990 with her first album. In this memoir, she tells her story on her terms, putting rumors to rest and coming clean about her mistakes. She speaks of her lifelong insecurities and how she persevered despite them.

Johnny Cash

Johnny Cash, *Cash: The Autobiography*, 1997.

American country music legend Johnny Cash talks about his hardworking childhood and his rise to country music stardom. Sparing no intimate details, he talks about his children and marriages, particularly to June Carter Cash. He also shares details about his relationships with other celebrities, from Elvis Presley to Bob Dylan to Billy Graham.

Frédéric Chopin

Adam Zamoyski, *Chopin: A New Biography*, 1979.

Historian Adam Zamoyski narrates the life of Frédéric Chopin, the nineteenth-century Romantic composer and pianist whose music and life have garnered intense fan devotion. Little has been known of Chopin's private life until now. Zamoyski unearths the secrets of the musician's life and places them within the context of his time.

Kurt Cobain

Charles R. Cross, *Heavier Than Heaven: A Biography of Kurt Cobain*, 2001.

Fans of *Nirvana* front man Kurt Cobain knew him primarily by his music. But Charles Cross used over four hundred interviews, his diary entries, and his suicide note to tell the paradoxical story of the rock star. He illuminates the meaning of the songs, tracing "Smells Like Teen Spirit" to a double date with Bikini Kill's Kathleen Hanna, Dave Grohl, and Tobi Vail, with whom Cobain was obsessed. Cross also discloses the disturbing prevalence of suicides in his family of origin and Cobain's dismaying swings from kindness to cruelty toward people and animals.

Sam Cooke

Peter Guralnick, *Dream Boogie: The Triumph of Sam Cooke*, 2005.

Blending gospel music with secular lyrics, American singer–songwriter Sam Cooke was one of the first soul musicians. His music and role in the civil rights movement sprang from a childhood in church. Music critic Peter Guralnick uses Cooke's life to depict American life in the 1950s and 1960s. His mysterious and violent death in 1963 has never been satisfactorily explained.

Fats Domino

Rick Coleman, *Blue Monday: Fats Domino and the Lost Dawn of Rock 'n' Roll*, 2005.

Tracing the history of the rock music genre's rise in New Orleans led R&B scholar Rick Coleman to conclude it wasn't Elvis Presley who was the father of rock 'n' roll. It was Fats Domino. His research into the legendary musician with early megahits like "Blueberry Hill" is a cultural biography of the era. In telling the story, Coleman reveals how the politics behind the record labels of the 1930s and 1940s skewed our understanding of our musical past.

Bob Dylan

Bob Dylan, *Chronicles: Volume One*, 2004.

American master Bob Dylan looks at the most critical points in his life and career. He helps readers see what he saw when he came to Manhattan alone in 1961 as a city of unlimited possibilities. With prose as captivating as his poetry, Dylan uncovers the thoughts and influences that shaped his life and art.

Ella Fitzgerald

Stuart Nicholson, *Ella Fitzgerald: A Biography of the First Lady of Jazz*, 1994.

Ella Fitzgerald, one of the most revered jazz singers of all time, was a private woman whose life was misunderstood. Stuart Nicholson reveals how this African American woman, raised in poverty, realized the American dream despite the rampant sexism and racism of her day. An authoritative discography by Phil Schaap also accompanies the biography.

Philip Glass

Philip Glass, *Words Without Music: A Memoir*, 2015.

American classical music composer Philip Glass was nominated for three Academy Awards. He is among the most popular late-twentieth-century composers with popular audiences. In this memoir, he shares growing up in Baltimore and his early days in music. While he tells stories of the famous people he has known, his passion for artistic creation steals the show.

Dave Grohl

Dave Grohl, *The Storyteller: Tales of Life and Music*, 2021.

You may know him as Nirvana's drummer or as the Foo Fighters' head. But Dave Grohl wants you to know him as he knows himself: a kid who dreamed of fame while growing up in Springfield, Virginia, who just happened to make it big after leaving home at eighteen to play with the band Scream, but who was later offered a place with an up-and-coming band named Nirvana. Beloved by fans for his humor and zest for life, Grohl shares his memories so you can see life through his eyes.

Lena Horne

James Gavin, *Stormy Weather: The Life of Lena Horne*, 2009.

From the Cotton Club to Hollywood, Lena Horne was renowned for her beauty and beautiful voice. But as James Gavin reveals, Horne was a wounded and angry woman who had endured a difficult childhood and struggled with racism. Despite her place as the first African American film star in the 1940s and 1950s, Horne was usually relegated to bit singing parts. Though she inspired many women singers to follow, she withdrew altogether from the public eye. Gavin was one of the few who managed to get an interview with her for this biography.

Elton John

Elton John, *Me: Elton John Official Autobiography*, 2019.

Born Reginald Dwight, Elton John grew up in a London suburb where he played piano and dreamed of becoming a star. As a young man, with his songwriting partner Bernie Taupin, he rose to the top of the American music charts in his early twenties. John gathered many famous friends and a serious drug habit along the journey. In this memoir, he writes about his experiences becoming clean, finding love with David Furnish, and becoming a father.

Quincy Jones

Quincy Jones, *Q: The Autobiography of Quincy Jones*, 2001.

Growing up on Chicago's South Side, Quincy Jones seemed destined for a life of pain, but when his father moved the family to Seattle, his life changed trajectory when he learned to play the trumpet. His genius on the instrument led to playing backup for Billie Holiday while in his teens. Though his musical talent was evident, his passion was arranging albums, and he worked for some of the business's biggest names, including Frank Sinatra, Ray Charles, and later Michael Jackson's blockbuster *Thriller*. He also composed the scores for many acclaimed films, such as *In the Heat of the Night* and *The Color Purple*. As a result, his life story reads like a who's who of twentieth-century entertainment.

Janis Joplin

Alice Echols, *Scars of Sweet Paradise: The Life and Times of Janis Joplin*, 1999.

Cultural critic and historian Alice Echols examines the meteoric rise and fatal fall of iconoclastic musician Janis Joplin, one of the greatest rock voices of the 1960s. Joplin thumbed her nose at the sweet, clean image that American women were encouraged to emulate and smashed expectations with her intense vocal style. However, the woman Echols reveals is not the woman the media portrays. Looking at Joplin's musical roots, she shows respect for the woman but has reservations about the wild, reckless lifestyle so common at the time.

Alicia Keys

Alicia Keys, *More Myself: A Journey*, 2020.

Megastar Alicia Keys writes about growing up in Hell's Kitchen and Harlem. She discloses her joys and sorrows and her triumphs and struggles in this honest memoir. Beginning with her tendency to people-please in her early career, she talks about lessons learned. For instance, public adulation means nothing if you don't value yourself. She also looks at those who surrounded her on her journey and reflects on their mixed influence.

Anthony Kiedis

Anthony Kiedis, *Scar Tissue*, 2004.

As a lyricist and lead singer of the band the Red Hot Chili Peppers, Anthony Kiedis has lived an extraordinary life. In this memoir, he describes how the band began in L.A. in 1983 with a unique blend of punk and funk. The craziness and the integrity of Kiedis's journey are as eye-opening and entertaining as the band.

Riley "B. B." King

Daniel de Visé, *King of the Blues: The Rise and Reign of B. B. King*, 2021.

Born in the Jim Crow South, "Blues Boy" or B. B. King lost his parents by age ten. Working as a sharecropper to earn a living, he began playing music and teaching himself his style, using local musicians and records by Blind Lemon

Jefferson and T-Bone Walker as inspiration. Over the next six decades, King performed 15,000 concerts in ninety countries. Daniel de Visé uncovers King's life, both the good and the bad.

John Lennon

Elizabeth Partridge, *John Lennon: All I Want Is the Truth*, 2005.

Beatle John Lennon was born in 1940 during a World War II air raid on Liverpool. His life never really settled down from its turbulent beginnings. Award-winning biographer Elizabeth Partridge covers his story from its fraught beginning to its tragically violent end.

Franz Liszt

Alan Walker, *Franz Liszt: The Virtuoso Years, 1811–1847* (Volume 1), 1983.

While Romantic composer and pianist Franz Liszt has been recognized as a romantic hero, the quality of his music needs to be better understood. Music scholar Alan Walker spent more than a decade unearthing unpublished material on Liszt all over Austria, Hungary, Weimar, and Budapest. In the process, he found that many previously published biographies of Liszt were largely fiction. This first volume of a three-volume set reveals Liszt as a child prodigy with a strong religious bent who later produced an astonishing body of work and performances. Walker also details his involvement with various nineteenth-century celebrities.

Bob Marley

Timothy White, *Catch a Fire: The Life of Bob Marley*, 1983.

Jamaican musician Bob Marley was a reggae music pioneer and an international icon. This biography, now in its fourth edition, chronicles Marley's life, but the updated material in this edition highlights the sizable impact his legacy has had around the world.

Paul McCartney

Barry Miles, *Paul McCartney: Many Years From Now*, 1997.

Using exclusive interviews conducted with McCartney over five years and with access to the McCartney archives, Barry Miles tells the story of the Beatles as Paul himself would tell it. Through Miles, Paul shares how he wrote much of the Beatles catalogue with John Lennon and where the ideas for the songs originated.

Felix Mendelssohn

R. Larry Todd, *Mendelssohn: A Life in Music*, 2003.

Nineteenth-century German composer Felix Mendelssohn, like Mozart, was a child prodigy. One of the most popular composers and performers of his day, he is now best known for popular songs like "The Wedding March" and "Hark, the Herald Angels Sing." After digging into Mendelssohn's letters, diaries, manuscripts, and paintings, R. Larry Todd provides a new look at his catalogue. And he reveals the effect antisemitism had on his work. Reading this biography will help readers see this musical genius in a new light.

Freddie Mercury

Leslie-Ann Jones, *Mercury: An Intimate Biography of Freddie Mercury*, 1997.

As the beloved vocalist and songwriter for the band Queen, Freddie Mercury became a superstar for his songs, voice, and flamboyant style. Unfortunately, he was also the first rock star to die from AIDS. Lesley-Ann Jones traveled the world to interview those who knew him before and during his years of fame.

Joni Mitchell

David Yaffe, *Reckless Daughter: A Portrait of Joni Mitchell*, 2017.

Music critic David Yaffe tells how the daughter of Canadian prairie farmers became a superstar on the folk music scene in the 1960s with hits like "Both Sides, Now." The self-taught musician was a central figure in the Laurel Canyon music scene in the 1970s, influencing a generation of musicians who followed her.

Bill Monroe

Richard D. Smith, *Can't You Hear Me Callin': The Life of Bill Monroe, Father of Bluegrass*, 2000.

Bluegrass journalist Richard D. Smith researched over 120 interviews across the years that delve into the life of reserved bluegrass icon Bill Monroe. Monroe starred in the Grand Ole Opry in Nashville, Tennessee, for over sixty years. His brilliant career influenced artists as diverse as Elvis Presley and Jerry Garcia, making Monroe one of the most influential musicians in the history of American popular music.

Keith Moon

Tony Fletcher, *Dear Boy: The Life of Keith Moon*, 1998.

The drummer of super-band The Who, Keith Moon, was as well known for his wild and reckless exploits offstage as he was for his drumming while on it. After conducting over 120 interviews with family, friends, and others who knew him, Tony Fletcher reveals that much of what we think we know about Moon isn't true. But what is true is stranger still.

Jim Morrison

Jerry Hopkins and Danny Sugerman, *No One Here Gets Out Alive*, 1980.

Jim Morrison, singer for the iconic rock band The Doors, was one of the most brilliant entertainers to emerge from the 1960s. Danny Sugerman, who worked closely with The Doors, works with journalist Jerry Hopkins to portray Morrison as a philosopher and poet who was also out of control.

Ferdinand Joseph Lamothe (Jelly Roll Morton)

Howard Reich and William Gaines, *Jelly's Blues: The Life, the Music, and Redemption of Jelly Roll Morton*, 2003.

Jazz icon Jelly Roll Morton was born in New Orleans in 1890. While he was a brilliant pianist and composer who helped found the Jazz Age, by the 1930s, he had fallen from grace in the popular imagination. But in 1992, a cache of Jelly Roll's papers was unearthed in New Orleans, which changed our understanding of the musician. Despite his poverty, he struggled to save his reputation, recover royalties lost to crooked publishers, and help other Black musicians do the same. Howard Reich reveals a brilliant man who fought and composed to the end.

Wolfgang Amadeus Mozart

Peter Gay, *Mozart: A Life*, 1999.

Acclaimed historian and biographer Peter Gay narrates the life of eighteenth-century Austrian composer Wolfgang Amadeus Mozart, widely regarded as the greatest musical genius in Western history. As a famous child prodigy, Mozart began playing the harpsichord at age three. As a composer, he excelled at symphonies, concertos, and opera.

Charlie Parker

Stanley Crouch, *Kansas City Lightning: The Rise and Times of Charlie Parker*, 2013.

Jazz critic Stanley Crouch profiles the father of bebop, the alto saxophone virtuoso Charlie Parker. Raised during the Great Depression, and tormented by drug addiction, Parker, also known as "The Bird," died at age thirty-four. For most of his adult life, he was torn between music and drugs and between his mother and his young wife. Crouch used interviews with many who knew him

to tell this first part of a two-part biography, which covers Parker's
early years.

Dolly Parton

Sarah Smarsh, *She Come By It Natural: Dolly Parton and the Women Who Lived Her Songs,* 2020.

Journalist Sarah Smarsh writes about Dolly Parton from a different perspective. She sees Dolly as a feminist icon whose songs validate women whose
voices are seldom heard. Smarsh also talks about how Dolly went from a poor
child in the Smoky Mountains to a self-made businesswoman with a philan-
thropic empire. And Dolly did it all on her terms. She dresses, talks, and sings
in an authentic manner that no one can duplicate, making her a beloved icon
for millions of fans. If you are interested in a memoir by Dolly Parton, see
Dolly: My Life and Other Unfinished Business, 1994.

Elvis Presley

Peter Guralnick, *Last Train to Memphis: The Rise of Elvis Presley,* 1994.

Legendary American singer and actor Elvis Presley changed the world with
hits like "Heartbreak Hotel" and "Hound Dog." Music critic Peter Guralnick
shows how Elvis changed not just America's musical landscape but also its
culture. This book covers the superstar's first twenty-four years until he left
for the army in 1958.

Prince Rogers Nelson ("Prince")

Prince, *The Beautiful Ones,* 2019.

Dan Peipenbring collaborated with Prince in the final months of the artist's
life, editing Prince's memories of his childhood and how he created his per-
sona and artistic vision. Taking photos from Prince's scrapbook, this memoir
takes us through his early years as a musician. Then, through pictures and
handwritten notes, we discover how Prince created *Purple Rain* and how he
evolved in the wake of this blockbuster work.

Keith Richards

Keith Richards, *Life,* 2010.

As songwriter, guitarist, and singer for the iconic rock band the Rolling Stones,
Keith Richards developed a reputation for hard living and debauchery. In
this book, he tells how he and the other band members met, the inspiration
for their songs, and the women they fought over. Richards's story, told with
honesty and wit, makes for fascinating reading.

Dmitri Shostakovich

Solomon Volkov, *Shostakovich and Stalin: The Extraordinary Relationship Between the Great Composer and the Brutal Dictator*, 2005.

Russian composer Dmitri Shostakovich was famous in the 1920s for his avant-garde compositions. But in the 1930s, Shostakovich was subjected to Stalin's notorious mistreatment of artists. Author Solomon Volkov, a Russian journalist and musicologist, says it could have been worse because Shostakovich insisted on speaking his truth, ignoring his peril. But the psychological price he paid was immense.

Paul Simon

Robert Hilburn, *Paul Simon: The Life*, 2018.

Paul Simon cooperated completely with Robert Hilburn while he was writing this biography. While growing up in Queens, Paul Simon loved baseball and music. When he was only twelve, he began making music with a buddy named Art Garfunkel. While the two broke records with their dreamy folk-pop sound and songs like "Bridge Over Troubled Water," their later split caused Simon pain. He continued making music that blended American with international music.

Frank Sinatra

James Kaplan, *Frank: The Voice*, 2010.

Old Blue Eyes was one of the first teen heartthrobs in America. His voice and charisma captivated a generation. Born in Hoboken, New Jersey, in 1915, Sinatra reached the peak of public adoration in the early 1950s when his public esteem plummeted. However, his performance in the movie *From Here to Eternity* resurrected his career. James Kaplan provides a two-volume biography of this enigmatic man. This first volume covers Sinatra's life from birth through 1954. The second volume, *Sinatra: The Chairman*, picks up from there until he died in 1988.

Saul Hudson (Slash)

Slash, *Slash*, 2007.

Lead guitarist for the mega band Guns N' Roses, Slash, was known for his reticent personality, and he kept his personal life private. In this autobiography, he tells how he was born in England but raised in L.A. While still young, he became a BMX rider of note but found his true calling when he discovered a discarded guitar in his grandmother's closet. From there, Slash and his friend Steven Adler stuck together as they connected with Axl Rose, Izzy Stradlin, and Duff McKagan to form one of history's most successful rock bands.

Bessie Smith

Jackie Kay, *Bessie Smith: A Poet's Biography of a Blues Legend*, 1997.

While growing up as a mixed-race child in Glasgow, Scotland, Jackie Kay discovered American blues singer Bessie Smith. She could instantly relate to this African American woman, born in 1894 and orphaned nine years later. Smith began by singing on street corners and then joined in traveling shows. Her first album, which she recorded with Columbia Records in 1923, sold 780,000 copies. Smith, a mystery until now, is captured by a lifelong fan.

Tina Turner

Tina Turner, *I, Tina: My Life Story*, 1986.

International superstar Tina Turner was born into a sharecropping family in Tennessee. For over five decades, she entertained, first with her husband Ike Turner and then in a much longer solo career. She's survived both lows and highs imagined by few. Her music has ranged from rhythm and blues to soul and rock. Turner writes this memoir at the height of her career.

Shania Twain

Shania Twain, *From This Moment On*, 2011.

Superstar Shania Twain had a painful and impoverished early life in rural Canada. She helped her mother and four siblings escape their violent father, fleeing to a battered women's shelter. Her parents later died together in a car crash, and Shania worked to keep her siblings together. As an adult, she rose to the top of the country music charts, but her troubles didn't end there. She describes heartbreaks and later happiness with the love of her life.

Hank Williams

Paul Hemphill, *Lovesick Blues: The Life of Hank Williams*, 2005.

Country music singer–songwriter Hank Williams lived a legendary country music life. Born in poverty with a congenital disability, he was raised almost entirely by his mother, learning to play music from a Black street singer. By his teens, he was an alcoholic who became a star of the Grand Ole Opry by the time he was in his twenties, using his sad and battered life as song material. Williams died alone, drunk, in the back of a car in 1953. He was twenty-nine years old.

Frank Zappa

Barry Miles, *Zappa: A Biography*, 1993.

Barry Miles knew Frank Zappa personally. He reveals that growing up in the 1940s, Zappa wanted to be a classical composer. But instead, he gained international fame as the head of the band the Mothers of Invention, who skewered American culture and politicians with clever satirical lyrics. Despite his zany reputation, Zappa was a family man who was married to the same woman for over thirty years. His influence on popular music has been immense.

Warren Zevon

Crystal Zevon, *I'll Sleep When I'm Dead: The Dirty Life and Times of Warren Zevon*, 2007.

Written by his former wife, Crystal, Warren Zevon, a rock star with a cult following, is revealed in his outrageous glory. Best known for his megahit "Werewolves of London," Zevon was notorious for his raucous lifestyle. Using over eighty interviews with other celebrities who knew Zevon, this tell-all biography delves into both the musician's misdeeds and his genius.

COLLECTIVE BIOGRAPHY

Clover Hope, *The Motherlode: 100+ Women Who Made Hip-Hop*, 2021.

From Roxanne Shanté to Cardi B, this book covers the famous and the respected but unknown. What they share is their music. The other details of their lives vary widely.

Mötley Crüe, *The Dirt: Confessions of the World's Most Notorious Rock Band*, 2014.

Making sure they lived up to the band's name, the four members of Mötley Crüe were determined to do the most drugs, drink the most alcohol, sleep with the most women, and get into the most fights of any band in history. What's impressive is that they succeeded and lived to talk about it. Vince Neil, Nikki Sixx, Tommy Lee, and Mick Mars each have sordid and sometimes heartbreaking tales about the mayhem they created and the people, famous or not, who went along for the ride.

Anita Pointer and Fritz Pointer, *Fairytale: The Pointer Sisters' Family History*, 2020.

The Pointer Sisters—June, Bonnie, Anita, and Ruth—had forty-eight years together as a musical act. The four sisters battled for attention and men from their early days in the civil rights and Black Power movements of the 1960s. Anita tells their story with help from their brother Fritz. The family journey from the south to the north, along with thousands of other Black families, is reflected in American society.

Andrew Ridgeley, *Wham!: George Michael & Me: A Memoir*, 2019.

Wham!, the pop music duo of George Michael and Andrew Ridgely, was one of the world's top bands in the 1980s. In this memoir, Ridgeley shares how the two men met as teenagers in 1975 and rose to the apex of the charts.

26

Stage and Screen

Alison Arngrim

Alison Arngrim, *Confessions of a Prairie Bitch: How I Survived Nellie Oleson and Learned to Love Being Hated*, 2010.

Millions remember hating the character Nellie Oleson on the *Little House on the Prairie* television show. But the actor who played her for seven years, Alison Arngrim, describes the experience as liberating. Arngrim was a shy young girl with eccentric parents, and playing Nellie gave her the confidence to be herself. She shares humorous stories of the behind-the-scenes quirks of her costars, including Michael Landon and Melissa Gilbert. But when her best friend, Steve Tracy, who played her husband on the show, died of AIDS, Arngrim found her second career as an activist.

Humphrey Bogart

Ann M. Sperber and Eric Lax, *Bogart*, 1997.

Starring in some of the most memorable Hollywood films, such as *Casablanca*, *Key Largo*, and *The Treasure of the Sierra Madre*, Humphrey Bogart was an A-list star for much of his forty-year career. He was best known for playing loners with edgy personalities. But Bogart was a man of conviction who worked hard and was faithful to his wife, actress Lauren Bacall. Ann M. Sperber passed away in 1991 while working on this book. Eric Lax, the author of a 1991 bestselling biography on Woody Allen, completed the project.

James Cagney

John McCabe, *Cagney*, 1997.

After shoving half a grapefruit in Mae Clarke's face in the movie *Public Enemy*, James Cagney was typecast as a gangster. The Irish American film star worked tirelessly to get different types of roles and finally succeeded in movies like *Yankee Doodle Dandy*. These roles suited the quiet, private actor much better. John McCabe narrates the life of Cagney, who played the bad guys but was a good guy in real life.

Charlie Chan

Yunte Huang, *Charlie Chan: The Untold Story of the Honorable Detective and His Rendezvous with American History*, 2010.
Beginning his career as a detective in Hawaii, Charlie Chan became a literary and Hollywood icon. English professor Yunte Huang demonstrates how Chan is still a symbol of America's cultural diversity. Using Chan as a thread, he weaves a history of American culture.

Joan Crawford

Peter Cowie, *Joan Crawford: The Enduring Star*, 2009.
Film historian Peter Cowie covers the life of legendary Hollywood film star Joan Crawford, who starred in such classics as *Grand Hotel* and *The Women*. Many biographies have highlighted her career's later years, but Cowie chooses to spotlight the earlier half. Using archives and over a hundred photographs, he provides a unique look at the iconic star.

Tina Fey

Tina Fey, *Bossypants*, 2011.
American actress, comedian, writer, and producer Tina Fey is well known for her years as a writer and cast member on *Saturday Night Live*. Since then, she has created and starred in the television series *30 Rock* and a series of films beginning with *Mean Girls* in 2004. In this memoir, she is characteristically funny in disclosing the normal and the odd events in her life.

Sally Field

Sally Field, *In Pieces*, 2018.
Beginning with her role as *Gidget*, American film star and director Sally Field has charmed audiences. Here she reveals what her public life was like behind the scenes. Her honesty will inspire others to believe that, even though life is difficult for everyone, it can be lived with integrity.

Carrie Fisher

Carrie Fisher, *The Princess Diarist*, 2016.
Before she died from cardiac arrest in 2016, actress, screenwriter, and author Carrie Fisher found the journals she had kept as a teenager while playing Princess Leah in the first film installment of the *Star Wars* franchise. Taking excerpts from the notebooks, she engagingly pieces together what happened on and off the set of one of the biggest blockbusters of all time. She also muses

on the insanity that having two famous entertainers for parents created in her life.

Michael J. Fox

Michael J. Fox, *Lucky Man: A Memoir*, 2002.

After becoming famous for his stint playing Alex P. Keaton on the 1980s sitcom *Family Ties* and then Marty McFly in the *Back to the Future* trilogy, which was followed by his portrayal of Mike Flaherty in *Spin City,* Michael J. Fox shocked the world by revealing he had Parkinson's disease. Here, he talks about his childhood in Canada and how he rose to fame. Fox provides a unique and hopeful perspective on his progressive neurological condition. He wrote a second memoir in 2020 called *No Time Like the Future* to update his fans on what he has learned and how he has coped.

Greta Garbo

Barry Paris, *Garbo: A Biography*, 1994.

In 1920s and 1930s Hollywood, Greta Garbo was at the peak of her stardom. But after retiring from films, Garbo became a recluse. For the last fifty years of her life, she rarely left her New York City apartment, not even to receive an Academy Award. Barry Paris used previously unpublished letters, taped conversations, and interviews to present the biography of this famed silver screen "enigma."

Judy Garland

Anne Edwards, *Judy Garland: A Biography*, 1975.

Judy Garland is an American icon. Anne Edwards goes far beyond the stories of drug and alcohol abuse to reveal a child star exploited, not just by Hollywood, but by her mother, who mercilessly used Garland's desire to help her family. The star of many movies, most notably *The Wizard of Oz,* Garland was also a sensitive soul who tried her hand at poetry. But, above all, she wanted to please, which was her gift and her downfall.

Audrey Hepburn

Sam Wasson, *Fifth Avenue, 5 A.M.: Audrey Hepburn*, Breakfast at Tiffany's, and the Dawn of the Modern Woman, 2010.

Film professor Sam Wasson reveals that Audrey Hepburn's life didn't live up to her image as a perfect, delicate glamour girl. Wasson focuses on her starring role as Holly Golightly in the blockbuster hit movie *Breakfast at Tiffany's* as a frame. The movie was based on the Truman Capote novella of the same name. Hepburn wasn't Capote's first choice. He wanted Marilyn Monroe, and

Hepburn herself had mixed feelings about accepting the part. Wasson goes on to demonstrate how the 1961 movie played a significant role in moving America out of the cultural norms of the 1950s to the changing social standards for women directly after the movie.

Katharine Hepburn

A. Scott Berg, *Kate Remembered*, 2003.
Acclaimed biographer A. Scott Berg covers the long life and seven-decade career of American entertainment icon and winner of four Academy Awards, Katharine Hepburn. When Berg was thirty-three and Hepburn was seventy-five, the two began a friendship that lasted until Hepburn died in 2003 at age ninety-five. Berg used those twenty years of intimate conversations to bring us the story of the private woman behind the illustrious career.

Alfred Hitchcock

Donald Spoto, *The Dark Side of Genius: The Life of Alfred Hitchcock*, 1983.
Biographer and theologian Donald Spoto narrates the life of the great English director of Hollywood horror and thriller films for both big and small screens, Alfred Hitchcock. He made more than forty films, many classics today like *Psycho, Rear Window,* and *The Birds.* Looking at the personal influences of the great director, Spoto sheds light on many of the brilliant choices Hitchcock made and clarifies his mysterious private life.

Buster Keaton

Dana Stevens, *Camera Man: Buster Keaton, the Dawn of Cinema, and the Invention of the Twentieth Century*, 2022.
In this combined biography and social history, film critic Dana Stevens traces the life of Buster Keaton. He began as a child star in a family vaudeville act. In his early twenties, Keaton joined the nascent Hollywood film industry as a director, star, stuntman, editor, and creator of classic silent films such as *The General.* Later, in his middle years, Keaton succumbed to alcohol addiction but reinvented himself in the earliest years of television. He rubbed shoulders with illustrious individuals like Harry Houdini, Lucille Ball, and F. Scott Fitzgerald.

Bruce Lee

Matthew Polly, *Bruce Lee: A Life*, 2018.
Award-winning author Matthew Polly profiles Bruce Lee, who brought Eastern culture to America and made it cool. After ten years of researching Lee's life, Polly looks at the myths surrounding Lee's life, including perhaps

the biggest of all—that Lee was a kung fu master who made a couple of movies to showcase his abilities. Following Lee from his childhood as a movie star in Hong Kong to his introduction to martial arts and his introduction to America, Polly goes on to detail his mysterious and unexpected death.

Julius Henry ("Groucho") Marx

Stephan Kanfer, *Groucho: The Life and Times of Julius Henry Marx*, 2000.

The five Marx brothers began their career as a wildly successful vaudeville act. Later, they took their talents to Broadway, where they made a splash with *The Cocoanuts* and *Animal Crackers*. But they reached superstar status with the movies *Duck Soup* and *A Night at the Opera*. The middle child, Groucho (Julius Henry), stood out from the rest. Biographer Stephan Kanfer profiles this most famous Marx brother, discussing how he wanted to be a doctor and tried, unsuccessfully, to have a happy family life.

Matthew McConaughey

Matthew McConaughey, *Greenlights*, 2020.

Oscar-winning actor Matthew McConaughey went through thirty-five years of his journals to find the common themes of his life and the lessons he's learned. In this memoir, he tells stories about his past, including failures and successes. He reveals himself to be as much a thoughtful maverick as the characters he's played.

Robert Mitchum

Lee Server, *Robert Mitchum: "Baby I Don't Care,"* 2001.

For almost fifty years, Robert Mitchum starred in unforgettable movie classics like *The Night of the Hunter* and *Cape Fear*. In many of these, he played cool, calm characters with an unsettling hint of violence just under the surface. But this wasn't entirely an act. Rebelling against mainstream acceptability, Mitchum spent time in prison for marijuana possession. He was the first Hollywood anti-hero and paved the way for later celebrities like James Dean and Clint Eastwood.

Isaac Mizrahi

Isaac Mizrahi, *I. M.: A Memoir*, 2019.

As a gay man growing up in a Syrian Jewish Orthodox family, Isaac Mizrahi was destined for a different life. Instead, after entering the fashion design industry, he became a cabaret performer and a TV personality. In his memoir, he discloses how all this came about, his problems as a gay man, and the incredible array of famous people he counts as friends.

Marilyn Monroe

Michelle Morgan, *Marilyn Monroe: Private and Undisclosed*, 2012.

Michelle Morgan, president of the U.K. Marilyn Monroe fan club, used exclusive interviews with everyone who knew Monroe and primary source material from Monroe's life to write about her life from her childhood as Norma Jeane to her tragic death. Unlike many of its predecessors, this portrait of Marilyn Monroe is fact-based and faithful to reality, not a scandalous tell-all. The seventy rare and previously unpublished photos also showcase the private side of Marilyn.

Mike Nichols

Mark Harris, *Mike Nichols: A Life*, 2021.

Highly lauded motion picture director Mike Nichols was born Igor Peschkowsky to Jewish parents in Berlin in 1931. Only eight years later, to escape the Nazis, he and his younger brother were sent to America alone. Mark Harris narrates how he was bullied and reviled once here, which gave him the impetus to achieve heights through movies like *Who's Afraid of Virginia Woolf* and *The Graduate*. By age thirty-five, he was at the pinnacle of success with fame and wealth.

Leonard Nimoy

Leonard Nimoy, *I Am Spock*, 1995.

The original *Star Trek* series fans could never get enough of Mr. Spock. Leonard Nimoy, the actor who portrayed him, discusses Spock in this memoir. Starring as Spock in the series, six motion pictures, and two episodes of *Star Trek: The Next Generation*, Nimoy also directed two of these movies. And he presents facets of Spock that no one else could.

Vincent Price

Victoria Price, *Vincent Price: A Daughter's Biography*, 1999.

Thanks to performances in movies like *House of Wax* and *The Pit and the Pendulum*, Vincent Price was one of Hollywood's biggest stars. He was also Victoria Price's father. In this touching book, she tells how she was born at the height of his career, when he was fifty-one years old. Although he was insanely busy with his many movie roles, Price maintained a close relationship with her until he married her stepmother, actress Coral Browne, who was determined to keep father and daughter apart. But later, the two renewed their close relationship. Victoria Price presents her famous father as only a devoted daughter can, and she reveals sides of him many never saw.

Arnold Schwarzenegger

Arnold Schwarzenegger, *Total Recall: My Unbelievably True Life Story*, 2012.

When successful Austrian bodybuilder Arnold Schwarzenegger moved to Los Angeles, he was twenty-one. Within ten years of arriving, he had become a millionaire businessman. Schwarzenegger was one of the world's biggest movie stars within twenty years. Then, in 2003, he started a new chapter in life as governor of California. In this memoir, he talks of how he achieved his spectacular successes, including his marriage to Maria Shiver, along with the things he regrets most, such as his secret affair.

William Shatner

William Shatner, *Up Till Now: The Autobiography*, 2008.

Before he was Captain Kirk on the original *Star Trek* series, William Shatner was already an impressive figure on the stage and small screen. Altogether, he has spent more than half a century performing. And he is loved by many. Since *Star Trek*, he has gone on to make albums, star in other TV series such as *Boston Legal*, and become a big hit on the talk show circuit. Here, he engagingly reveals all the fun he's had and what makes him tick.

Will Smith

Will Smith, *Will*, 2021.

Is there anyone on the planet who doesn't know who Will Smith is? Raised in West Philadelphia, he became a major rap star, then a wildly successful actor and producer. He tells his story here with the help of bestselling author Mark Manson. Throughout the book, Smith speaks plainly. While discussing his phenomenal career success, he also honestly describes where he's messed up and his struggles to improve. While he still has a way to go, his story is impressive.

Barbara Joan "Barbra" Streisand

William J. Mann, *Hello Gorgeous: Becoming Barbra Streisand*, 2012.

By age twenty-one, Barbra Streisand, a poor kid from Brooklyn, was the top selling female recording artist in America. Hollywood biographer William Mann talks about her whirlwind rise to the top. Recreating the New York City of the early 1960s, Mann explains how Bob Fosse and Jerome Robbins used the Broadway production of *Funny Girl* to showcase Streisand's talents. He also highlights her vulnerability and her relationships with associates and lovers.

Cicely Tyson

Cicely Tyson, *Just As I Am*, 2021.

In her nineties, American actress and fashion model Cicely Tyson writes of her seventy-plus years in film and on stage. She writes of the fame and the accolades. But Tyson is equally as honest about the pain she has endured. And through it all, she gives glory to her God.

Rudolph Valentino

Emily W. Leider, *Dark Lover: The Life and Death of Rudolph Valentino*, 2003.

Rudolph Valentino, a star of early Hollywood movies, was one of America's earliest heartthrobs. Valentino was an Italian immigrant whose androgynous sexuality and dark good looks made him both idolized and deplored. After his death at age thirty-one following surgery for appendicitis and a perforated ulcer, there was international hysteria that included several suicides. Leider looks at the societal factors that turned Valentino into a lightning rod of sexual intensity.

Esther Williams

Esther Williams, *The Million Dollar Mermaid: An Autobiography*, 1999.

As a teenager, Esther Williams was a competitive swimmer who set national records and planned to compete in the 1940 Summer Olympics. Unfortunately, the games were canceled when World War II began. But while she was swimming in an aquacade, she was discovered by a Hollywood agent. At MGM studios, she learned to project glamour and sex appeal. But still, she found her private life challenging to manage. She shares it all in this memoir.

27

Novelists and Short Story Writers

Jane Austen

Paula Byrne, *The Real Jane Austen:*
A Life in Small Things, 2013.

Paula Byrne uses an unconventional approach to tell of the life of literary legend Jane Austen. Instead of telling her story chronologically, Byrne uses moment, scenes, and objects from her personal life and her novels to shed light on Austen's daily life. Austen traveled widely and the different landscapes and political climates she encountered influenced her work in unexpected ways.

Clive Barker

Stephen Jones, *Clive Barker's Shadows in Eden*, 1991.

Stephen Jones looks at the personality and life of bestselling American horror fiction writer Clive Barker. Using interviews, reviews, and discussions, Jones also includes many photographic and artistic illustrations.

Pearl Buck

Hilary Spurling, *Burying the Bones:*
Pearl Buck's Life in China, 2010.

Pearl Buck garnered international fame with her novel *The Good Earth*, which depicts China during the era in which she grew up. British writer Hilary Spurling tells the story of the American writer, who was the daughter of a Presbyterian missionary who moved the family to China when Buck was small. Her father was a humorless figure who spent all his money on his missionary work. Her mother did her best to make her children's lives comfortable. But the backdrop of a China long gone, in which Buck grew up, is itself almost a character in her work.

Angela Carter

Edmund Gordon, *The Invention of Angela Carter:*
A Biography, 2017.

Edmund Gordon had complete access to Angela Carter's manuscripts, letters, and journals. In addition, he interviewed friends and family to piece together this portrait of one of the late twentieth century's most unconventional writers. Her work was informed by her adventurous life. Although she died from lung cancer at age fifty-one, she had already changed the face of literature with iconoclastic works like *The Bloody Chamber*.

John Cheever

Susan Cheever, *Home Before Dark: A Biographical Memoir of John Cheever by His Daughter*, 1984.

Using her famous father's unpublished letters and journals, along with her memories, Susan Cheever writes a tribute to her father, the beloved short story writer and novelist John Cheever. While Cheever wrote about the suburban culture in which he lived, his battle with alcoholism deeply affected his family, including his daughter Susan who tells about it all in this memoir.

Agatha Christie

Agatha Christie, *Agatha Christie: An Autobiography*, 1977.

Crime novelist and playwright Agatha Christie is one of the world's best selling authors. Before her death in 1976, she wrote this memoir, which finally revealed her private life for her legions of fans. She covers it all, her early childhood, her marriages, and her archaeological expeditions. For a third-person account of her life, you can read Gillian Gill's *Agatha Christie: The Woman and Her Mysteries*.

Charles Dickens

Claire Tomalin, *The Invisible Woman: The Story of Charles Dickens and Nelly Ternan*, 1990.

In *The Invisible Woman*, literary biographer Claire Tomalin focuses on the little-known story of Charles Dickens's affair with Nelly Ternan, which began when he was middle-aged and she was an eighteen-year-old actress. Their affair led to the breakup of Dickens's marriage and then lasted until he died.

Isak Dinesen

Judith Thurman, *Isak Dinesen: The Life of a Storyteller*, 1982.

Judith Thurman's classic work on Isak Dinesen sorts out the life and art of the Danish author of *Out of Africa*. Dinesen's work has mystical elements and a beauty that led to her being nominated twice for a Nobel Prize.

Daphne du Maurier

Margaret Forster, *Daphne du Maurier: The Secret Life of the Renowned Storyteller*, 1993.

Novelist and biographer Margaret Forster uncovers the woman behind the blockbuster novel *Rebecca*. Du Maurier was extremely reticent about disclosing the details of her life. Forster unpacks her difficult childhood and marriage as well has her enigmatic sexuality.

George Eliot

Kathryn Hughes, *George Eliot: The Last Victorian*, 1998.

Writing under the pen name George Eliot, Mary Ann Evans produced nineteenth-century classics such as *Middlemarch* and *Silas Marner*. The pen name was a necessity because Victorian readers were not yet ready to accept female writers. British journalist Kathryn Hughes chronicles the unconventional life that Eliot lived, including her scandalous affair with writer and editor George Henry Lewes. Eliot's work was so popular that she was friends with respected male writers of the day. Hughes looks at her work in context of the Victorian era in which she lived.

Annie Ernaux

Annie Ernaux, *The Years*, 2008.

Award-winning and bestselling French author Annie Ernaux crafted a different kind of autobiography when she wrote this book. She goes through her life, from 1941 to 2006, highlighting photos, books, songs, radio, TV, advertising, news headlines, and personal stories that were important to her year by year. The result helps us remember our own past as we compare her memories with those of our own.

Penelope Fitzgerald

Hermione Lee, *Penelope Fitzgerald: A Life*, 2013.

Master biographer Hermione Lee traces the life of the twentieth-century British novelist Penelope Fitzgerald. Her novels, such as *Offshore* and *The Blue Flower*, were short and subtle but were nevertheless intriguing works of genius. Interestingly, Fitzgerald published her first novel at age sixty and didn't become famous until she was eighty. She enjoyed playing the part of a harebrained old lady, while she was really razor-sharp.

Frank Herbert

Brian Herbert, *Dreamer of Dune: The Biography of Frank Herbert*, 2003.

As the eldest son of the creator of *Dune*, Brian Herbert talks honestly about his father's life of intense genius. While *Dune* is Herbert's best known, he also wrote over twenty books including *The Green Brain* and *The White Plague*. Life wasn't easy for Herbert. After growing up in Washington State and trying his hand at various careers, he endured years of poverty while establishing himself as a writer.

Georgette Heyer

Jennifer Kloester, *Georgette Heyer: Biography of a Bookseller*, 2011.

As one of the best selling and most popular authors of the twentieth century, Georgette Heyer, was an anomaly in that she never gave a single interview and never appeared in public. Yet through the years she churned out regency romances and detective fiction that is still widely read today.

John le Carré

John le Carré, *The Pigeon Tunnel: Stories from My Life*, 2016.

Born David John Moore Cornwell, British espionage novelist John le Carré published this first memoir just four years before his death in 2020. After serving in British intelligence in the Cold War, he began to write his novels. With his vast experience traveling the globe in sometimes dangerous situations, le Carré's accounts of his life are at times disturbing, sometimes riveting, and sometimes surprisingly funny.

Gabriel García Márquez

Rodrigo García, *A Farewell to Gabo and Mercedes: A Son's Memoir*, 2021.

When famed magical realism writer Gabriel García Márquez came down with a cold, Rodrigo García watched as his mother, Mercedes Barcha, resigned herself to his loss. At the time, García Márquez was eighty-seven years old and in the grip of dementia. García then began keeping a record of the passing days, and his father became the focus of this loving and touching memoir.

Jean Genet

Edmund White, *Genet: A Biography*, 1993.

The infamous French writer Jean Genet was an iconoclast who deliberately set out to shock society. As a young man, he was a criminal who took up the mantle of activist for the marginalized and downtrodden. He was also a male prostitute, and his life of crime never came to an end. His early experiments in the theater of the absurd garnered the attention of international celebrities. And his novels, calculated to jar conventional expectations, changed the landscape of literature forever.

Günter Grass

Günter Grass, *Peeling the Onion*, 2006.

Nobel Prize–winning German author Günter Grass writes about his life as a young boy in Danzig through the publication of his internationally acclaimed novel *The Tin Drum*. He was rejected at age fifteen when he volunteered for the Nazi submarine corps, but two years later, he was drafted into the Waffen SS. Captured in the final weeks of the war, he wound up in an American POW camp. After the war, he made his way to Paris and began his career. This memoir is the first of a trilogy.

Thomas Hardy

Michael Millgate, *Thomas Hardy: A Biography Revisited*, 1982.

Hardy scholar Michael Millgate revises his original biography of the British literary giant, considering new information that has challenged previous depictions of his life. Hardy was self-educated. His relations with women were sometimes difficult, but he occasionally collaborated with aspiring women authors. Using his own techniques, he kept his mind sharp so he could produce works of literature well into old age.

Ernest Hemingway

Ernest Hemingway, *A Moveable Feast*, 1964.

During the 1920s, before he became a giant in the American literary landscape, Ernest Hemingway lived in Paris, where he frequently rubbed shoulders with Gertrude Stein, James Joyce, and Scott and Zelda Fitzgerald. During those days of writing in cafes, Hemingway found his writing voice. This memoir was written near the end of his life of writing such classics as *A Farewell to Arms* and *For Whom the Bell Tolls*.

Zora Neale Hurston

Zora Neale Hurston, *Dust Tracks on a Road: An Autobiography*, 1942.

American folklorist and acclaimed author Zora Neale Hurston wrote this autobiography at the apex of her career. The Harlem Renaissance writer who penned such works as *Mules and Men* and *Their Eyes Were Watching God* writes in her singular style about her life from a childhood in an all-Black Florida town to becoming one of the leading intellectuals of her day.

Shirley Jackson

Ruth Franklin, *Shirley Jackson: A Rather Haunted Life*, 2016.

Shirley Jackson lived the twentieth-century American middle-class dream. At least that's what she and women like her were told. As the wife of a college professor, Jackson took care of her home and family, but in addition to that, she wrote gothic works that biographer Ruth Franklin sees as "belonging to the great tradition of Hawthorne, Poe, and James." Her works like *We Always Lived in the Castle* and *The Haunting of Hill House* give credence to Franklin's argument.

Henry James

Leon Edel, *Henry James: The Master, 1901–1916*, 1972.

This last of a five-volume biography of American author Henry James can be read alone, as it summarizes the information found in all four volumes that preceded it. It highlights the last fifteen years of James's life, mostly lived in London, where he socializes with George Bernard Shaw, Virginia Woolf, and a young Winston Churchill. It also discusses his long-time friendship with author Edith Wharton.

Stephen King

Stephen King, *On Writing: A Memoir of the Craft*, 2000.

As one of the best selling authors of all time, master horror writer Stephen King begins with his childhood, raised by his single mother. After talking about how he wanted to be a writer from a young age, the author of novels such as *Carrie* and *The Stand* explains to aspiring writers what he sees as the most important facets of the writing craft. He ends the book right after his near-fatal accident, when he was struck by a vehicle while out walking on a rural road in Maine.

Anne Lamott

Anne Lamott, *Bird by Bird: Some Instructions on Writing and Life*, 1994.

When she was a child, writer Anne Lamott watched her brother struggle to complete a report on birds that was due in school the next day. While he had been given three months to complete his work, he had started the day before and was understandably panicking. Her father calmly instructed him to take it "bird by bird." Lamott uses that advice to provide her own guide on how to write along with a generous sprinkling of stories and anecdotes from her life to spice things up.

D. H. Lawrence

Frances Wilson, *Burning Man: The Trials of D. H. Lawrence*, 2021.

Using *The Divine Comedy* to structure her biography of early twentieth-century British novelist D. H. Lawrence, Frances Wilson follows Lawrence through his journeys around the world, focusing on the period between 1915 and 1925, which was his most prolific. She uses three scenes in particular, his crises in Cornwall, Italy, and New Mexico. She also looks at the people who stood against him, like his wife, Frieda; Maurice Magnus; and Mabel Dodge Luhan.

Doris Lessing

Doris Lessing, *Under My Skin: Volume One of My Autobiography, to 1949*, 1994.

Self-educated intellectual Doris Lessing, the author of *The Golden Notebook*, was one of the most brilliant writers of the twentieth century. As the daughter of British colonial parents, she grew up in Persia and Southern Rhodesia. Using her uncanny ability to articulate the deep nuances of thought and feeling, she traces her growth of consciousness, sexuality, and political views. Lessing went on the be awarded the Nobel Prize for Literature in 2007.

H. P. Lovecraft

S. T. Joshi, *H. P. Lovecraft: A Life*, 1996.

Indian American literary scholar S. T. Joshi writes the life story of Howard Phillips Lovecraft with understanding, yet honesty. He details Lovecraft's abhorrent racism and his regrettable treatment of his wife. But he also spends a great deal of time telling the stories behind the stories, providing commentary on them as well.

Somerset Maugham

Selina Hastings, *The Secret Lives of Somerset Maugham: A Biography*, 2009.

For a time, Somerset Maugham was the most famous writer in the world. Digging into his personal correspondence and previously unknown interviews, Selina Hastings tells the story of his secret life that helped him create his great works like *Of Human Bondage*. She depicts his childhood as a lonely orphan living with detached relatives, which left him searching the rest of his life for love and closeness. She explores his lovers, including many men, and the celebrities that peppered his life.

Herman Melville

Hershel Parker, *Herman Melville: A Biography: 1819–1851* (Volume 1), 1996.

This first volume of a two-book biography chronicles the first forty years of Melville's life. Melville was a son of wealthy New Yorkers whose father lost not one but two family fortunes. His family pulled him out of private boarding school at age twelve and put him to work in a bank and a fur store. But at age twenty-one, he left to sail on the Pacific as a whaleman. His early books *Typee* and *Omoo* about life in the South Sea Islands made him rich and famous. After a few commercial failures, he began to write *Moby Dick*, which is where this book ends.

Flannery O'Connor

Brad Gooch, *Flannery: A Life of Flannery O'Connor*, 2009.

Biographer Brad Gooch writes of American original Flannery O'Connor, whose novels and stories reflected her sincere Catholic belief but were, at the same time, dark and witty critiques of society. Gooch details her many literary friendships with celebrity writers such as Robert Lowell, Walker Percy, Thomas Merton, and Elizabeth Bishop. Even though for much of her life she suffered from ill health that eventually confined her to her mother's farm, O'Connor lived a life passion.

Edgar Allan Poe

Kenneth Silverman, *Edgar A. Poe: Mournful and Never-Ending Remembrance*, 1991.

Edgar Allan Poe is a towering figure in America's literary canon. His poems, stories, and novels are not only required reading for many students' but they are also voluntarily read with gusto. Pulitzer Prize–winning biographer Kenneth Silverman reveals that Poe was also one of the nation's first professional writers: he wrote reviews and criticism to earn extra money. According to Silverman, Poe's many struggles, including poverty and alcoholism, resulted from a lack of self-worth, which triggered a self-destructive spiral.

Marcel Proust

Jean-Yves Tadié, *Marcel Proust: A Life*, 1996.

Proust scholar Jean-Yves Tadié profiles the life of Marcel Proust, whose novel *A Remembrance of Things Past* is considered one of the greatest literary works of the twentieth century. Using primary sources, Tadié provides an engaging look at the author's life and his social and cultural milieu.

Philip Roth

Blake Bailey, *Philip Roth: The Biography*, 2021.

A celebrated author of literary works, Philip Roth grew up in a lower-middle-class Jewish community. From there, he rose to the height of fame in postwar America for his masterful short stories and novels. Biographer Blake Bailey looks at Roth's stories and real-life romances, including his decades-long relationship with the actress Claire Bloom. In addition, he looks at his rivalrous friendships with luminaries Saul Bellow, John Updike, and William Styron. Roth died in 2018.

Mary Shelley

Muriel Spark, *Mary Shelley*, 1987.

Scottish novelist Muriel Spark presents the life of Mary Shelley, the famed author of the novel *Frankenstein, or Modern Prometheus*. Shelley was a daughter of women's rights writer Mary Wollstonecraft. At age seventeen, she eloped with the poet Percy Bysshe Shelley. It was while staying with him and Lord Byron that she began the novel that became *Frankenstein*. Spark defends Shelley's place in the British literary pantheon.

Lee Smith

Lee Smith, *Dimestore: A Writer's Life*, 2016.

In her novels and short stories, Lee Smith portrays the mountain culture of the Southern Appalachian region, because that's what she knows. Growing up in Grundy, Virginia, Smith spent a lot of time in her father's dime store making up stories about the dolls there and listening to the chitchat of his customers. At age nine, she was writing and selling her stories for a nickel apiece. In this memoir Smith talks about her own story with the same clarity and vivacity that she uses in her fiction.

Nicholas Sparks

Nicholas Sparks and Micah Sparks, *Three Weeks with My Brother*, 2004.

Bestselling author Nicholas Sparks writes of a three-week journey around the world with his brother, Micah. The two set off in their late thirties, to spend some time together as the only remaining members of their family. As they travel to the Australian outback and to Easter Island, as well as many other places, they reflect on childhood memories and celebrate life and companionship.

John Steinbeck

William Souder, *Mad at the World: A Life of John Steinbeck*, 2020.

Biographer William Souder provides a full-length narrative of the life of Nobel Laurate John Steinbeck. Notoriously irascible and taciturn, Steinbeck was nevertheless sympathetic to the plight of the working people whose cause he first took up during the Great Depression and the Dust Bowl years when destitute people flooded into the California agricultural country only to be mercilessly used. Despite his good intentions, Steinbeck had trouble keeping his private life in order. But his brilliance is unmistakable. Steinbeck also wrote a memoir of his own, his highly regarded *Travels with Charley: In Search of America*.

James Tiptree Jr.

Julie Phillips, *James Tiptree, Jr.: The Double Life of Alice B. Sheldon*, 2006.

Science fiction writer James Tiptree Jr. wrote classics such as *Houston, Houston, Do You Read?* and *The Women Men Don't See*, which earned him a reputation for his understanding of female characters. He maintained relationships with writers such as Philip K. Dick and Ursula Le Guin, strictly through correspondence. Using extensive research, Julie Phillips put together the real identity of Tiptree: a woman named Alice B. Sheldon, whose real life was even more interesting than her alter ego's.

J. R. R. Tolkien

Humphrey Carpenter, *J. R. R. Tolkien: A Biography*, 1977.

English biographer and radio broadcaster Humphrey Carpenter was authorized to create this biography of the beloved Oxford professor of Middle English and creator of *The Hobbit*, *The Lord of the Rings*, and *The Silmarillion*. Tolkien was born in South Africa during the colonial period and lost both his parents at an early age. Brought up in England with little money, he was later a soldier in World War I. He was a member of the Inklings, a group of writers in Oxford that included C. S. Lewis, who regularly met to discuss life and work. Carpenter had unrestricted access to all Tolkien's papers and interviewed friends and family to provide this biography.

Leo Tolstoy

Henri Troyat, *Tolstoy*, 1965.

French historian Henri Troyat brings together the contradictions in the life of one of the world's greatest writers, Leo Tolstoy. Though Tolstoy was an aristocrat, he admired and defended peasants; while he largely disliked women, he portrayed them masterfully in novels like *Anna Karenina*. Troyat explains how Tolstoy finally became a teacher of morality with his religious conversion.

Mark Twain

Justin Kaplan, *Mr. Clemens and Mark Twain: A Biography*, 1966.

Life in the Gilded Age was one of contradictions for American literary legend Samuel Clemens, aka Mark Twain. Justin Kaplan set this biography up almost as that of two separate people. First there was the Midwestern Mark Twain who wrote books like *Huckleberry Finn* and wrote biting and hilarious satire, who had common sense and who despised ostentation. But then there was also Samuel Clemens, who married an heiress and lived an exorbitant lifestyle in the East. The conflict in the author, Kaplan asserts, neatly encapsulates the conflict between morality and ambition in American society. Mark Twain also wrote several autobiographical works of note including *Life on the Mississippi* and *Roughing It*.

John Updike

Adam Begley, *Updike*, 2014.

One of twentieth-century America's most highly regarded writers of novels, poems, short stories, and criticism was John Updike, who began his career at the *New Yorker*. Biographer Adam Begley tells how Updike's works were often semiautobiographical and were based on his small-town and suburban experiences. While narrating Updike's life, Begley also discusses his work, including *The Witches of Eastwick* and the *Rabbit* series.

Alice Walker

Evelyn C. White, *Alice Walker: A Life*, 2004.

The first Black woman to win a Pulitzer Prize, for her novel *The Color Purple*, Alice Walker began life as the eighth child of Georgia sharecroppers. Evelyn C. White used interviews and in-depth research to tell how Walker began writing and attended college. Her work has continued to champion African American and women's causes.

Evelyn Waugh

Paula Byrne, *Mad World: Evelyn Waugh and the Secrets of Brideshead*, 2009.

Twentieth-century English author Evelyn Waugh wrote the classic novel *Brideshead Revisited*. Biographer Paula Byrne tells of his glamourous and colorful family, who were the inspirations for his work. She also shares generous information on his friends the Mitford sisters and on the "Bright Young People."

H. G. Wells

Claire Tomalin, *The Young H. G. Wells: Changing the World*, 2021.

Science fiction writer H. G. Wells was famous for inventive books like *The Time Machine* and *The War of the Worlds*. Yet all his well-regarded works were written by the time he was forty. Literary biographer Claire Tomalin tells how this child of two servant-class people educated himself through scholarships and hard work. But his poor health made all his accomplishments difficult. His first book, *The Time Machine*, was borne of his own desire to escape reality.

Eudora Welty

Eudora Welty, *One Writer's Beginnings*, 1983.

Pulitzer Prize–winning author Eudora Welty was famous for her honest, humorous, and plainspoken depictions of life in the American South in the twentieth century. In her memoir, she talks about her family and their impact on her writing. While Welty spent most of her life out of the spotlight because of her preference for privacy, she did the world a favor in investigating her family history and how it all affected her creativity. She is known for novels like *The Optimist's Daughter* and short stories like "Why I Live at the P.O."

Edith Wharton

Hermione Lee, *Edith Wharton*, 2007.

Using previously unavailable materials, biographer Hermione Lee presents a new examination of Edith Wharton, one of America's greatest writers. Born to an upper-class family in 1862, Wharton moved to Europe early on and lived for most of her life in France. Famously friends with literary notables like Henry James and Aldous Huxley, she also worked tirelessly on relief efforts during World War I. Lee breaks through the stereotypical portrayals of Wharton to bring us the real woman.

Tobias Wolff

Tobias Wolff, *This Boy's Life: A Memoir*, 1989.

Fiction and nonfiction writer Tobias Wolff reveals how his parents' divorce and their decision for Tobias's brother and father to stay together, while Wolff remained with his mother, affected him. He and his mother were extraordinarily close until she remarried, and he had to fight to keep his self-respect in the face of his stepfather's hostility. His difficult adolescence, with its mistakes and triumphs, helped him become a successful writer.

Jacqueline Woodson

Jacqueline Woodson, *Brown Girl Dreaming*, 2014.
American writer Jacqueline Woodson is known for her poems and books for all age levels, including *Feathers* and *Miracle's Boys*. Here, Woodson writes about life growing up in South Carolina and New York in the 1960s and 1970s. Using poetry to capture her feelings in each time and place, she shares the experiences that made her the writer she is today.

Virginia Woolf

Lyndall Gordon, *Virginia Woolf: A Writer's Life*, 1984.
British academic and literary biographer Lyndall Gordon narrates the life of British writer Virginia Woolf. Woolf was the celebrated writer of classics such as *To the Lighthouse* and *Mrs. Dalloway*, and Gordon covers her life from herupper-crust childhood through her death by suicide.

COLLECTIVE BIOGRAPHY

Lucasta Miller, *The Brontë Myth*, 2001.
Using an unusual approach to uncover the lives of the famed Brontë family, Lucasta Miller reads biographies of the sisters starting with Elizabeth Gaskell's *Life of Charlotte Brontë* and proceeding on through biographies down through the intervening years. Miller finds that each generation of writers reinvents the sisters anew. Her attempt to straighten out the facts provides new insights into the lives of these remarkable women.

Poets and Playwrights

Maya Angelou

Maya Angelou,
***The Collected Autobiographies of Maya Angelou*, 1995.**
Most know of American Poet Laureate Maya Angelou's first memoir, *I Know Why the Caged Bird Sings*, published in 1969. After that, she published five more well-regarded memoirs. As a poet, she has a gift for rendering the experiences in her life with clarity and verve. Angelou also shares memories and recipes in *Hallelujah! The Welcome Table*, 2004.

Elizabeth Bishop

Megan Marshall, *Elizabeth Bishop:*
***A Miracle for Breakfast*, 2017.**
Celebrated twentieth-century American poet Elizabeth Bishop is captured in this biography by her former Harvard poetry workshop student, Megan Marshall. Bishop, who was shy, lived out of the spotlight. Marshall uncovers dark aspects of her childhood and the relationships she maintained with various lovers and friends, including Marianne Moore and Robert Lowell.

Elizabeth Barrett Browning

Margaret Forster, *Elizabeth Barrett Browning:*
***A Biography*, 1988.**
Using previously unavailable correspondence, literary critic Margaret Forster says Browning was a strong woman who kept to herself before meeting her husband, the poet Robert Browning, because she wished to write on her terms. Her blank verse poem "Aurora Leigh" is a feminist work that was rejected by critics but loved by the public. Forster discusses how, in the poet's later years living in Italy, Browning became interested in spiritualism.

Charles Bukowski

Howard Sounes, *Charles Bukowski:*
***Locked in the Arms of a Crazy Life*, 1998.**
Biographer Howard Sounes uncovers the facts from the life of Charles Bukowski, the poet and author of autobiographical novels on whom the Hollywood movie *Barfly* is based. In his early life, Bukowski was an alcoholic

postal worker. Then, in middle age, he became a writer of immense talent. Sounes draws on private letters, unpublished works, and interviews with his friends, family, and lovers to tell his story.

George Gordon (Lord Byron)

Phyllis Grosskurth, *Byron: The Flawed Angel*, 1997.

Early-nineteenth-century British Romantic poet Lord Byron was a celebrity of rock-star status. As a bisexual man, he traveled most of Europe, leaving a wake of lovers and a series of fatherless children behind him. His only legitimate child was the mathematical genius Ada Lovelace. Scandal piled deep around him before his death at age thirty-six.

Geoffrey Chaucer

John Gardner, *The Life and Times of Chaucer*, 1977.

Novelist and academic John Gardner, himself the notable author of the novel *Grendel*, retells the life of fourteenth-century English writer Geoffrey Chaucer, the author of *The Canterbury Tales*. This biography stands out because Gardner is a translator of Middle English poetry, so combining the well-known facts of Chaucer's life with criticism and educated guesswork makes the man come alive in a way that few biographies manage.

Annie Dillard

Annie Dillard, *Pilgrim at Tinker Creek*, 1974.

As a young woman, Annie Dillard spent a year living near Tinker Creek in Virginia. Her beautiful and stunningly written account of animals, plants, water, and light will help you see the natural world differently. In addition, Dillard is an award-winning poet. Her other memoirs include *An American Childhood* and *The Writing Life*.

Tove Ditlevsen

Tove Ditlevsen, *The Copenhagen Trilogy: Childhood; Youth; Dependency*, 1967.

Danish poet Tove Ditlevsen wrote three autobiographical novels in her fifties. The set is considered her masterpiece. The first, *Childhood*, tells of her conviction as a child that she would be a poet. The second, *Youth*, talks of her coming of age and discovering sex and a career. And the final one, *Dependency*, talks about her ghastly first marriage and drug addiction. Ditlevsen died by suicide in 1976.

T. S. Eliot

Peter Ackroyd, *T. S. Eliot*, 1984.

Anglo-American poet, playwright, and critic Thomas Stearns Eliot had a tremendous influence on the literary world in the twentieth century. While Eliot was notoriously private, award-winning author Peter Ackroyd researched extensively to uncover the character of this man who, despite being a religious and political conservative, managed to usher in modern poetry.

Robert Frost

Jay Parini, *Robert Frost: A Life*, 1998.

Many already know that Robert Frost, one of the twentieth century's most famous American poets, was a private man. Jay Parini, a scholar, poet, and biographer, takes a fresh look at Frost's complexity. After examining the poet's archives, Parini uncovers the factors behind his choices to help the reader better understand the poems he left behind.

Langston Hughes

Arnold Rampersad, *The Life of Langston Hughes: 1902–1941: I, Too, Sing America* (Volume 1), 1986.

Literary critic Arnold Rampersad memorializes Harlem Renaissance poet Langston Hughes by celebrating the poet's most significant early works. Using archival collections, Rampersad follows Hughes around the globe to the Soviet Union, Mexico, Africa, Japan, and other far-flung places. He discusses what makes Hughes's work great and the influence he left on those in his wake.

Mary Karr

Mary Karr, *Lit: A Memoir*, 2009.

Acclaimed poet and memoirist Mary Karr wrote this book as a sequel to her first two memoirs, *The Liar's Club* and *Cherry*. In this one, she talks of her struggles with alcohol and being a mother. The book was widely praised for its writing and has been called a work of art.

John Keats

Walter Jackson Bate, *John Keats*, 1963.

Literary critic Walter Jackson Bate fleshes out the early life of nineteenth-century Romantic English poet John Keats. Bate sees the great challenge of poets of every age as honoring the towering poets before them while still producing fresh and original work. He sees in Keats a poet who succeeds in this challenge and, thus, serves as a model for poets who follow him.

Robert Lowell

Kay Redfield Jamison, *Robert Lowell, Setting the River on Fire: A Study of Genius, Mania, and Character*, 2017.

Pulitzer Prize winner Robert Lowell was a brilliant twentieth-century American poet who suffered from manic–depressive illness (now called bipolar disorder). Kay Redfield Jamison is a clinical psychologist whose primary area of expertise is bipolar disorder. She uses previously inaccessible medical records to tell Lowell's story and examine the relationship between the disorder and creativity.

Christopher Marlowe

Charles Nicholl, *The Reckoning: The Murder of Christopher Marlowe*, 1992.

What happened to Christopher Marlowe, the brilliant and controversial young Elizabethan playwright? English author and literary detective Charles Nicholl tells the familiar story of how Marlowe went drinking with some pals one day in 1593 and was stabbed to death in an argument over the bill. But is that the real story? Questions have always hung about the affair. And, in his reconstruction of the events of that fateful night, Nicholl unveils much more than a sordid murder.

Edna St. Vincent Millay

Nancy Milford, *Savage Beauty: The Life of Edna St. Vincent Millay*, 2001.

Jazz Age poet Edna St. Vincent Millay was a modern girl famous for defying convention. Most scandalously, she smoked in public and had many lovers of both sexes. But it was for her poetry that she garnered the most attention and praise. Biographer Nancy Milford writes of her troubled life.

Pablo Neruda

Adam Feinstein, *Pablo Neruda: A Passion for Life*, 2004.

Gabriel García Márquez declared Nobel-winning Chilean poet Pablo Neruda "the greatest poet of the twentieth century—in any language." Adam Feinstein narrates the poet's life, covering his politics, his writing, and his lovers.

Fernando Pessoa

Richard Zenith, *Pessoa: A Biography*, 2021.

Portuguese poet Fernando Pessoa always believed in his greatness, even though he feared the insanity that stalked his family. Writing under many different names (heteronyms), each with its own alter ego, Pessoa was relatively unknown in his lifetime. So when 25,000 of his papers turned up in a trunk, Richard Zenith had the sources necessary to craft this surprising biography and to document his literary genius.

Sylvia Plath

Heather Clark, *Red Comet: The Short Life and Blazing Art of Sylvia Plath*, 2020.

Many Sylvia Plath fans already know about the author's life from her autobiographical novel *The Bell Jar*, her stunning poems, and her shocking suicide while married to acclaimed British poet Ted Hughes. But Heather Clark goes far beyond the surface-level facts surrounding Plath to present a more nuanced biography. While sympathetic to Plath, she also looks forthrightly at the other people in her life so that all sides are represented fairly.

Ezra Pound

Humphrey Carpenter, *A Serious Character: The Life of Ezra Pound*, 1988.

Acclaimed and controversial twentieth-century poet, critic, editor, and educator Ezra Pound is one of the most famous intellectuals of his time. But, as English biographer Humphrey Carpenter relates, in 1945, Pound was arrested for broadcasting Axis propaganda in Rome during World War II, resulting in treason charges. Later, he spent thirteen years in a psychiatric hospital in Washington, D.C.

Aleksandr Pushkin

T. J. Binyon, *Pushkin: A Biography*, 2002.

In the first half of the nineteenth century, Aleksandr Pushkin was one of Russia's greatest poets. He also wrote novels, plays, and short stories. After living a wildly extravagant life, he died in a duel at age thirty-eight. English scholar Timothy John Binyon uncovers the real life of this romantic hero while also bringing nineteenth-century Russia to life.

William Shakespeare

Bill Bryson, *Shakespeare: The World as Stage*, 2007.

Bestselling American author Bill Bryson, author of *A Walk in the Woods*, provides a biography of The Bard that anyone can read and enjoy. Not only does Bryson cover the few facts we know about Shakespeare, but he also hops around Elizabethan England to acquaint readers with the time and place. Then he explains Shakespearean scholarship's conclusions and controversies.

Percy Bysshe Shelley

Richard Holmes, *Shelley: The Pursuit*, 1974.

Richard Holmes, the acclaimed literary biographer, made his name with this biography of the early-nineteenth-century English Romantic poet Percy Bysshe Shelley. Whereas before, Shelley had always been portrayed as a mild and ethereal dreamer, Holmes presents him in an entirely different light. Instead of a victim of his delicate temperament, as Holmes sees him, he was a rebel, determined to do what he wanted no matter who he hurt. Nevertheless, he admits Shelley's work is brilliant, inspiring such poets to follow as W. B. Yeats and Allen Ginsburg.

Tom Stoppard

Hermione Lee, *Tom Stoppard: A Life*, 2020.

Using her trademark meticulous research, Hermione Lee profiles British playwright Tom Stoppard from his birth in Czechoslovakia, his childhood in India, and everywhere he lived afterward to flesh out the story of this wildly successful writer. She interviews everyone who has worked with Stoppard, from Trevor Nunn to Steven Spielberg, to try to uncover this elusive man behind the shows.

Tennessee Williams

James Grissom, *Follies of God: Tennessee Williams and the Women of the Fog*, 2015.

As a young man, James Grissom wrote a letter to writer Tennessee Williams asking for advice. To his surprise, Williams, struggling to make it in theater and whose work had been called "overrated," asked Grissom to come for a visit. As a result of their conversation, Williams sent Grissom on a trip to meet up with the women who had inspired him to see what they thought of Williams and his work. The extraordinary women included Lillian Gish, Maureen Stapleton, and Jessica Tandy. As a result, Grissom reveals a side of Williams that no one else could.

William Butler Yeats

R. F. Foster, *W. B. Yeats, A Life: I: The Apprentice Mage, 1865–1914*, 1997.

In this extraordinarily well researched biography, Roy Foster overturns the popular perception of the famed late-nineteenth- and early-twentieth-century Irish poet. From a bourgeois childhood in Ireland, Yeats explored ideas, lifestyle choices, love affairs, drugs, and occultism and emerged as one of the most original poets of the age. This volume ends when Yeats is fifty years old, during World War I. Yeats also wrote six autobiographical works collectively called *Autobiographies*.

Children's Storytellers and Legendary Figures

Louisa May Alcott

John Matteson, *Eden's Outcasts: The Story of Louisa May Alcott and Her Father,* 2007.

As the author of classic novels like *Little Women, Little Men,* and *Jo's Boys,* Louisa May Alcott is internationally recognized. However, many don't know that her father, Bronson Alcott, was an idealist who was a close friend of Emerson and Thoreau and an esteemed educator. Professor John Matteson uncovers the tense relationship between the ambitious but loving Louisa and her perfectionist but equally loving father.

King Arthur

David Day, *The Search for King Arthur,* 1995.

Canadian author David Day explores the roots of the King Arthur legends. Beginning with the records of the historic Roman Artorius, he covers every iteration of the tales of Arthur and his companions, from Merlin to Guinevere.

L. Frank Baum

Evan I. Schwartz, *Finding Oz: How L. Frank Baum Discovered the Great American Story,* 2009.

As the writer of the iconic children's series *The Wizard of Oz,* L. Frank Baum broke records with his books. Evan I. Schwartz tells how the events and people in Baum's life inspired the works. The Emerald City was based on the Chicago World's Fair of 1893, and his mother-in-law, women's rights leader Matilda Joslyn Gage, was the inspiration for both good and evil witches. Overall, this book takes you through American culture's late nineteenth through the early twentieth centuries and demonstrates how Baum used the American Dream as fuel for his imaginative works.

Roald Dahl

Roald Dahl, *Boy: Tales of Childhood,* 1984.

As the creator of children's classics such as *Charlie and the Chocolate Factory* and *James and the Giant Peach,* Roald Dahl astounded his readers with his imaginative and quirky characters and plot lines. However, many don't know he wrote equally successful dark short stories and plays for adults. Before all that, though, Dahl was a boy growing up in England. In this memoir, he talks in his usual hilarious style about growing up.

Queen Guinevere

Nichole Evelina, *The Once and Future Queen: Guinevere in Arthurian Legend*, 2017.

For fifteen years, biographer Nichole Evelina researched Arthurian legends. Looking at portrayals of Queen Guinevere in popular works across the centuries from Celtic times to the present, Evelina finds that the legendary queen reflects the attitudes toward women in general for each period.

Helen of Troy

Bettany Hughes, *Helen of Troy: The Story Behind the Most Beautiful Woman in the World*, 2005.

British historian Bettany Hughes searches for the real Helen of Troy. Helen's story goes back three thousand years to when she was purportedly the most beautiful woman in the world, "the face that launched a thousand ships," tipping off the Trojan War when she left her Greek husband, King Menelaus, for the Trojan prince, Paris. That's the legend, according to Homer, but what's the real story? While searching for examples of stories about Helen in Greece, North Africa, and Asia Minor, Hughes pieces together a portrait of one of the most famous women in history.

John Henry

Scott Reynolds Nelson, *Steel Drivin' Man: John Henry, the Untold Story of an American Legend*, 2006.

Most Americans are familiar with the song about folk hero John Henry who could plow through solid rock faster than any steam drill. But was he a real person? Scott Reynolds investigates the question and determines that John Henry is based on a Black convict from Virginia who was sent to work on the mile-long Lewis Tunnel for the C&O Railroad. Along with telling the true story (the convicts really did beat the steam drill), he also tells the story of how the legends grew and details the many versions of the popular song.

Jim Henson

Brian Jay Jones, *Jim Henson: The Biography*, 2013.

Without Jim Henson, the world would be bereft of Big Bird, Kermit the Frog, Bert and Ernie, Miss Piggy, and other characters that have made our lives, and those of our children, brighter. Brian Jay Jones had the complete cooperation of Henson's family to gather material for this biography. Henson died at fifty-three, leaving behind grieving fans of *Sesame Street* and *The Muppet Show*. He also produced the cult movies *The Dark Crystal* and *Labyrinth*.

Beatrix Potter

Linda Lear, *Beatrix Potter: A Life in Nature*, 2006.

We all know Peter Rabbit and his siblings Flopsy, Mopsy, and Cottontail, but most of us know little about their creator, Beatrix Potter. While her charming children's stories delighted her contemporaries, they were more than just stories. Potter was the first female naturalist, and her primary aim was to convince people to value the natural world and preserve it. Linda Lear looks at her art, her life, and her legacy.

Fred Rogers

Maxwell King, *The Good Neighbor: The Life and Works of Fred Rogers*, 2018.

In this first full-length biography of Fred Rogers, Maxwell King covers the story of *Mister Rogers' Neighborhood*, beloved by millions of children for decades in the mid to late twentieth century. Using interviews, oral histories, and archives, he focuses on Rogers's hard work and dedication in creating his show.

Charles Schulz

David Michaelis, *Schulz and Peanuts: A Biography*, 2007.

While everyone knows about Charlie Brown and the Peanuts gang, most know little about their creator, Charles Schulz. Biographer David Michaelis shows how Schulz used these characters to teach us that, under the veneer of adulthood, we are still children with insecurities. Schulz never recovered from the shock of leaving for boot camp to head to war-torn Europe in 1942, just three days after his mother died from cancer.

Theodore Geisel (Dr. Seuss)

Brian Jay Jones, *Becoming Dr. Seuss: Theodore Geisel and the Making of an American Imagination*, 2019.

Theodore Geisel was the author of the much-loved children's books *Horton Hears a Who*, *The Cat in the Hat*, and *The Grinch Who Stole Christmas*. But he began as a political cartoonist who pilloried despots like Hitler. While his rhymes may seem effortless, they took Geisel a great deal of time to perfect. His devotion to the smallest of his readers made reading fun for millions of children.

Dare Wright

Jean Nathan, *The Secret Life of the Lonely Doll: The Search for Dare Wright*, 2004.

Many women of a certain age remember the book with the pink-and-white gingham cover called *The Lonely Doll*. The book was a sensation when it came out and sold many copies. So when journalist Jean Nathan came upon the cover image in 1997, she sought the book out. Later, she tracked down Dare Wright, the book's author, finding her living in an old public hospital in Queens, New York. Then, she managed to stitch together the fascinating life of this enigmatic artist.

30

Popular Culture and Comedians

Alison Bechdel

Alison Bechdel, *The Secret to Superhuman Strength*, 2021.
In this graphic memoir, American cartoonist Alison Bechdel looks at her past obsessions with fitness and all the crazes that came and went with it. Starting in the 1960s with Jack LaLanne through today's spin classes, Bechdel covers the clothes, gear, and activities we've been through to improve ourselves. As she gets older, though, she turns to other sources for answers to life's questions, like Eastern philosophers and writers.

Carol Burnett

Carol Burnett, *This Time Together: Laughter and Reflection*, 2010.
Beloved by millions of fans, Carol Burnett talks about her friendships through the years with entertainment greats such as Jimmy Stewart and Julie Andrews. *The Carol Burnett Show*, winner of twenty-five Emmys over its eleven-year run, provides many of her amusing anecdotes. In addition, Burnett reveals the creativity and camaraderie that went into them.

Daniel Boone

John Mack Faragher, *Daniel Boone: The Life and Legend of an American Pioneer*, 1992.
Historian John Mack Faragher narrates the story of America's frontier hero, Daniel Boone. Using available sources from the time and popular legend, Faragher pieces together the life of Boone while placing his story in the context of the people with whom he lived, making this one of the most reliable biographies of Boone available.

Gabrielle ("Coco") Chanel

François Baudot, *Chanel*, 1996.
French designer Coco Chanel influenced culture worldwide through her designs and the wealth she used to support notable names like playwright Jean Cocteau, composer Igor Stravinsky, and poet Pierre Reverdy. However, many don't know she was the daughter of French peasants and was raised in a convent orphanage. Although when Chanel was a young woman, women were

still expected to wear corsets and long skirts, she changed all that, encouraging them to cut their hair, get suntans, and even wear slacks. Later, she designed haute couture and perfumes like Chanel No. 5.

Roger Ebert

Roger Ebert, *Life Itself: A Memoir*, 2011.

Pulitzer Prize–winning American film critic and screenwriter Roger Ebert began his career as a film reviewer for the *Chicago Sun-Times* in 1967. He was also famous for his twenty-three years as cohost of *Siskel & Ebert & the Movies,* a television series that ran on PBS. Before his thyroid cancer death in 2006, Ebert published his book about his life, the good, the bad, the addictions, and his spiritual beliefs. He also shares stories of friendships with celebrities and his viewpoints on famous directors and stars.

Bobby Fischer

Frank Brady, *Endgame: Bobby Fischer's Remarkable Rise and Fall—from America's Brightest Prodigy to the Edge of Madness*, 2011.

Bobby Fischer was a child prodigy with an IQ of 181, placing him well above the genius range. By age fourteen, he was the youngest chess master in U.S. history and the first American to win the World Chess Championship. After defeating Soviet champion Boris Spassky in 1972, Fischer became a U.S. media sensation, with millions of dollars' worth of scholarships offered to him. But, as Frank Brady reports, Fischer turned to an apocalyptic religion and began making antisemitic statements, even though his mother was Jewish. His paranoia increased throughout the 1990s to 2005, when he turned down another lucrative offer.

Woody Guthrie

Woody Guthrie, *Bound for Glory*, 1943.

American songwriter and folk singer Woody Guthrie wrote hundreds of songs but is best known for "This Land Is Your Land." Born in Oklahoma and driven to California during the Dust Bowl and the Great Depression, Guthrie traveled with migrant workers learning folk songs. He influenced many musicians, including Bob Dylan. Here he tells his own migrant story of traveling through America.

Harry Houdini

William Kalush, *The Secret Life of Houdini: The Making of America's First Superhero*, 2006.

Almost a century after his death, Harry Houdini is still one of the most famous magicians. Houdini was the son of Hungarian immigrants and began his career on the vaudeville circuit, making escapes from handcuffs and straitjackets. He later moved to increasingly dangerous acts, such as escapes from waterproof containers, helping him grow wealthy. He died in 1926, most likely from a burst appendix.

Colin Jost

Colin Jost, *A Very Punchable Face: A Memoir*, 2020.

You know him from *Saturday Night Live*, as a regular on Weekend Update. But Colin Jost has lived a surreal life that makes his comedic outlook understandable. While he graduated from Harvard, he seems to view the world as a series of bizarre situations for which he happens to be present. Strange incidents and outlook aside, he's a brilliant comedian with a stellar résumé who has opened for Dave Chappelle and hosted the Emmy Awards.

Jack Kirby

Mark Evanier, *Kirby: King of Comics*, 2007.

Fantasy and adventure comics were Jack Kirby's specialties. In the 1940s, he remade the signature look of most comic strips and began producing a string of work featuring characters like Captain America, The X-Men, The Hulk, and The Fantastic Four. His story is told here by American comic book and screen writer Mark Evanier, who knew Kirby personally.

Stan Lee

Danny Fingeroth, *A Marvelous Life: The Amazing Story of Stan Lee*, 2019.

Pop culture critic Danny Fingeroth worked with Stan Lee for over thirty years. In this comprehensive biography, he uses this relationship to provide a behind-the-scenes look at Lee's time at Marvel Comics. Inventing over five hundred iconic comic characters, such as Spider-Man and Iron Man, Lee is internationally famous for comic books, movies, and television series based on his brainchildren.

Alice Roosevelt Longworth

Stacy A. Cordery, *Alice: Alice Roosevelt Longworth, from White House Princess to Washington Power Broker*, 2007.

The eldest daughter of Teddy Roosevelt, Alice Roosevelt Longworth made waves as a teenager in Washington with her gambling and public cigarette smoking. She was a fixture in the nation's power center for seventy years. She was always in the spotlight in a life that spanned most of the twentieth century; she earned the nickname "the other Washington monument." She was sharped-tongued but had apolitical astuteness that caused even the powerful to listen to what she had to say. During her marriage to the speaker of the house, Nicholas Longworth, she had many lovers.

Bunny Mellon

Meryl Gordon, *Bunny Mellon: The Life of an American Style Legend*, 2017.

Rachel "Bunny" Mellon was a twentieth-century gardener, philanthropist, and art collector who designed the White House Rose Garden. She died at age 103 in 2014. Meryl Gordon used her letters, diaries, appointment calendars, and interviews with people who knew her to describe this American style icon.

Matthew Polly

Matthew Polly, *American Shaolin: Flying Kicks, Buddhist Monks, and the Legend of Iron Crotch: An Odyssey in the New China*, 2007.

Watching the 1970s TV series *Kung Fu* as a kid, Matthew Polly, a bullied weakling, dreamed of traveling to a Shaolin Temple in China to be trained as an unbeatable fighter like Caine in the show. He later horrified his parents when he dropped out of Princeton to travel to China to realize his dream. While the temple itself was now a tourist trap run by Communist Party flunkies, the monks still taught the ancient fighting forms. But could an American like him succeed?

Robert Ripley

Neal Thompson, *A Curious Man: The Strange & Brilliant Life of Robert "Believe It or Not!" Ripley*, 2013.

In the early twentieth century, a shy and awkward young cartoonist became a millionaire after turning his global search for the superlative, the odd, and the outrageous into a successful franchise of cartoons, radio shows, and television specials. But Ripley didn't just capitalize on the eccentrics he covered; he aimed to make them respected. In many ways, he created the entertainment world we know today.

Martin Short

Martin Short, *I Must Say: My Life as a Humble Comedy Legend*, 2014.

Comedian Martin Short lets us in on his secrets to a happy life. From his early years in show business working for Second City Toronto to his years on *Saturday Night Live*, Short shares his friendships with celebrities Steve Martin, John Candy, and others. He shares the happy times, like hosting big parties in his L.A. home with his beloved wife Nancy, and he tells of the painful times, like when he lost her. Throughout, he maintains his characteristic humor and warmth.

Jessica Simpson

Jessica Simpson, *Open Book*, 2020.

Jessica Simpson has seen pop stardom's highs and lows in America. Her memoir talks of being sexually abused as a young girl in 1980s Texas. Later, after unsuccessfully auditioning for the *Mickey Mouse Club* at age thirteen, she landed a record contract with Columbia and married 98 Degrees member Nick Lachey. Once she divorced him, she began what she describes as an emotionally abusive relationship with John Mayer. Throughout it all, she felt intense pressure to support her family and maintain the perfect weight, which resulted in periods of alcohol abuse. The book ends happily with her husband Eric Johnson, their children, and a successful clothing line.

Hans Sloane

James Delbourgo, *Collecting the World: Hans Sloane and the Origins of the British Museum* 2017.

Wealthy London physician Hans Sloane was indispensable in creating the British Museum in 1759. Before the museum opened, he had managed to amass a vast collection of curiosities from all over the world, including artifacts, novelties, and even human beings, which made him a controversial figure.

Patti Smith

Patti Smith, *Just Kids*, 2010.

When Patti Smith left her New Jersey home for New York City, she knew no one and had no place to stay. By chance, she met a young photographer named Robert Mapplethorpe, and the two began a tender, special relationship taking care of each other. As they began to grow up in NYC in the late '60s and '70s, they lived for a while in the fabled Chelsea Hotel and met many famous artists, rock stars, and assorted hangers-on. Smith's artistry comes through in her writing.

Adrian Tomine

Adrian Tomine, *The Loneliness of the Long-Distance Cartoonist*, 2020.

American comic Adrian Tomine self-published his *Optic Nerve*, which was the beginning of a brilliant career. Yet, despite numerous awards and significant recognition, he questions whether turning a childhood hobby into a job was good. It's not his life he's questioning. It's comic books and the culture that goes with them.

Gore Vidal

Jay Parini, *Empire of Self: A Life of Gore Vidal*, 2015.

Author Jay Parini had been friends with Gore Vidal for three decades before the celebrity author's death in 2012. He writes about Vidal's dazzling life, which included relationships with everyone from Eleanor Roosevelt to Truman Capote. Vidal was as famous for his skirmishes with notables like William F. Buckley Jr. and *The New York Times* as he was for his serious work. Before his death, he was a novelist, essayist, screenwriter, historian, and pioneer of gay rights.

31

Scientists, Inventors, and Mathematicians

George Washington Carver

John Perry, *George Washington Carver*, 2011.

Though he was born into slavery, George Washington Carver was raised by his owners as their child after his mother's kidnapping during the Civil War. Later, he was the first Black person to graduate from Iowa State. Carver turned down a job offer from Thomas Edison, with an exorbitant salary, to continue his work at the Tuskegee Institute. He spent over four decades teaching the institute's poor Black students. But Carver was also a chemist, botanist, and inventor whose experiments with peanuts, sweet potatoes, and soybeans revolutionized Southern agriculture.

Marie Curie and Pierre Curie

Lauren Redniss, *Radioactive: Marie & Pierre Curie: A Tale of Love and Fallout*, 2010.

Artist and writer Lauren Redniss takes us into the world of the Curies, especially Marie, through more than one hundred collages. She uses photos, images, clippings, and drawings to complement the text in this account of and immersion in the Curies' lives.

Charles Darwin

Adrian Desmond and James Moore, *Darwin: The Life of a Tormented Evolutionist*, 1991.

Desmond and Moore provide a definitive look at Charles Darwin's life, from childhood through death. But the book focuses on his voyage aboard the *Beagle* and his later struggles to develop his theory of evolution. Darwin suffered personally for breaking with his day's theology and popular worldview. The authors dig deep into how Darwin affected the world and how the world, in turn, affected him.

Charles Darwin, *The Voyage of the Beagle*, 1839.

Charles Darwin chronicles his five-year voyage aboard the *Beagle* in this personal journal beginning in 1831. He captures the events and sights that caught his attention, from an Argentina civil war to geological formations. After

The Origin of Species was published, the material gathered from this voyage changed the world forever.

Jennifer Doudna

Walter Isaacson, *The Code Breaker: Jennifer Doudna, Gene Editing, and the Future of the Human Race*, 2021.
Jennifer Doudna defied the messages she received growing up that girls couldn't be scientists. As an adult, she became a geneticist who helped develop CRISPR, a tool capable of editing DNA. While the discovery could transform human life as we know it, Doudna has asked hard questions about how the tool should and shouldn't be used.

Thomas Alva Edison

Randall E. Stross, *The Wizard of Menlo Park: How Thomas Alva Edison Invented the Modern World*, 2007.
Thomas Edison's technological genius is still legendary. He invented or helped to invent the phonograph, incandescent light, power and distribution systems, and motion picture cameras, an impressive list that changed the world forever. But as Randall E. Stross reveals after conducting meticulous research, his highest genius may have been self-promotion.

Albert Einstein

A. Douglas Stone, *Einstein and the Quantum: The Quest of the Valiant Swabian*, 2013.
When people think of Albert Einstein today, they usually think of his Theory of Relativity. But according to A. Douglas Stone, Einstein had more to do with the development of quantum physics than Max Planck or Niels Bohr. Einstein finally renounced his interest in quantum theory because he was attached to his belief in the objective and eternal nature of material reality.

Rana el Kaliouby

Rana el Kaliouby, *Girl Decoded: A Scientist's Quest to Reclaim Our Humanity by Bringing Emotional Intelligence to Technology*, 2020.
Rana el Kaliouby became a computer scientist despite her traditional upbringing in Egypt and Kuwait. After divorcing her husband, she moved to America with her children. She cofounded Affectiva, which seeks to help artificial intelligence technology—AI—become more emotionally intelligent in dealing with human interactions. In this memoir, she confronts her emotions as she aims to humanize technology for everyone's benefit.

Philo T. Farnsworth

Evan I. Schwartz, *The Last Lone Inventor: A Tale of Genius, Deceit, and the Birth of Television*, 2002.

Evan I. Schwartz narrates the story of the man behind television—Philo T. Farnsworth. At age twenty, Farnsworth ran a lab above a San Francisco garage and filed for patents. He was a genius who soon caught the attention of RCA magnate David Sarnoff, who wanted to control television like he controlled radio. The clash of these two men, the thinker and the businessman, had a profound and lasting effect on culture.

Michael Faraday

Alan W. Hirshfeld, *The Electric Life of Michael Faraday*, 2006.

Michael Faraday was a profoundly religious man who wanted to discover God through the scientific study of divine creation. He was a friend of Charles Darwin and inspired Thomas Edison with his discoveries about electricity and magnetism. While providing details on Faraday's private life, Alan W. Hirshfeld also makes his most significant contributions understandable to those without a scientific background.

Richard Feynman

James Gleick, *Genius: The Life and Science of Richard Feynman*, 1992.

Acclaimed biographer and science writer James Gleick delivers a comprehensive portrait of revered twentieth-century physicist Richard Feynman. Feynman worked on the Manhattan Project with Robert Oppenheimer as a young man at the dawn of the Atomic Age. Feynman's professional discoveries were legendary, but his eccentric and enthusiastic personality was part of his celebrity.

Buckminster Fuller

Alec Nevala-Lee, *Inventor of the Future: The Visionary Life of Buckminster Fuller*, 2022.

Twentieth-century American architect, inventor, and futurist Buckminster Fuller was a recognized genius during his lifetime. Alec Nevala-Lee supplies the first comprehensive look at the life of Fuller, with its contradictions and brilliance. His ideas have influenced everything from the sustainability movement to Silicon Valley's tech industry. Nevala-Lee also explores Fuller's personal life and encounters with famous people, from Frank Lloyd Wright to Steve Jobs.

Galileo Galilei

Dava Sobel, *Galileo's Daughter: A Historical Memoir of Science, Faith, and Love*, 1999.

Before he became a famous scientist, Galileo had wanted to enter a monastery. Of his three illegitimate children, the eldest, a daughter, entered a convent at age thirteen and took the name of Suor Maria Celeste. Throughout her life, she maintained correspondence with her father, which Dava Sobel translated into English. These letters shed new light on his personality. Famously forced by the church to spend the end of his life under house arrest for his belief that the Earth revolved around the Sun, Galileo serves as an icon of the schism between science and religion.

Kurt Gödel

Stephen Budiansky, *Journey to the Edge of Reason: The Life of Kurt Gödel*, 2021.

Twentieth-century logician Kurt Gödel made history with his proof that mathematical systems must contain propositions that are true but not provable. Historian Stephen Budiansky writes about his rich relationships with other scientists and intellectuals. Budiansky also discusses the debilitating attacks of paranoia that ultimately ended Gödel's life.

Werner Heisenberg

David C. Cassidy, *Uncertainty: The Life and Science of Werner Heisenberg*, 1991.

Modern physicist Werner Heisenberg was an indispensable contributor to the development of quantum physics. But his decision to remain in Nazi Germany throughout World War II is as controversial as his involvement in developing an atomic bomb for Hitler. David C. Cassidy narrates the story of this significant scientist.

Homer H. Hickam Jr.

Homer H. Hickam Jr., *Rocket Boys: A Memoir*, 1998.

"Sonny" Hickam Jr., a NASA engineer of distinction, writes this memoir of growing up in Coalwood, West Virginia, in the 1950s. As the son of a coal miner, Hickam and three of his friends were inspired by watching the Soviet satellite *Sputnik* fly overhead, inspiring them to launch a rocket themselves. Despite a lack of money and community members' interference, the boys successfully launched a rocket they had designed and put together from scrap materials.

Robert Hooke

Lisa Jardine, *The Curious Life of Robert Hooke: The Man Who Measured London*, 2003.
British historian Lisa Jardine explores the life of seventeenth-century engineer, surveyor, architect, and inventor Robert Hooke, a brilliant man who helped Christopher Wren rebuild London after the Great Fire of 1666. Hooke never became as famous as he should have, primarily because he couldn't get along with people like Sir Isaac Newton. But his numerous achievements led Jardine to tell his story.

David Hosack

Victoria Johnson, *American Eden: David Hosack, Botany, and Medicine in the Garden of the Early Republic*, 2018.
Professor Victoria Johnson brings David Hosack, an intimate of many American founding fathers, to life. Hosack was born in New York City and returned after receiving his education in Europe. His fascination with plants and his experiments using them for medical research drew the attention of Thomas Jefferson, James Madison, and Lafayette. In 1810, he opened the Elgin Botanic Garden, the first of its kind in America.

Katherine Johnson

Katherine Johnson, *My Remarkable Journey: A Memoir*, 2021.
As a Black child in the Allegheny Mountains of West Virginia, Katherine Johnson was a prodigy. Here she writes of how she attended school and was encouraged to become a research mathematician by an African American professor. Later, she became a human computer who helped NASA make its first space flights. President Barack Obama honored her at age ninety-seven with the Presidential Medal of Freedom. Her life was presented in the movie *Hidden Figures*.

Ernest Lawrence

Michael Hiltzik, *Big Science: Ernest Lawrence and the Invention that Launched the Military–Industrial Complex*, 2015.
In the 1930s, a young scientist in Berkeley, California named Ernest Lawrence invented the cyclotron. The device changed our understanding of the fundamental ways nature is constructed and ushered in the nuclear age. Without Lawrence, there would be no Large Hadron Collider or CERN.

Henrietta Swan Leavitt

George Johnson, *Miss Leavitt's Stars: The Untold Story of the Woman Who Discovered How to Measure the Universe*, 2005.
American science writer George Johnson writes about an overlooked human computer working at the Harvard Observatory. Radcliff-educated Henrietta Swan Leavitt discovered a law to use variable stars, whose brightness changes periodically, to measure cosmic distances. In the process, she ended the debate on the size of the universe.

Gregor Mendel

Robin Marantz Henig, *The Monk in the Garden: The Lost and Found Genius of Gregor Mendel, the Father of Genetics*, 2000.
Nineteenth-century scientist Gregor Mendel set the mathematical foundations for genetics while living as a priest in a monastery in Eastern Europe. There, he taught and experimented with botany. His work trying to determine the origins of various varieties of pea plants led to his work with genetics. Science writer Robin Marantz Henig teases out the facts among the myths that surround Mendel's life.

Isaac Newton

Richard S. Westfall, *Never at Rest: A Biography of Isaac Newton*, 1980.
Focusing on Sir Isaac Newton's scientific achievements, Richard S. Westfall spends a great deal of time on his development of calculus, optics, and universal gravitation. He also covers the private life of one of the most brilliant scientific minds in history.

Hakeem Muata Oluseyi

Hakeem Oluseyi and Joshua Horwitz, *A Quantum Life: My Unlikely Journey from the Street to the Stars*, 2021.
Born James Edward Plummer, Oluseyi changed his name after his acceptance into the Stanford physics department's Ph.D. program. His tale of growing up in extreme poverty and abuse in areas ranging from tough inner cities to rural Mississippi is eye-opening. When his genius and love of science weren't helpful, he learned to forge a new identity as a "gangsta nerd" to get by. He sold drugs while studying science. To reach success in physics, he had to deal with a crack cocaine addiction he had developed in college. But now he investigates the mysteries of the universe.

Ivan Pavlov

Daniel P. Todes, *Ivan Pavlov: A Russian Life in Science*, 2014.
Remember Pavlov's dogs? As it turns out, he never taught them to salivate with a bell. That's just one of the facts about the famous Russian psychologist that Daniel Todes spent twenty years researching. He was born to a priestly family in imperial Russia. Pavlov worked as a psychologist but became involved in politics as a dissident under Lenin. While many mistakenly remember him as a behaviorist, he wanted to understand the emotional and intellectual content of consciousness.

George Price

Oren Harman, *The Price of Altruism: George Price and the Search for the Origins of Kindness*, 2010.
George R. Price was a twentieth-century American geneticist who wanted to solve the evolutionary riddle of altruism. Science writer Oren Harman narrates his life, which reached its professional height while working on the Manhattan Project. Harman details Price's conversion to Christianity and his suicide in a squatter's flat after giving all his possessions away to the homeless.

Cassandra Quave

Cassandra Leah Quave, *The Plant Hunter: A Scientist's Quest for Nature's Next Medicines*, 2021.
Dr. Cassandra Quave narrates this memoir of her adventures as a world-traveling ethnobotanist. She weaves her fascination with the incredible benefits of plants with the equally impressive story of how she has searched for them, often over difficult terrain, despite only having one leg due to congenital disabilities. She provides compelling evidence that plants may become our saviors in the end.

Ramanujan

Robert Kanigel, *The Man Who Knew Infinity: A Life of the Genius Ramanujan*, 1991.
American author Robert Kanigel tells the story of Indian mathematical genius Ramanujan. Before World War I, Ramanujan attended Cambridge University under the tutelage of G. H. Hardy. Kanigel uses the relationship between the two men to explain number theory. In using the languages of symbols and mathematics, the biography makes the topic accessible to the general reader.

Hermann Rorschach

Damion Searles, *The Inkblots: Hermann Rorschach, His Iconic Test, and the Power of Seeing*, 2017.
In 1917, psychiatrist Hermann Rorschach developed an experiment to test Freud's theory that humans are driven more by what they see than what they say. Rorschach was also an artist who was influenced by the modern art movement. His test, which involves ten inkblots designed to reveal the inner workings of people's minds, is still in use today. Damion Searles uses previously unknown or unavailable material to share the life and work of the creator of this brilliant synthesis of art and science.

Jonas Salk

Charlotte DeCroes Jacobs, *Jonas Salk: A Life*, 2015.
Many know that Jonas Salk created the world's first successful polio vaccine. He became, in the years following, a beloved public figure. Yet Salk, raised in a New York City tenement, wanted the scientific community's recognition. Sadly, he never got it. Professor Charlotte DeCroes Jacobs reveals that Salk, a quiet, private man, was disliked by many of his peers from the start. She tells how his single-minded pursuit of helping humanity cost both him and his family personally.

Tim Samaras

Brantley Hargrove, *The Man Who Caught the Storm: The Life of Legendary Tornado Chaser Tim Samaras*, 2018.
Tim Samaras never attended college, yet he chased tornados, America's monster storms, using brilliant tools he invented. He astonished scientists with his discoveries. Samaras couldn't stop himself from taking ever-greater risks in his pursuit of knowledge. Brantley Hargrove tells the story of a man whose obsessions were only matched by the natural fury he pursued.

Adam Savage

Adam Savage, *Every Tool's a Hammer: Life Is What You Make It*, 2019.
Adam Savage, the Discovery Channel's *Mythbusters* star, chronicles stories from his lifetime of making, breaking, and remaking an astonishing array of projects. This memoir encourages readers to do the same, with conversations with other creators and artists.

Claude Shannon

Jimmy Soni and Rob Goodman, *A Mind at Play:*
How Claude Shannon Invented the Information Age, **2017.**

Michigan native Claude Shannon was a founder of the digital revolution. From his work at MIT and his participation with scientists such as Alan Turing in battling the Nazis, he helped create the Information Age. Jimmy Soni and Rob Goodman relay the life of this brilliant polymath.

William Smith

Simon Winchester, *The Map That Changed the World:*
William Smith and the Birth of Modern Geology, **2001.**

Acclaimed British author Simon Winchester tells the little-known story of a canal digger named William Smith, who discovered in 1793 that he could use excavated fossils to map the underside of the Earth. He spent the next twenty-two years making a hand-painted map of his findings. He wound up in debtor's prison after falling victim to a plagiarist. Winchester relates how ten years after his achievement, Smith was finally rewarded by the Geological Society of London.

E. Sreedharan

M. S. Ashokan, *Karmayogi:*
A Biography of E. Sreedharan, **2015.**

Karmayogi was an Indian engineer and technocrat known for efficiency and productivity. During his career, he was responsible for the Kolkata Metro, the Konkan Railway, and the impressive Dehli Metro. He managed all this while working only an eight-hour day. M. S. Ashokan tells the inspirational story of this private man renowned in modern India for his work ethic.

Nikola Tesla

W. Bernard Carlson, *Tesla:*
Inventor of the Electrical Age, **2013.**

People remember Nikola Tesla for his eccentric personality and interests. But biographer W. Bernard Carlson focuses on Tesla's prolific creativity and inventions. As a young man, he became one of the world's first celebrity scientists while demonstrating his electrical displays. But rather than being a mystical genius as purported, Carlson, through careful research, reveals him to be an idealist who used showmanship and mythmaking to sell his ideas.

Alan Turing

Andrew Hodges, *Alan Turing: The Enigma*, 1983.

British mathematician Alan Turing broke the German Enigma cipher, giving the Allies the upper hand in World War II. Before the war, Turing focused on creating a universal computing machine (a theoretical machine) that laid the foundation for the computer science revolution. Despite his genius and contributions to science, Turing was arrested for his homosexuality, which was illegal in 1950s Britain. After participating in a forced conversion therapy program, Turing died by suicide in 1954. His story is told here by British mathematician and gay rights advocate Andrew Hodges.

Neil deGrasse Tyson

Neil deGrasse Tyson, *The Sky Is Not the Limit: Adventures of an Urban Astrophysicist*, 2000.

As a young man growing up in the Bronx, Neil deGrasse Tyson was both an athlete and a science nerd. While participating in sports, he also set up a telescope to explore the night sky. After graduating from Harvard and earning a Ph.D. in astrophysics from Columbia, Tyson became the director of the Hayden Planetarium. In this memoir, he discusses his thoughts on science and the universe while encouraging us all to reach for our dreams.

Edith Widder

Edith Widder, Ph.D., *Below the Edge of Darkness: A Memoir of Exploring Light and Life in the Deep Sea*, 2021.

Marine biologist Edith Widder tells how temporary blindness in college led to her fascination with light, leading to a career in bioluminescence. On her first excursion into the deep ocean, eight hundred feet down, she was amazed by all the explosions of light she saw. What, Widder wondered, was going on? Here, she takes her readers into the bizarre world of the deep seas and their eerie lifeforms, large and small. She also describes the equipment upon which her life depends as she explores this little-known ecosystem.

Wilbur Wright and Orville Wright

James Tobin, *To Conquer the Air: The Wright Brothers and the Great Race for Flight*, 2003.

At the dawn of the twentieth century, there was an international race to be the first to put humans in flight. Most were betting on Samuel Langley of the Smithsonian Institution, who had the financial backing of the U.S. War Department. But instead, it was two unknown brothers, Wilbur and Orville Wright, owners of an Ohio bicycle shop, who faced tremendous difficulties finally putting the first airplane in flight. Award-winning author James Tobin narrates how they did it on an obscure spit of land off the North Carolina coast.

COLLECTIVE BIOGRAPHY

Howard Markel, *The Secret of Life: Rosalind Franklin, James Watson, Francis Crick, and the Discovery of DNA's Double Helix,* 2021.

Professor Howard Markel explores the relationships between the first scientists to discover the double helix structure of DNA—James Watson, Francis Crick, and the overlooked Rosalind Franklin. The race to discover the structure was feverishly pursued by these three as well as Maurice Wilkins and Linus Pauling. In recounting the work involved, Markel focuses on how Franklin's contributions were overlooked due to the participants' personalities and their misogyny and antisemitism.

32

Thinkers and Commentators

Henry Adams

Henry Adams, *The Education of Henry Adams*, 1918.

Henry Adams was born into a distinguished Boston family, which gave him the luxury of pursuing his interests. In this classic memoir, he records his efforts to understand the world as he saw it, including his criticism of the nineteenth-century education system and its theory. His work is considered a masterful handling of the intellectual concerns of his day, bringing together his avenues of exploration in determining the individual's place in history and society.

Eula Biss

Eula Biss, *Having and Being Had*, 2020.

Celebrated writer Eula Biss divides her life into two parts: before she owned a washing machine and after. From this starting point, she examines capitalism and its effects on our lives, especially on her own.

Edmund Burke

David Bromwich, *The Intellectual Life of Edmund Burke: From the Sublime and Beautiful to American Independence*, 2014.

According to many, the father of modern conservatism is eighteenth-century British statesman, thinker, and writer Edmund Burke. But his ideas were more subtle and complex than recent history would lead you to believe. In this intellectual biography, David Bromwich examines Burke's thinking. Burke regarded service as intertwined with morality, and Bromwich attempted to clarify his ideas. Civil liberty was foremost in his mind, and he was a champion of the oppressed.

Joan Didion

Joan Didion, *The White Album: Essays*, 1979.

Through looking at the crazy world around her, from Charles Manson to shopping malls, literary journalist Joan Didion tries to understand her spiritual perplexity. This work is now considered a classic autobiography.

W. E. B. Du Bois

David Levering Lewis, *W. E. B. Du Bois, 1868–1919: Biography of a Race*, 1993; and *W. E. B. Du Bois: The Fight for Equality and the American Century, 1919–1963*, 2001.

David Levering Lewis spent years researching the life of W. E. B. Du Bois, who was born just after the end of the American Civil War. Du Bois was an influential sociologist, historian, author, and activist who changed how Americans, particularly African Americans, saw themselves through works like *The Souls of the Black Folk*.

Friedrich Engels

Tristram Hunt, *Marx's General: The Revolutionary Life of Friedrich Engels*, 2009.

British historian Tristram Hunt delves into the life of Friedrich Engels, who, with Karl Marx, established the philosophical basis for international communism. Although Engels was born into money and worked in the cotton industry to maintain his upper-middle-class life in England, he also co-wrote *The Communist Manifesto*. Engels wasn't just Marx's sidekick. He was also a respected thinker who predicted the world of unfettered capitalism and globalization we live in today. Hunt examines whether Engels is responsible for the communist overreaches of the early twentieth century or whether his ideas were distorted by those who put them into practice.

Sigmund Freud

Élisabeth Roudinesco, *Freud: In His Time and Ours*, 2014.

Using new archival material, Élisabeth Roudinesco revisits Freud's life, recreating the early days of his practice amid fin de siècle Vienna. Freud, who sought to uncover the mysteries of the human mind, was blind to his own subconscious influences. While he contributed significantly to our understanding of ourselves, he has been misunderstood himself.

Margaret Fuller

Megan Marshall, *Margaret Fuller: A New American Life*, 2013.

Award-winning author Megan Marshall portrays nineteenth-century intellectual Margaret Fuller, who was Thoreau's first editor, Emerson's friend, and the first female war correspondent. Marshall follows Fuller from Boston to New York, where her front-page column in the *New York Tribune* showcased her activism for America's urban poor and its prostitutes. Fuller's life ended in scandal when she, her young lover, and their son died in a shipwreck off Fire Island.

Martin Heidegger

**Rüdiger Safranski, *Martin Heidegger:
Between Good and Evil*, 1994.**

Literary scholar Rüdiger Safranski examines the checkered life of Martin
Heidegger, one of the most influential twentieth-century philosophers to
come out of Germany. While Heidegger paved the way for the work of Sartre
and Foucault, he also began as a propagandist for the Nazi regime. Safranski
explains Heidegger's philosophical thought and what makes it great.

William James

**Robert D. Richardson, *William James:
In the Maelstrom of American Modernism*, 2006.**

The oldest child in the extraordinary James family, William was known
for his contributions to psychology, philosophy, education, and religion. In
many ways, he shaped the intellectual climate of the modern era. Robert D.
Richardson spent ten years exploring personal letters, journals, and school
records to show us how William James became such a towering figure.

Immanuel Kant

Manfred Kuehn, *Kant: A Biography*, 2001.

Philosophy professor Manfred Kuehn provides this full-length biography of German philosopher Immanuel Kant. Born in 1724, Kant was an
Enlightenment philosopher widely thought to be one of the greatest philosophers of all time.

George F. Kennan

**John Lewis Gaddis, *George F. Kennan:
An American Life*, 2011.**

In the late 1940s, diplomat George F. Kennan wrote two documents that laid
out the United States "containment theory" regarding the Soviet Union. The
influence of his ideas changed the world during the Cold War era. This authorized biography is based on interviews with Kennan and his archives.

John Maynard Keynes

**Robert Skidelsky, *John Maynard Keynes, 1883–1946:
Economist, Philosopher, Statesman*, 2003.**

Professor of political economy Robert Skidelsky produced a three-volume
work about acclaimed twentieth-century economist John Maynard Keynes.
This book abridges the entire work into one volume that examines Keynes's
whole life as well as his intellectual development. His ideas had a tremendous

impact on the post–World War II economy, and Skidelsky also explains these influences.

Anne Morrow Lindbergh

Anne Morrow Lindbergh, *Gift from the Sea*, 1955.

Anne Morrow Lindbergh was married to famous pilot Charles Lindbergh. In the early days of their marriage, she traveled with him on survey flights around the North Atlantic. After their children were born, Lindbergh devoted her time to their family. She wrote this classic meditation on life and relationships after a solo visit to the coast. The beautifully written work became an instant bestseller.

Machiavelli

Miles J. Unger, *Machiavelli: A Biography*, 2011.

Italian Renaissance diplomat and civil servant Niccolò Machiavelli is famous today for his political guide, *The Prince*. A friend of Leonardo da Vinci and Michelangelo, Machiavelli depicted the world as he saw it. As a diplomat, he dealt with the corrupt Pope Alexander VI and Cesare Borgia, who served as a model for *The Prince*. Miles J. Unger presents Machiavelli as a thoughtful observer of human nature.

Karl Marx

Mary Gabriel, *Love and Capital: Karl and Jenny Marx and the Birth of a Revolution*, 2011.

Biographer Mary Gabriel reveals the private life of Karl Marx by focusing on his marriage to his wife, Jenny. Marx was an intellectual and revolutionary, often on the run from governments, but he was also a devoted husband and father. Gabriel shows the human face of a renowned and reviled thinker who brought the world *The Communist Manifesto*.

Margaret Mead and Gregory Bateson

Mary Catherine Bateson, *With a Daughter's Eye: A Memoir of Margaret Mead and Gregory Bateson*, 1984.

Legendary anthropologists Margaret Mead and Gregory Bateson had a child named Mary Catherine, who herself grew up to be a prominent cultural anthropologist. In this memoir, daughter Mary describes what it was like to grow up with such singular and esteemed parents.

Mary Pipher

Mary Pipher *A Life in Light: Meditations on Impermanence,* **2022.**

Psychologist and author of *Reviving Ophelia* Mary Pipher presents her memoir through a series of essays. In them, she explores her difficult childhood and how it shaped the woman she became. The coping skills she developed are generously shared with her readers, providing them with a way to manage their challenges.

Baruch de Spinoza

Steven Nadler, *A Book Forged in Hell: Spinoza's Scandalous Treatise and the Birth of the Secular Age,* **2011.**

Seventeenth-century Dutch philosopher Baruch de Spinoza influenced the Enlightenment, liberal politics, and Jewish Zionism. Steven Nadler demonstrates that while Spinoza's *Theological-Political Treatise* was roundly condemned as heretical and blasphemous, it was also responsible for Thomas Paine's *Common Sense* and the Declaration of Independence. Spinoza asserted that the Bible is not the literal word of God and that modern states should rest on religious and intellectual freedom, which was scandalous for his time.

Henry David Thoreau

Laura Dassow Walls, *Henry David Thoreau: A Life,* **2017.**

Best known today as the author of *Walden*, Henry David Thoreau was a member of Ralph Waldo Emerson's small intellectual circle in Concord, Massachusetts. In addition to writing, he was a naturalist, manual laborer, inventor, and political activist. Using both the published and unpublished papers Thoreau left behind, Laura Dassow Walls aspires to present every side of the writer, from the death of his brother during childhood to his own death at age forty-four.

Sherry Turkle

Sherry Turkle, *The Empathy Diaries: A Memoir,* **2021.**

MIT psychologist Sherry Turkle writes about our psychological relationship to the technology we use. The machines we employ shape us in ways we seldom see. In this memoir, she writes of her coming of age as the child of an absent scientist and a secretive mother. Her career as a woman in a world of men was also a challenging code to crack. She writes of this selective culture and how she learned to survive and thrive while working in it.

Alfred North Whitehead

Alfred North Whitehead, *Dialogues of Alfred North Whitehead*, 1956.

Writer Lucien Price collected conversations and interviews with world-famous polymath Alfred North Whitehead. Then he edited them into a biography using Whitehead's words to convey his thinking on topics as mundane as living well and as astounding as his insights into philosophy and science. Whitehead's influence on modern thought is immense, and this book demonstrates why.

Ludwig Wittgenstein

Ray Monk, *Ludwig Wittgenstein: The Duty of Genius*, 1990.

Philosophy professor Ray Monk traces the life of Ludwig Wittgenstein, considered by many to be the greatest philosopher of the twentieth century. Wittgenstein was the youngest of eight children born to a wealthy Viennese couple in the fin de siècle era. He grew up with luminaries from the arts, science, and business as frequent guests, including Sigmund Freud and Johannes Brahms. Ray Monk brings this charismatic figure to life and makes his philosophical teaching understandable.

COLLECTIVE BIOGRAPHY

Katherine Briggs and Isabel Briggs Myers

Merve Emre, *The Personality Brokers: The Strange History of Myers–Briggs and the Birth of Personality Testing*, 2018.

Most people know about the Myers–Briggs Type Indicator (MBTI). Many people know their own four-letter personality indicator combination of the sixteen possible combinations. The indicator has become a more-than-two-billion-dollar industry serving counselors, schools, and businesses. The test is inextricably tied up with its creators, a mother–daughter duo who were homemakers, novelists, and amateur psychologists. They came up with the original quizzes to validate the work of C. G. Jung. But the test has never been validated, and experts are at a loss as to why its acceptance is so widespread. English professor Merve Emre looks at its history to uncover why.

33

Health and Medicine

Eben Alexander

Eben Alexander, *Proof of Heaven:*
A Neurosurgeon's Journey into the Afterlife, 2012.

Neurosurgeon Dr. Eben Alexander didn't believe that near-death experiences were possible until he had one himself. As a rare illness attacked his brain, the part that controls thought and emotion stopped working, leaving him comatose for seven days. Then, just as his doctors gave up on him, he returned to consciousness and recovered completely. But the most fantastic part of the story is Alexander's experiences while his brain wasn't working.

Frank Bruni

Frank Bruni, *The Beauty of Dusk:*
On Vision Lost and Found, 2022.

Journalist Frank Bruni woke up one morning in 2017 with blurred vision. He was dismayed to find that during the night he had had a stroke that cut off the blood to one of his optic nerves. To make matters worse, there was no cure, and his other eye could suffer the same fate, rendering him completely blind. His memoir examines his response to this new reality and how losing one sort of vision resulted in gaining another.

Elizabeth Blackwell and Emily Blackwell

Janice P. Nimura, *The Doctors Blackwell:*
How Two Pioneering Sisters Brought Medicine to Women
and Women to Medicine, 2021.

Many people have heard of Elizabeth Blackwell. She has been rightly applauded as the first woman to receive an M.D. in America. But what's less known is that her younger sister Emily soon joined her and became a better physician. Janice P. Nimura sets forth the achievements of both sisters, who traveled together and opened the New York Infirmary for Indigent Women and Children, the first hospital ever staffed by women.

Susannah Cahalan

Susannah Cahalan, *Brain on Fire:*
My Month of Madness, 2012.

This bestselling memoir tells how author Susannah Cahalan woke up one day, at age twenty-four, strapped to a hospital bed with no idea how she had gotten there. She had been an ordinary young woman embarking on adult life when she was suddenly labeled a violent, psychotic flight risk. She had no idea what had happened until she was later diagnosed with a rare autoimmune disease of the brain.

Ben Carson

Ben Carson, *Gifted Hands: The Ben Carson Story*, 2009.

Before he became involved in politics and served as the secretary of housing and urban development under the Trump Administration, Ben Carson was a brilliant pediatric surgeon. He was the first to separate occipital craniopagus twins, in 1987. Carson confides how his single mother raised him and his brother in an inner-city apartment. His peers called him the class dummy, but his mother insisted he read library books, which led to his eventual recognition for his considerable intellect. In addition, he became convinced that he could accomplish anything if he trusted God and stayed determined.

Norman Cousins

Norman Cousins, *Anatomy of an Illness as Perceived by the Patient*, 1979.

American essayist and editor Norman Cousins began a revolution in health care with this memoir. In it, he describes how he worked with his doctor to beat the odds when he was diagnosed with a life-threatening collagen disease that had no known cure. Using his ability to laugh, hope, and persevere, Cousins inspired the world and proved the mind's ability to aid in healing the body.

Paul Farmer

Tracy Kidder, *Mountains Beyond Mountains*, 2003.

Pulitzer Prize–winning author Tracy Kidder shares the inspiring story of Dr. Paul Farmer, who was raised in a bus and on a boat. Farmer went on to teach at Harvard and became an infectious-disease specialist, an anthropologist, and a practicing physician who traveled the world hoping to solve seemingly insurmountable health problems. Farmer died in 2022.

Miriam Feldman and Nick Feldman

Miriam Feldman, *He Came in With It: A Portrait of Motherhood and Madness*, 2020.

Craig O'Rourke and Miriam Feldman lived the perfect life in their L.A. home. Both were artists, and they had four wonderful children. But when their son

Nick was diagnosed with schizophrenia as a teenager, their lives began to fall apart. One day Miriam found drawings and journals Nick kept as he began to succumb to his illness. As she goes through them, she begins to piece together what is going on in his mind. This leads her to conclude that there is no such thing as a perfect family.

Galen of Pergamum

Susan P. Mattern, *The Prince of Medicine: Galen in the Roman Empire,* 2013.

One of the most famous physicians of antiquity, Galen of Pergamum (129 to ca. 216 C.E.), lived an amazing life. He began his career taking care of wounded gladiators. Then he later went on to serve in a small group of court physicians attending Marcus Aurelius and his family. As a Greek intellectual living in the Roman Empire, Galen studied many subjects, from philosophy to medicine. History professor Susan P. Mattern discusses this significant physician's legacy.

Josie George

Josie George, *A Still Life: A Memoir,* 2021.

In telling the story of her life with a disabling, chronic illness, Josie George takes her readers to her small home in the British Midlands, where she lives with her son. Primarily confined to her house for most of her life, Josie has learned to see the beauty in small things.

Jan Grue

Jan Grue, *I Live a Life Like Yours: A Memoir,* 2018.

At age three, Jan Grue was diagnosed with muscular atrophy in his native Norway. He reflects on disability, society, and what it means to be human while narrating how he went from being a boy with what he felt was a limited future to becoming a college professor, husband, and father.

Jeremy Leon Hance

Jeremy Leon Hance, *Baggage: Confessions of a Globe-Trotting Hypochondriac,* 2020.

Freelance environmental journalist Jeremy Leon Hance has anxiety and OCD. While this would be tough on anyone, Hance must face his issues while traveling to places like Guyana, where bats, flesh-eating ants, and drunken tour guides must be contended with. With his partner for company, he manages to meet his challenges—most of the time. His humorous stories can inspire others to face their fears and get on with their lives.

Carl Hart

Dr. Carl Hart, *High Price: A Neuroscientist's Journey of Self-Discovery That Challenges Everything You Know About Drugs and Society*, 2013.

Columbia University's first tenured Black professor in the sciences, neuroscientist Carl Hart, knows the physical and mental harm drugs can do to a person. But unlike many of his colleagues, Hart also understands the challenges of many people who struggle with addiction because he was raised in poor neighborhoods where drugs could be an escape from crushing poverty or an escape through selling them for money. So, he chose to examine the relationship between drugs, pleasure, and motivation among people and in the brain. As a result, his memoir will change how readers think about poverty, race, and addiction.

Sarah Hepola

Sarah Hepola, *Blackout: Remembering the Things I Drank to Forget*, 2015.

Alcohol made life worth living for Sarah Hepola. She regularly closed down bars and often couldn't remember what she said or how she met the men she wound up with. She laughed about it in public, but in private, she was increasingly uneasy with the effects the drinking had on her. In this memoir, she discusses choosing to embark on a new adventure—sobriety.

Daisy Hernández

Daisy Hernández, *The Kissing Bug: A True Story of a Family, an Insect, and a Nation's Neglect of a Deadly Disease*, 2021.

You've probably heard of the Zika virus, but have you heard of Chagas? The disease, also known as the kissing bug disease, is the more common of the two in the United States. Yet we rarely hear about Chagas. So after discovering her aunt had died from the disease in New Jersey, Hernández searches to find out why the parasitic illness is ignored and to learn about its dangers.

Marya Hornbacher

Marya Hornbacher, *Wasted: A Memoir of Anorexia and Bulimia*, 1997.

While it's not often in the news today, for years, anorexia and bulimia, two of the most common eating disorders, were rampant. Marya Hornbacher recalls her five hospital stays and the price she paid to become thinner. The disease sometimes proves fatal, but Hornbacher learned to get well on her own.

John Hunter

Wendy Moore, *The Knife Man: Blood, Body Snatching, and the Birth of Modern Surgery*, 2005.

Modern medicine owes an outstanding debt to the eccentric medical pioneer John Hunter, says journalist Wendy Moore. When Hunter started practicing, bloodletting was the conventional treatment for everything, yet it cured little. But Hunter was so well respected that he treated Benjamin Franklin, Lord Byron, Adam Smith, and Thomas Gainsborough. Hunt used body snatching to obtain cadavers for study, and he infected himself with venereal disease so he could understand it better. His methods may make many uncomfortable today, but we are better off for his discoveries.

Suleika Jaouad

Suleika Jaouad, *Between Two Kingdoms: A Memoir of a Life Interrupted*, 2021.

After she graduated from college, Suleika Jaouad was diagnosed with leukemia and given a thirty-five percent chance of survival. For the next four years, she spent much time in the hospital while writing about her experiences for *The New York Times*. After years of chemo and a bone marrow transplant, she was cured. But now she had another problem; she didn't know how to live. So, with her pet terrier mutt for company, she began to visit the people who had written to her while she was in the hospital. Her story is a thought-provoking look at the line between sickness and health.

Chloé Cooper Jones

Chloé Cooper Jones, *Easy Beauty: A Memoir*, 2022.

Born with sacral agenesis, a rare congenital condition, Chloé Cooper Jones lives with great physical pain. But in addition to the discomfort, she also lives with judgments for her appearance, which include her short height and unsteady gait, differences that cause her to be overlooked or underestimated. But once she has a child, Jones decides to travel the world. She records her adventures here with grace and wit.

Helen Keller

Dorothy Herrmann, *Helen Keller: A Life*, 1998.

Helen Keller, famous for her work on behalf of the disabled, was deaf, mute, and blind. In this biography, Dorothy Herrmann explores Keller's famous relationship with her teacher Annie Sullivan. Then she discusses Keller's later successes and failures in college, in her career, and in love.

Helen Keller, *The Story of My Life*, 1902.

Helen Keller talks about her first twenty-two years. She tells how she lost sight and hearing through an early childhood illness. Using the famous incident at the water pump when Annie Sullivan spelled "W-A-T-E-R" while the liquid rushed over her hand, Keller tells of learning to communicate. She finishes with her Radcliffe College honors graduation.

Rosemary Kennedy

Kate Clifford Larson, *Rosemary: The Hidden Kennedy Daughter*, 2015.

The Kennedys were at the apex of American wealth and political power from the late nineteenth through the twentieth centuries. Joe and Rose had nine children. One of them, the beautiful Rosemary, hid a secret—she was mentally disabled. While the Kennedys sought to care for her, they didn't want the world to know one of their children wasn't perfect. As she became more difficult to handle, Joe decided to have her lobotomized at age twenty-three. Then they placed her in a home in Wisconsin. It wasn't until JFK ran for president and visited her that the family decided to make her a part of their lives again. After that, the family donated money and attention to individuals with disabilities.

Riva Lehrer

Riva Lehrer, *Golem Girl: A Memoir*, 2020.

Born with spina bifida in 1958, Riva Lehrer spent her childhood as a patient, working with doctors who wanted to make her better. She believed she was flawed and needed to be fixed or she would never live a normal life. But when she joined a group of artists, writers, and performers building a Disability Culture as an adult, she asked whether she could paint them. In painting them, she transformed the way she saw herself.

Billy Milligan

Daniel Keyes, *The Minds of Billy Milligan*, 1981.

Billy Milligan was the first person ever acquitted of criminal activity because of insanity. After being arrested for kidnapping and raping three women, Milligan was discovered to have multiple personality disorder and was found to have twenty-four distinct personalities. More than one of these were criminals, some were children, some were women, and one was called the "Teacher" who kept them all together. Daniel Keyes, the award-winning author of *Flowers for Algernon*, tells his story.

Henry Molaison

Luke Dittrich, *Patient H. M.:*
***A Story of Memory, Madness, and Family Secrets*, 2016.**

Lobotomy was an experimental procedure performed on countless Americans beginning in the 1930s. Believing their method could cure everything from schizophrenia to homosexuality, a group of surgeons subjected humans to practices that would never be allowed today. One of the most famous patients was Henry Molaison, officially known as Patient H. M., a twenty-seven-year-old farm worker who was lobotomized for epilepsy by author Luke Dittrich's grandfather. Dittrich reveals that the operation didn't heal H. M. but took away his memory. Nevertheless, for the next sixty years, he was one of history's most studied humans. Dittrich uses his story to examine a disturbing period in American medicine.

Martin Pistorius

Martin Pistorius, *Ghost Boy: The Miraculous Escape*
***of a Misdiagnosed Boy Trapped Inside His Own Body*, 2011.**

In 1988, at age twelve, Martin Pistorius lost his voice and then stopped eating. Then he withdrew and slept, refusing to interact with family and friends. Finally, after eighteen months, he could no longer speak or walk. While his doctors didn't know what was wrong, they told his parents he had a degenerative disease with little consciousness and had less than two years to live. While his parents were heartbroken, they did their best to cope. What they didn't know was that Martin was not lacking consciousness; his mind was clear. And he survived to tell of his harrowing experiences.

David Poses

David Poses, *The Weight of Air: A Story of the Lies*
***about Addiction and the Truth about Recovery*, 2021.**

In writing about his mental illness and addiction, David Poses is brutally honest in depicting his years in and out of detox, rehab, twelve-step programs, and a halfway house. He was on the verge of suicide when he finally found an evidence-based treatment for opioid addiction. He contends that traditional treatments don't help. Instead, they make things worse.

Oliver Sacks

Oliver Sacks, *Uncle Tungsten:*
***Memories of a Chemical Boyhood*, 2001.**

Oliver Sacks's parents were both doctors, rare for London in the 1930s and 1940s. They raised their equally brilliant children, Oliver and his older brother, Dave, called "Uncle Tungsten" by the family. Oliver discloses his unhappiness as a young Jewish boy in a brutal British boarding school and how he feared he might share his brother's mental illness. But this heart-warming memoir shares how the two brothers used chemistry to escape their problems.

Elyn R. Saks

Elyn R. Saks, *The Center Cannot Hold: My Journey Through Madness*, 2007.

When she was eight years old, growing up in Miami during the 1960s, Elyn Saks had her first hints that something wasn't quite right. As a student at Oxford University, she had her first full-blown schizophrenic episode. Later, at Yale Law School, she was found singing on the roof of the law school library at midnight after having a complete breakdown. Yet, despite her subsequent hospitalization, she managed to complete law school and go on to become an endowed professor. Now studying to be a psychoanalyst to specialize in mental health law, she discusses her ordeals and triumphs.

David Small

David Small, *Stitches: A Memoir*, 2009.

David Small is the award-winning author of children's books like *Imogene's Antlers* and *The Gardener*. When he was fourteen years old, he awoke from what he thought was minor surgery to discover that his vocal cord had been cut. It turned out he had throat cancer and was not expected to live much longer. He couldn't talk, and his parents made his life much more difficult than it needed to be, which resulted in his leaving home at sixteen with only his dream of becoming an artist.

Jill Bolte Taylor

Jill Bolte Taylor, *My Stroke of Insight: A Brain Scientist's Personal Journey*, 2006.

At age thirty-seven, Harvard-trained brain scientist Jill Taylor endured a stroke. As a scientist, she was fascinated by the changes taking place in her abilities and perceptions. Since the stroke occurred on the left side, she lost her ability to walk, talk, read, write, and remember. Then her consciousness shifted to the right and she felt "at one with the universe." She has since recovered completely. She tells the astounding tale of the unique functioning of each side of our brains from her unique perspective.

34

Grief and Life Challenges

Chimamanda Ngozi Adichie

Chimamanda Ngozi Adichie, *Notes on Grief,* 2021.
Globally recognized author of *Half of a Yellow Sun*, Chimamanda Ngozi Adichie, wrote this memoir after her father died in 2020 from kidney failure during the COVID-19 pandemic. Adichie remembers the man who raised her in Nigeria.

Sherman Alexie

Sherman Alexie, *You Don't Have to Say You Love Me: A Memoir,* 2017.
Award-winning author of *Smoke Signals* and *The Absolutely True Diary of a Part-Time Indian*, Sherman Alexie, grapples with his childhood after the death of his mother when she was seventy-eight. He uses seventy-eight poems, seventy-eight essays, and family photos to focus on what life was like for him to be raised on an Indian reservation with three siblings by two alcoholic parents with no money. The mother portrayed is beautiful and...complicated.

Chang Bunker and Eng Bunker

Yunte Huang, *Inseparable: The Original Siamese Twins and Their Rendezvous with American History,* 2018.
In 1824, a British merchant "discovered" a pair of thirteen-year-old twins conjoined at the sternum and sharing a liver. Yunte Huang tells the story of how the pair made it to Boston five years later, first as museum exhibits and then as showmen who traveled rural America. The brothers married two White sisters and had twenty-one children between the two of them. They also had control of enslaved people. Huang examines their sensational story from the perspective of an Asian American.

Jennings Michael Burch

Jennings Michael Burch, *They Cage the Animals at Night,* 1984.
In this touching memoir, former foster child Jennings Michael Burch tells of how he was dropped off at an orphanage as a child by his mother. He moved so frequently from one foster home to another that he never had a chance to

form relationships. Sometimes he would return to his family of origin, but the situation was always precarious. Somehow, he learned to reach out for love along the way. This is the story of how he grew up.

Cadillac Man

Cadillac Man, *Land of the Lost Souls: My Life on the Streets*, 2009.

Cadillac Man spent the sixteen years before writing his memoir living on New York City's streets. All the while, he was recording the events of his daily life in journals. Here, he puts them together to create a portrait of what his life has been like—the bad and the unexpected good.

Alexis Marie Chute

Alexis Marie Chute, *Expecting Sunshine: A Journey of Grief, Healing, and Pregnancy after Loss*, 2017.

When artist and author Alexis Marie Chute lost her son Zachary at birth, she was devastated. She could not work for an entire year, which she calls her "Year of Distraction." But when she became pregnant again, she set out to recover her lost identity so she could be there for her next child. Her journey through the process and all its problems may inspire anyone who has lost a child.

Dasani Coates

Andrea Elliott, *Invisible Child: Poverty, Survival, and Hope in an American City*, 2021.

Dasani Coates was born in Brooklyn early in the twenty-first century. She spent her childhood in and out of various homeless shelters. Pulitzer Prize–winning author Andrea Elliott writes of how Dasani and her seven siblings stuck together to survive hunger, violence, and parental addiction. At age thirteen, Dasani was enrolled in a boarding school in Pennsylvania, giving her a chance at a new life. Elliott follows her story for eight years and highlights the difficulties of reconciling the two worlds in which she lived.

Jill Ker Conway

Jill Ker Conway, *The Road from Coorain*, 1989.

The first woman president of Smith College, historian Jill Ker Conway writes of growing up in the harsh Australian outback, where she had to work like a man on her parent's sheep ranch. Despite the lonely landscape, Conway was happy until her world was upended when her father died. As she moved with her mother to Sydney, attended school, and tried to help her increasingly dependent mother, she ultimately learned to care for herself.

Margaret Erle

Gabrielle Glaser, *American Baby: A Mother, A Child, and the Shadow History of Adoption*, 2021.

In the 1960s, birth control was difficult to get, and abortion was illegal. So, in 1961, when sixteen-year-old Margaret Erle found out she was pregnant, her family sent her to a maternity home. She never got to hold her newborn son, the baby was adopted out, and that was the end of the story. The child, David, grew up wondering why he had been given away. Margaret married his father and went on to have other children, but the thought of her firstborn haunted her. As an adult, David searched for his birth parents, and they discovered that he had spent his early childhood just a few blocks away. Gabrielle Glaser writes of the nation's sealed adoption records and of the fight of other adopted children to reunite with their families of origin.

Eleni Gatzoyiannis

Nicholas Gage, *Eleni*, 1983.

At age forty-one, Eleni Gatzoyiannis refused to give in to her small Greek town's traditions and the communist insurgents in civil war–torn Greece of 1948. Instead of sacrificing her children to be sent to a "camp" inside the Iron Curtain, she helped her son and his three sisters escape. She was imprisoned, tortured, and executed for her defiance. Investigative reporter Nicholas Gage returned to Greece from New York, where his mother Eleni had sent him, to uncover her heartbreaking fate.

Sue Klebold

Sue Klebold, *A Mother's Reckoning: Living in the Aftermath of Tragedy*, 2016.

The word Columbine has become code for school shootings in America. On April 20, 1999, Eric Harris and Dylan Klebold killed twelve students and one teacher, wounding twenty-four others before dying by suicide. Sixteen years after the tragedy, Dylan's mother, Sue Klebold, tells her story. She questions everything about herself and her relationship with her son. There are no easy answers, but Klebold hopes to help others struggling with tragedies and help parents see the signs that their children are in trouble before it is too late.

Christopher Knight

Michael Finkel, *The Stranger in the Woods: The Extraordinary Story of the Last True Hermit*, 2017.

In 1986, when he was twenty years old, Christopher Knight drove from his home in Massachusetts to Maine and disappeared. For the next thirty years, he lived alone in the woods, surviving below-freezing temperatures in the winter, partially by breaking into nearby cabins for food, clothes, and needed supplies. For years, the community had no idea who the thief was. When Knight was caught and forced to return to regular civilization, journalist Michael Finkel came to know him and tried to get to the bottom of what would make someone live the way he did.

David Sheff and Nic Sheff

David Sheff, *Beautiful Boy:*
A Father's Journey Through His Son's Addiction, 2007.

The elder son, varsity athlete, and honor student Nic Sheff was every parent's dream until he became addicted to crystal meth. His father, journalist David Sheff, desperately searched for treatments. He searched his soul for what he may have done to cause it. And finally, he recounts his wrenching experiences going through a parent's worst nightmare.

J. D. Vance

J. D. Vance, *Hillbilly Elegy:*
A Memoir of a Family and Culture in Crisis, 2016.

As the first family member to graduate from the prestigious Yale Law School, J. D. Vance reckons with his family story. While he was raised by his grandparents, who moved hopefully from Kentucky to Ohio after World War II to break away from Appalachia's poverty, he finds that their "hillbilly" legacy of alcoholism and poverty was not so easy to escape. And the research uncovers his family's story to be unfortunately common.

Jeannette Walls

Jeannette Walls, *The Glass Castle: A Memoir,* 2005.

In this astonishing memoir, Jeannette Walls writes of her parents' unconventional way of raising her and her three siblings. Life could be an adventure, when the children were young, as they camped, moved from place to place, listened to her father's stories, and watched her mother paint. But as time went on, they moved to her father's West Virginia hometown, where every bit of the romance and excitement of their earlier life vanished. Their mother did nothing to help the children, and their father often disappeared, taking the family's meager resources with him. Jeannette and two of her siblings managed to leave and create decent lives for themselves.

Tara Westover

Tara Westover, *Educated: A Memoir,* 2018.

As a child of religious survivalists in Idaho, Tara Westover never went to public school or saw a doctor. Her education came from helping her mother with herbal remedies and helping her father in his junk yard. But at 17, Tara left home to attend school at Brigham Young University and went on to finish her education at Cambridge University in the U.K. At these institutions, she faces the truth about her violent—but still loved—family.

35

Inspirational Tales

Mitch Albom

Mitch Albom, *Tuesdays with Morrie:*
An Old Man, a Young Man, and Life's Greatest Lesson, 1997.

Author Mitch Albom wrote this memorial of his beloved college professor, Morrie Schwartz. When Mitch looked Morrie up twenty years after graduating college, he found that his mentor was dying from ALS. From then until Morrie died, Albom visited him every Tuesday, because that's what they had done while Albom was in college. He finds throughout his visits that Morrie still has a lot to teach.

Cecilia Aragon

Cecilia Aragon, *Flying Free: My Victory Over Fear to Become the First Latina Pilot on the US Aerobatic Team*, 2020.

Growing up in a Midwestern town as the daughter of immigrants in the 1960s, Cecilia Rodriguez Aragon was bullied and overlooked by teachers, which convinced her she was a loser doomed to failure. She went on to use mathematical techniques to overcome her terror, becoming a member of the world-famous U.S. Unlimited Aerobatic Team, which required her to jump out of airplanes in front of millions of people. But her career didn't stop there. She also worked as a test pilot to help design experimental aircraft.

Derek Black

Eli Saslow, *Rising Out of Hatred:*
The Awakening of a Former White Nationalist, 2018.

Derek Black was the son of Don Black, the founder of the Internet hate site Stormfront, and the godson of KKK Grand Wizard David Duke. Derek could easily have stepped into his father's role until attending a liberal arts college exposed him to the people he had been taught to hate. Since then, he has renounced his White nationalist views. In this book, he reveals why.

E. R. Braithwaite

E. R. Braithwaite, *To Sir, With Love*, 1959.

When Black instructor E. R. Braithwaite entered a tough London school to teach delinquent adolescents, his work was cut out for him. He insisted on manners. The students were required to call him "Sir" and to address the girls in the class as "Miss." He taught them the basic rules of self-respect, which turned into respect for others. It didn't happen quickly and wasn't easy, but it was worth every bit of effort in the end.

Albert B. Facey

A. B. Facey, *A Fortunate Life*, 1981.

Living his life in Australia, Albert B. Facey became a renowned author when he published this autobiography at age eighty-seven. He writes of growing up without parents in Western Australia, then trying to survive as an itinerant worker, losing his farm during the Depression, then losing a son to war and finally his cherished wife. Yet despite his life of hardships, he felt he was truly blessed in the end.

James Gregory

James Gregory, *Goodbye Bafana: Nelson Mandela, My Prisoner, My Friend*, 1995.

When James Gregory was growing up, South Africa was under apartheid. But as a White Afrikaner growing up on a farm in Transkei, that was all right with him. The system, which kept twenty-five million Black people from voting, education, or land ownership, wasn't a problem for Gregory. But because he had learned to speak Xhosa and Nguni while growing up, he decided to become a prison guard on Robben Island, where Black prisoners were held. It was there he met Nelson Mandela. He tells how their relationship led Gregory to advocate for a free and democratic South Africa.

Anthony Ray Hinton

Anthony Ray Hinton, *The Sun Does Shine: How I Found Life and Freedom on Death Row*, 2018.

From 1985 to 2015, Anthony Ray Hinton spent his time on death row in an Alabama prison for two murders he didn't commit. He quickly found out that without money and with Black skin, his prospects for acquittal were almost nonexistent. But Hinton decided not to let circumstances beat him. Instead, he resolved to become the best person he could be and in doing so served as an inspiration for other inmates. Fifty-four of these prisoners were executed near his cell. But at age fifty-nine, he won his freedom with the help of Bryan Stevenson, the civil rights attorney who wrote *Just Mercy*. He writes here of the power of faith and forgiveness.

William Kamkwamba

William Kamkwamba, *The Boy Who Harnessed the Wind: Creating Currents of Electricity and Hope*, 2009.

In Malawi, where William Kamkwamba grew up, poverty was the norm, and science was mostly unknown. But William read a book called *Using Energy* that gave him the idea of making a windmill to bring electricity and water to his village. So even though his dreams of attending school ended during a famine, William used old science textbooks, scrap metal, and parts to construct a windmill that first brought electricity and then ran water to his home. In doing so, he inspired the world.

Randy Pausch

Randy Pausch, *The Last Lecture*, 2008.

Shortly after Carnegie Mellon computer science professor Randy Pausch was diagnosed with terminal cancer, he gave a lecture entitled "Really Achieving Your Childhood Dreams." In it, he summed up all he had come to believe about living. Through it, he continues to inspire millions.

Jessie Bennett Sams

Jessie Bennett Sams, *White Mother*, 2016.

At age seven, twin sisters Veanie and Mingie Bennett lived in Florida with only a paralyzed and terminally ill father. They had no mother at all. To survive, they had to steal their food and fight for their lives. But when they wound up on the White side of town one day, they met Mrs. Rossie Lee. That one event likely saved their lives. Here "Veanie," Jessie Bennett Sams, tells their story of hope and love.

Silvia Vasquez-Lavado

Silvia Vasquez-Lavado, *In the Shadow of a Mountain: A Memoir of Courage*, 2022.

Life held many challenges for Silvia Vasquez-Lavado, including being a Latina woman in Silicon Valley's macho world and dealing with the aftereffects of childhood abuse. She also felt compelled to hide her sexual orientation and alcoholism. To counteract the stress, she began to climb mountains. Gathering a group of young female survivors like herself, she organized a trip to scale Mount Everest. Here, she describes the incredible journey to the top.

36

Spirituality and Faith

Karen Armstrong

Karen Armstrong, *The Spiral Staircase: My Climb Out of Darkness*, 2004.

Karen Armstrong, the author of *The Case for God* and *A History of God*, is a well-respected author. At age seventeen, she entered a convent and began seven of the unhappiest years of her life. Here she tells the story of how she went from a crumbling faith to rediscovering the divine through studying comparative religion.

Augustine of Hippo

Augustine of Hippo, *The Confessions of St. Augustine*, ca. 398 C.E.

Fourth-century theologian and Latin philosopher Augustine of Hippo, also called St. Augustine, is considered one of the greatest Christian thinkers in history. His writings had a profound impact on the direction western Christianity developed. His influence continued through the medieval period. He is also considered by many to be a "theological father" of the Protestant Reformation.

Dietrich Bonhoeffer

Dietrich Bonhoeffer, *Letters and Papers from Prison*, 1951.

The Nazis executed German Lutheran pastor and theologian Dietrich Bonhoeffer in 1945 for his part in a plot to assassinate Hitler. His letters, written while he awaited execution, show his concern and care for his family.

John Calvin

William J. Bouwsma, *John Calvin: A Sixteenth-Century Portrait*, 1987.

Historian William J. Bouwsma writes the life of the founder of Calvinism. Rather than the typical portrayal of him as a dour tyrant bent on ridding the world of fun, Bouwsma helps the reader see that Calvin was a sympathetic figure in the context of his time. Bouwsma clarifies the influences of humanism and late Renaissance culture on both the man and the faith he founded. His teachings and followers ushered in the modern world and its focus on individualism, capitalism, science, democracy, and secularization.

Thomas Cranmer

Diarmaid MacCulloch, *Thomas Cranmer: A Life*, 1996.
Archbishop Thomas Cranmer led England through the tumultuous reign of Henry VIII. He played a delicate balancing act as a religious leader and statesman and was the guiding hand behind the Anglican *Book of Common Prayer*.

David

Joel Baden, *The Historical David: The Real Life of an Inverted Hero*, 2013.
Professor of the Hebrew Scriptures Joel S. Baden looks honestly at the historical David, the first king of Israel. Baden finds David doesn't clean up as well as the biblical accounts would have us believe. But the David he finds is every bit as interesting and even more complex.

Dorothy Day

Jim Forest, *All Is Grace: A Biography of Dorothy Day*, 2011.
Dorothy Day was the founder of the Catholic Worker movement. After giving birth out of wedlock to her daughter Tamar in 1927, she converted to Catholicism. Jim Forest researched her journals and letters to find how she combined her faith with her work for the poor. She was also a pacifist who was arrested for her part in protests.

Jonathan Edwards

George M. Marsden, *Jonathan Edwards: A Life*, 2003.
History professor George M. Marsden recreates the colonial world in which American preacher Jonathan Edwards was raised. Edwards struggled to reconcile his Puritan heritage with the secular, modern world of the Enlightenment. Edward's controversial sermon, "Sinners in the Hands of an Angry God," sparked the Great Awakening of the eighteenth century.

St. Francis of Assisi

Omer Englebert, *St. Francis of Assisi: A Biography*, 1979.
Using careful scholarship to uncover the facts about St. Francis of Assisi, Omer Englebert also creates a spiritual narrative. Moreover, he succeeds in making Francis accessible and inspiring to modern readers.

Gangaji

Gangaji, *Hidden Treasure:*
***Uncovering the Truth in Your Life Story*, 2011.**

In telling her life story, Gangaji (born Antoinette Roberson Varner) seeks to help her readers uncover the truths their own stories have to offer them. She describes how, as a disillusioned child of the American South, she traveled to India, where she found her being through her studies with Papaji.

God

Jack Miles, *God: A Biography*, 1995.

American author Jack Miles uses the Hebrew Scriptures and his experiences as a Jesuit-trained scholar to bring us the life of God by narrating how God evolves through his interactions with his creations.

Greg Graffin

Greg Graffin, *Anarchy Evolution: Faith, Science,*
***and Bad Religion in a World Without God*, 2010.**

The lead singer of the punk band Bad Religion is also a professor of life sciences at UCLA. Greg Graffin writes about his life and how science saved him from mistakes as a teenager. He discusses the effects of dishonesty in religions on our lives while detailing his own.

Billy Graham

Billy Graham, *Nearing Home:*
***Life, Faith, and Finishing Well*, 2011.**

The world-famous and politically influential twentieth-century evangelist Billy Graham died in 2018 at age ninety-nine. He wrote this memoir while in his nineties. In it, he discusses the things that surprised him about growing old. He says, "…growing old in age is natural, but growing old with grace is a choice." He discusses how growing old in grace is possible through Christian faith. For a historical biography that covers Graham's entire life, see Grant Wacker's *One Soul at a Time: The Story of Billy Graham*, published in 2019.

Ruth Bell Graham

Ruth Bell Graham, *It's My Turn*, 1982.

The wife of twentieth-century evangelical pastor Billy Graham discusses what it was like to be married to the world's most successful and influential evangelist. She reflects on raising their five children in North Carolina's western mountains.

Hildegard of Bingen

Fiona Maddocks, *Hildegard of Bingen: The Woman of Her Age*, 2001.

Twelfth-century German abbess, visionary, poet, composer, and naturalist Hildegard of Bingen was a rare and controversial woman for her time. Fiona Maddocks used Hildegard's writings to craft this fascinating biography.

Angela Himsel

Angela Himsel, *A River Could Be a Tree: A Memoir*, 2018.

Growing up as one of eleven children in a fundamentalist Christian home in Indiana, Angela Himsel fervently believed in the brand of Christianity that her parents espoused. At age nineteen, she decided to study at the Hebrew University in Jerusalem to learn more about the Scriptures. Instead, Himsel found herself questioning her worldview. She eventually found her spiritual home by way of a mikvah in Manhattan. She explains how she moved from being a fundamentalist Christian to becoming a practicing Jew in this memoir.

Jasmine L. Holmes

Jasmine L. Holmes, *Mother to Son: Letters to a Black Boy on Identity and Hope*, 2020.

Wanting to help her son Wynn in his faith and his life, Jasmine L. Holmes wrote these letters to prepare him for the unfairness he should expect in life. Being a Black man would inevitably lead him to encounter racism, but Holmes wants him to know that if he keeps himself rooted in his relationship with Jesus Christ, he can make it through.

Jesus

Paula Fredriksen, *Jesus of Nazareth, King of the Jews: A Jewish Life and the Emergence of Christianity*, 1999.

Professor of Scripture Paula Fredriksen begins her life of Jesus with the crucifixion because it is the only undisputed historical fact known about him. From there, she investigates the place and the time in which he lived, with its religious and political practices, to piece together how Jesus was proclaimed Messiah. For a gospel-based biography written by a respected Christian journalist, see *The Jesus I Never Knew*, by Philip Yancey.

Pope John Paul II

George Weigel, *The End and the Beginning:*
Pope John Paul II—The Victory of Freedom, the Last Years,
***the Legacy*, 2010.**

This book is the second of Weigel's biographies of Pope John Paul II. The first was titled *Witness to Hope: The Biography of Pope John Paul II.* This second volume tells of the Pope's fight against communism, which helped bring down European communism, and the fall of the Soviet Union, changing world history. Weigel also discusses the crippling disease that plagued him in his final years as he struggled to deal with mounting accusations of corruption in the Catholic Church.

C. S. Lewis

C. S. Lewis, *Surprised by Joy:*
***The Shape of My Early Life*, 1955.**

This partial autobiography tells of twentieth-century apologist, scholar, and beloved author C. S. Lewis and his conversion from atheism to Christianity. In it, he shares his search early in life for joy or longing. Readers may confuse the "Joy" in this title with his later wife, Joy Gresham. He discusses his wife and her wrenching death in *A Grief Observed.*

Martin Luther

Herman Selderhuis, *Martin Luther:*
***A Spiritual Biography*, 2017.**

Reformation scholar Herman Selderhuis seeks to expose the spiritual roots and beliefs that compelled Luther to nail the *Ninety-Five Theses* to the cathedral in Mainz, setting off the Protestant Reformation. Rather than seeing Luther as a hero or a heretic, Selderhuis shows a sincere and devoted man of God.

Nisargadatta Maharaj

Nisargadatta Maharaj, *I Am That:*
***Talks with Sri Nisargadatta Maharaj*, 1973.**

Indian sage Sri Nisargadatta Maharaj is a teacher of Advaita or non-dualism. This book brought him international fame and following. In it, he shares dialogues with followers who were seeking to shed their false identities. His message is that to end personal suffering, a person must penetrate their authentic being and experience it directly. According to Nisargadatta Maharaj, it is not a matter of changing but of uncovering what you already are.

Father Joe Maier

Greg Barrett, *The Gospel of Father Joe: Revolutions and Revelations in the Slums of Bangkok*, 2008.
Father Joe Maier entered the squatter slums of Bangkok in the 1970s to fight poverty. His tools were pencils, paper, crayons, and anger. Since then, his Human Development Foundation and Mercy Centre have educated thousands of children. Some of these children have gone on to become international scholars.

Moses Maimonides

Joel Kraemer, *Maimonides: The Life and World of One of Civilization's Greatest Minds*, 2008.
Maimonides was born in Muslim-ruled Spain in 1138. As a Jew, he compiled the *Mishneh Torah,* on which all following Jewish legal codes were based. In Egypt, he became a physician and worked for Sultan Saladin. People studied his medical works for centuries in Hebrew and Latin. He was also a master of scientific and philosophical thought. He led a remarkable life before dying in Cairo in 1204.

Cotton Mather

Kenneth Silverman, *The Life and Times of Cotton Mather*, 1984.
Cotton Mather is most famous today for his role in the Salem witch trials. But that emphasis leads to misunderstandings about the real man. Kenneth Silverman helps readers see that the early American Congregationalist minister believed he was put on earth to do good. He published more than four hundred works in his efforts to live up to his ideals.

D. L. Moody

Kevin Belmonte, *D. L. Moody—A Life: Innovator, Evangelist, World Changer*, 2014.
Nineteenth-century evangelist Dwight L. Moody brought a new gospel message to the U.K. and the U.S. He influenced a British prime minister and seven U.S. presidents. He even started a mission in Chicago's "Little Hell" before the Civil War, which president-elect Abraham Lincoln visited.

Dena Moes

Dena Moes, *The Buddha Sat Right Here: A Family Odyssey Through India and Nepal*, 2019.
The Moeses' California family included Dena, a Yale-educated midwife, her

husband Adam, a Buddhist yogi, and their daughters, teenaged Bella and the enthusiastic preteen Sophia. They decided they needed a change. So, they took up their backpacks for an eight-month excursion to India and Nepal. While there, they met the Dalai Lama and Amma, the Divine Mother. They also visited the tree where the Buddha found his enlightenment.

Thomas More

Peter Ackroyd, *The Life of Thomas More*, 1998.
English novelist and biographer Peter Ackroyd tells the story of the sixteenth-century chancellor of England, head of the Church of England, and Catholic martyr Sir Thomas More. In telling More's story, Ackroyd also provides a history of life in England under King Henry VIII. More, the author of *Utopia*, has been called "The Man for All Seasons."

Muhammad

Mohamad Jeara, *Muhammad, the World-Changer: An Intimate Portrait*, 2021.
Using details previously known only to Muslim scholars, Mohamad Jeara unveils the life of Muhammad, the founder of Islam, in the context of his own time and culture. Women nurtured and inspired him, some from the Jewish and Christian faiths. As a result, not only did he change his tribal culture and unleash one of the most significant religious movements in history, but he also escaped both slavery and assassination.

Takashi Nagai

Paul Glynn, *A Song for Nagasaki: The Story of Takashi Nagai: Scientist, Convert and Survivor of the Atomic Bomb*, 1989.
Takashi Nagai was a survivor of the atomic bomb dropped on Nagasaki, Japan, on August 9, 1945. The radiation exposure left the Catholic convert with leukemia. However, he sought to help others physically and spiritually for the rest of his life. His story provides insights into Japanese history and culture, making it an intriguing look at a man revered there today.

Eugene H. Peterson

Winn Collier, *A Burning in My Bones: The Authorized Biography of Eugene H. Peterson, Translator of* The Message, 2021.
Collier explains what made Eugene Peterson, American pastor and translator of *The Message*, so unique and beloved. She reveals his unique combination of gratitude for the life he was given and an irrepressible desire to get to know God personally.

Radhanath Swami

Radhanath Swami, *The Journey Home: Autobiography of an American Swami*, 2008.

Born in Chicago in 1950, Richard Slavin began a spiritual quest as a teenager, taking him to remote caves in the Himalayas. In this autobiography, he tells how he found union with the Divine through yoga. Radhanath Swami covers the stages he went through to achieve self-awareness. Today he travels the world teaching from his community in Mumbai, India.

Sabeeha Rehman

Sabeeha Rehman, *Threading My Prayer Rug: One Woman's Journey from Pakistani Muslim to American Muslim*, 2016.

Author, blogger, and speaker Sabeeha Rehman relates her experience as a bride in an arranged marriage over forty years ago. Raised as a secular Muslim in Pakistan, she finds love and fulfillment in her marriage and becomes a conservative, devout Muslim in the United States. Here Rehman writes about her struggles and joys and talks about her work to raise interfaith communication and understanding. In addition, she has an insider perspective on the backlash faced by American Muslims after the 9/11 attacks.

Jana Riess

Jana Riess, *Flunking Sainthood: A Year of Breaking Sabbath, Forgetting to Pray, and Still Loving My Neighbor*, 2011.

Religious journalist Jana Riess spent a year adhering to twelve spiritual practices to become saintlier. Thinking the exercise will be easy, she's surprised that she can't maintain any of the practices, even gratitude or fasting, perfectly.

Kevin Roose

Kevin Roose, *The Unlikely Disciple: A Sinner's Semester at America's Holiest University*, 2009.

As a sophomore at Brown University, Kevin Roose fit right in. But he was intrigued when he had a chance encounter with a group of students from Liberty University, in Lynchburg, Virginia. So, the following year, he transferred to Liberty as a full-time student. Founded by the late Rev. Jerry Falwell, LU is a prominent conservative Baptist university. The culture shock for Roose was great, but he was determined to treat the students, professors, and ministers respectfully. As a result, his thought-provoking account makes an entertaining read for both believers and non-believers.

Joseph Smith

Richard Lyman Bushman, *Joseph Smith: Rough Stone Rolling*, 2005.

At age twenty-three, Joseph Smith published the *Book of Mormon*. By the time of his violent death fifteen years later, he had founded cities and a new religion and had amassed thousands of followers. Richard L. Bushman, a practicing member of the Church of Jesus Christ of Latter-day Saints and a Ph.D. recipient from Harvard, writes of Smith's life and death and his contributions to Christian theology.

Howard Storm

Howard Storm, *My Descent into Death: A Second Chance at Life*, 2000.

Many people are familiar with the stories of near-death experiences, or NDEs. People typically find themselves out of their bodies, surveying scenes below before entering a tunnel of light. But Howard Storm, an atheist and self-proclaimed misanthrope had a disturbingly different experience in 1985. Instead of loving beings of light, Storm was greeted by sadistic beings of evil. Before being sent back to his body, Storm was allowed to go to heaven, where his many questions about this life were answered. Now a Christian minister, Storm imparts his insights to anyone who will listen.

Joni Eareckson Tada

Joni Eareckson Tada, *The God I Love: A Lifetime of Walking with Jesus*, 2003.

As a teen, Joni Eareckson was an ordinary, athletic girl before an accident left her quadriplegic. Tada published her first memoir as she made a name for herself from art she created using her mouth to hold her writing implements. This book updates Joni's life after thirty years as a person with paralysis. She married and developed her disability ministry in the intervening years. Here she shares her struggles and her joys.

Tim Tebow

Tim Tebow, *Shaken: Discovering Your True Identity in the Midst of Life's Storms*, 2016.

After having a successful beginning to his pro football career, Tim Tebow experienced a series of setbacks that would have been devastating for many. But Tebow writes of how his life and all its events have strengthened his faith. He hopes, through this book, to do the same for his readers.

Teresa of Avila

Cathleen Medwick, *Teresa of Avila: The Progress of a Soul*, 1999.

Sixteenth-century Christian mystic Teresa of Avila entered a convent while she was young. While she is most known for ecstatic states, which left her paralyzed and mute for hours at a time, the writing she was required to compose regarding them helps make her accessible today. A lesser-known side of Teresa was her ability as an administrator who reformed the Carmelite nuns.

William Tyndale

S. Michael Wilcox, *Fire in the Bones: William Tyndale—Martyr, Father of the English Bible*, 2004.

Before the Protestant Reformation, reading the Bible was available only to those who understood Latin, primarily priests and scholars. Ordinary people were forbidden to read the Holy Book. William Tyndale translated the Bible into English. For this crime, he was hunted by both church and the state. His story and martyrdom read like a thriller.

Swami Vivekananda

Swami Nikhilananda, *Vivekananda: A Biography*, 1989.

As the first Indian to bring India's spiritual message to the West, Swami Vivekananda taught Vedanta, the non-duality of the Godhead, and the oneness of all existence. His life is traced here by Swami Nikhilananda, a scholar who founded the Ramakrishna–Vivekananda Center of New York.

Qian Julie Wang

Qian Julie Wang, *Beautiful Country: A Memoir of an Undocumented Childhood*, 2021.

Her parents were both professors in China. But when they arrived in New York City's Chinatown with seven-year-old Qian in 1994, they took the stress of being undocumented sweatshop workers out on each other. Qian, who spoke no English, was ignored by teachers and students. But she discovered the library and learned English from the Berenstain Bears, whom she considered her first American friends. Life turned even darker when her mother collapsed from an illness and her father became even more distant. She tells the story of how she survived in this touching and harrowing memoir.

Simone Weil

Simone Weil, *Waiting for God*, 1950.

Social activist, Christian mystic, and philosopher Simone Weil wrote these

essays based on ideas she gathered from her correspondence with the
Reverend Father Perrin. This work is considered a classic of moral genius.

Paramhansa Yogananda

Paramhansa Yogananda, *Autobiography of a Yogi*, 1946.

Indian yogi and guru Paramhansa Yogananda is one of the most famous
spiritual teachers of the twentieth century. In his autobiography, he tells of
the many gurus and other spiritual adepts he met in his lifetime. Through his
supreme devotion to God and interactions with other gurus, he pierces many
mysteries surrounding existence. It is a fascinating look at the marvels that
humans can achieve. To help others in their spiritual quests, Yogananda spent
his last years in the West teaching meditation and Kriya Yoga.

Brigham Young

John G. Turner, *Brigham Young: Pioneer Prophet*, 2012.

Religious studies professor John G. Turner chronicles the life of Brigham
Young, who led an uneventful life until Joseph Smith, founder of the Church
of Jesus Christ of Latter-day Saints, was murdered in 1844. Young led the
remaining followers to Utah, where the charismatic leader set himself up
in the tradition of biblical patriarchs and prophets. By the time of his death,
he had married over fifty times, fought off the U.S. Army, and significantly
increased the size of the Mormon movement.

COLLECTIVE BIOGRAPHY

Agnes Smith and Margaret Smith

Janet Soskice, *The Sisters of Sinai: How Two Lady Adventurers Discovered the Hidden Gospels*, 2009.

When two middle-aged identical twins from Scotland went to the Holy Land
in 1892, they made a magnificent discovery in the library of St. Catherine's
Monastery at Mount Sinai. While looking in a palimpsest, they found the
remains of one of the earliest known copies of the Gospels written in ancient
Syriac, the language of Jesus.

37

Foodies

William Alexander

William Alexander, *52 Loaves: One Man's Relentless Pursuit of Truth, Meaning, and a Perfect Crust*, 2010.

William Alexander once tasted the perfect bread in a restaurant. Determined to create a perfect loaf of his own, Alexander commits himself to baking peasant bread every week until he meets his goal. Not content to rely on the local markets for his ingredients, he also grows, harvests, winnows, threshes, and mills the wheat to use in the process. As he documents his efforts, he also reflects on humanity's ties to bread and the desire to create something perfect.

Anthony Bourdain

CNN, *Anthony Bourdain Remembered*, 2019.

Celebrity chef and author of *Kitchen Confidential* Anthony Bourdain died in June 2018, leaving his fans bereft. In this tribute to his life, his fans, fellow chefs, and other notable figures speak of the effect Bourdain and his practice of culinary diplomacy had on them.

Bill Buford

Bill Buford, *Heat: An Amateur's Adventures as Kitchen Slave, Line Cook, Pasta-Maker, and Apprentice to a Dante-Quoting Butcher in Tuscany*, 2006.

American journalist Bill Buford documents learning to cook, beginning under chef Mario Batali at his three-star New York restaurant Babbo. After rising from kitchen slave to cook, he works under masters of Italian cooking in Italy. Part memoir and part biography of Batali, this book provides insight into what goes on behind the scenes to produce truly great food.

David Chang

David Chang, *Eat a Peach: A Memoir*, 2020.

The son of Korean immigrants, David Chang grew up in Virginia, where he always felt like an outsider. After graduation, he borrowed money from his father to start a restaurant, and in 2004, he opened Momofuku in Manhattan's East Village. By 2018, he owned restaurants worldwide and had a Netflix show and a podcast. In this memoir, he shares how he grew his business and the obstacles he has overcome.

John Chapman

William Kerrigan, *Johnny Appleseed and the American Orchard: A Cultural History*, 2012.

The American frontier hero Johnny Appleseed was a real man named John Chapman. Historian William Kerrigan spent fifteen years researching Chapman in libraries from New England to the Midwest. He also hiked, biked, and kayaked along the same paths Chapman trod. Here, Kerrigan separates facts from the fables. For example, despite Chapman's efforts to promote the apple tree, a changing marketplace caused grafting, rather than planting from seed, to win the day.

Julia Child

Julia Child, *My Life in France*, 2006.

When Julia Child first moved to France with her husband, Paul, in 1948, she could neither speak French nor cook. But she began taking cooking classes at the Cordon Bleu, where she discovered her passion. She reminisces about her growing fame as she published her cookbook *Mastering the Art of French Cooking* and starred in the television show *The French Chef*. Bob Spitz provides a third-person biography of Child in *Dearie: The Remarkable Life of Julia Child*, 2012.

M. F. K. Fisher

M. F. K. Fisher, *As They Were*, 1982.

In these autobiographical essays, M. F. K. Fisher writes about her life as a food writer, adored for her style. She helps readers see that simple pleasures like food make life worth living. Her most famous work is her 1942 guide to survive and thrive in trying times *How to Cook a Wolf*.

Linda Greenlaw

Linda Greenlaw, *The Lobster Chronicles: Life on a Very Small Island*, 2002.

After writing *The Hungry Ocean*, a book about swordfishing, and performing in the movie *The Perfect Storm*, Linda Greenlaw returned to Isle au Haut, a tiny island off the coast of Maine. Thirty of the island's seventy permanent residents were Greenlaw's relatives. She talks about the island's quirky inhabitants and life in such tight and exclusive quarters. And along the way, she shares the best way to cook and serve a lobster.

Vallery Lomas

Vallery Lomas, *Life Is What You Bake It:*
Recipes, Stories, and Inspiration to Bake Your Way
***to the Top: A Baking Book*, 2021.**

Former lawyer Vallery Lomas became a baker after she won the third-season contest on *The Great American Baking Show*. But when her season of the show was pulled due to Me Too accusations against one of the judges, she managed to get her press coverage. In this book, she shares one hundred recipes for delicious food influenced by her childhood in Louisiana and her time in Paris.

COLLECTIVE BIOGRAPHY

Alice Arndt, ed., *Culinary Biographies: A Dictionary*
of the World's Great Historic Chefs, Cookbook Authors
and Collectors, Farmers, Gourmets, Home Economists,
Nutritionists, Restaurateurs, Philosophers, Physicians,
Scientists, Writers, and Others Who Influenced
***the Way We Eat Today*, 2006.**

This reference book covers famous and unknown culinary figures and their relationships to food. Editor Alice Arndt includes articles written by various contributors on all the individuals whose culinary relevance is catalogued here. The volume includes three indices.

Adrian Miller, *The President's Kitchen Cabinet: The Story*
of the African Americans Who Have Fed Our First Families,
***from the Washingtons to the Obamas*, 2017.**

Adrian Miller talks about the Black chefs, cooks, butlers, stewards, and servers for the first family from George and Martha Washington to Barack and Michelle Obama. He names 150 of these folks and provides stories from their service.

38

Athletes and Sports Figures

Henry Aaron

Howard Bryant, *The Last Hero: A Life of Henry Aaron*, 2010.
Following Jackie Robinson's barrier-breaking career, Henry Aaron used his success as a baseball hitter to fight racism in baseball and American culture. Using exclusive interviews and painstaking research, Howard Bryant chronicles Aaron's rise to the top and his uneasy relationship with fame.

Andre Agassi

Andre Agassi, *Open: An Autobiography*, 2009.
Andre Agassi changed the face of tennis forever when he entered the pros at age sixteen, sporting long, frosted hair and pierced ears. He struggled on the pro circuit but captured the 1992 Wimbledon title cup. After this, he became a globally recognized superstar athlete. Here, Agassi reflects on his incredible career, his relationships with other tennis stars, and his failed romances, including the one with actress Brooke Shields. He also talks about how he finally found love with tennis pro Steffi Graf.

Muhammad Ali

Muhammad Ali, *The Greatest: My Own Story*, 1975.
One of the most endearing athletes in twentieth-century America, Muhammad Ali, was in his own words "The Greatest." Nobel Prize–winning novelist Toni Morrison edited the story he shares here. In it, Ali tells of the racism and discrimination he endured growing up in the American South and how he found his calling in boxing. The heavyweight champion discusses his antiwar activities and how his showmanship drew fans, and he even shares his poetic works.

Arthur Ashe

Arthur Ashe and Arnold Rampersad,
***Days of Grace: A Memoir*, 1993.**
American tennis professional Arthur Ashe was the first African American ranked as the number one tennis player in the world. In all, he won three Grand Slam titles. In *Days of Grace*, he talks about his tennis career and

social activism, including his role as a spokesperson for Haitian refugees. Ashe died of AIDS-related pneumonia in 1986.

Simone Biles

Simone Biles, *Courage to Soar: A Body in Motion, a Life in Balance*, 2016.

Internationally acclaimed gymnast Simone Biles was a foster-care child growing up in Spring, Texas. She went on to earn nineteen medals, fourteen of which were Olympic gold. Here she talks about her religious faith and the courage and perseverance that led to her success. She encourages others to work hard and follow their dreams as well.

Roberto Clemente

David Maraniss, *Clemente: The Passion and Grace of Baseball's Last Hero*, 2006.

Hall of Famer Roberto Clemente played eighteen seasons of major league baseball. While playing for the Pittsburgh Pirates, he won four batting titles and led his team to championships in 1960 and 1971. Biographer David Maraniss describes Clemente on the diamond and off. He also tells of his tragic but heroic death in an airplane crash on New Year's Eve 1972, en route to deliver supplies and food to Nicaraguan earthquake victims.

Tom Daley

Tom Daley, *Coming Up for Air: What I Learned from Sport, Fame and Fatherhood*, 2021.

British diver Tom Daley, an Olympic gold medalist in the men's synchronized 10 meter platform event, is also the winner of four additional Olympic diving medals. In his memoir, he reveals the experiences and resilience that led to his successes. Married to screenwriter and activist Dustin Lance Black, Daley also tells of how he found the courage to speak about his sexuality and what his family means to him.

Joe DiMaggio

Richard Ben Cramer, *Joe DiMaggio: The Hero's Life*, 2000.

American journalist Richard Ben Cramer presents an eye-opening look at one of baseball's legends, Joe DiMaggio. As an immigrant playing for the New York Yankees in the 1930s, DiMaggio was seemingly gifted at everything he touched, from the diamond to love. But Cramer reveals there was more to DiMaggio than good looks and athletic grace.

Brett Favre

Jeff Pearlman, *Gunslinger: The Remarkable, Improbable, Iconic Life of Brett Favre*, 2016.

Sportswriter Jeff Perlman profiles NFL legend Brett Favre, who was the quarterback for the Green Bay Packers for twenty years. Using over five hundred interviews, Pearlman follows the athlete from his rough childhood through his time at Southern Mississippi and his professional career, which began with the Atlanta Falcons. But his life was far from perfect, especially off the field, where he struggled with addiction, infidelity, and his reluctance to leave the sport.

William Finnegan

William Finnegan, *Barbarian Days: A Surfing Life*, 2015.

Elite surfer and war correspondent William Finnegan recounts his extraordinary life as a globetrotting thrill seeker. During his childhood in California and Hawaii, the bookish Finnegan began surfing and quickly became obsessed. He writes of his experiences as a young man growing up in a tough culture and how his camaraderie with fellow surfers helped him. He tells incredible stories of chasing waves in Polynesia, Fiji, Tonga, New York, and Africa.

Tyson Fury

Tyson Fury, *Behind the Mask: My Autobiography*, 2019.

British World Heavyweight Champion Tyson Fury writes of his birth in Manchester, where he weighed in at just one pound. Despite his odds-defying success at boxing, Tyson was later stripped of his titles due to alcohol and cocaine abuse. But Fury wasn't finished. He writes of how he fought his demons and Deontay Wilder to win the WBC heavyweight title.

Lou Gehrig

Jonathan Eig, *Luckiest Man: The Life and Death of Lou Gehrig*, 2005.

Legendary first baseman Lou Gehrig was called the Iron Horse. Using interviews with those who knew him, in addition to previously unavailable correspondence, biographer Jonathan Eig presents a side of Gehrig few know. Growing up in New York City, the future Yankee was a shy young man. He found his calling in baseball, but at the height of his fame, Gehrig suffered symptoms from ALS, the disease later named after Gehrig that claimed his life.

Sergei Grinkov and Ekaterina Gordeeva

Ekaterina Gordeeva, *My Sergei: A Love Story*, 1996.

Former Soviet—then Russian—figure skater Ekaterina "Katia" Gordeeva writes of her life with her husband and skating partner Sergei Grinkov. The couple were 1988 and 1994 Olympic champions and won world championships in pairs skating four times. But in 1995, Grinkov had a heart attack while practicing with Katia on the ice. He died later, at age twenty-eight. Here is her touching memoir about their life and their love.

Jack Johnson

Geoffrey C. Ward, *Unforgivable Blackness: The Rise and Fall of Jack Johnson*, 2004.

Author and screenwriter Geoffrey C. Ward narrates the extraordinary life of the first Black heavyweight champion in history, Jack Johnson, who won the title in 1908. Johnson lived his life on his terms at a time in America when White people ran everything. He had money, fame, and marriages to three White women. For the marriages, the federal government imprisoned him for one year and exiled him for seven for this "crime." Ward presents Johnson as more than a record breaker; he was determined to live life on his terms, no matter the cost.

Michael Jordan

Roland Lazenby, *Michael Jordan: The Life*, 2014.

After following Michael Jordan's stratospheric career for almost thirty years, basketball journalist Roland Lazenby renders a well-rounded profile of the legendary player. Conducting hundreds of interviews with Jordan and people who know him, Lazenby covers his years growing up in North Carolina, his college career, and his most compelling moments on the court. The Jordan he uncovers is incredibly ambitious and, at times, reckless.

Billie Jean King

Billie Jean King, *All In: An Autobiography*, 2021.

Recipient of the Presidential Medal of Freedom in 2009, Billie Jean King was a tennis champion who won an incredible twenty Wimbledon championships and thirty-nine Grand Slam titles. But she is most memorable for her defeat of Bobby Riggs in the Battle of the Sexes. King tells how her determination and success led to viewpoints on cultural watersheds like the women's movement, the civil rights movement, and the LGBTQ+ rights movement. In addition, she gives insights and encouragement for those wishing to be true to themselves in the face of societal barriers.

Sandy Koufax

Jane Leavy, *Sandy Koufax: A Lefty's Legacy*, 2002.

Jane Leavy dives into the life of reclusive Brooklyn Dodgers pitcher Sandy Koufax. Why she asks, did this three-time Cy Young award winner hide from the public after reaching the top? In seeking to answer this question, she looks at how he viewed himself. In uncovering Koufax's motivations, she reveals a lot about how we turn people into heroes.

Eric Liddell

Duncan Hamilton, *For the Glory: Eric Liddell's Journey from Olympic Champion to Modern Martyr*, 2016.

Duncan Hamilton tells the story of Olympic sprinter Eric Liddell, who was memorialized in the Academy Award–winning film *Chariots of Fire*. His devotion to his Christian beliefs led Liddell to refuse to run on Sundays. This drew the ire of the British press because his decision not to run likely cost him a medal in the 1924 Paris Olympics. But he went on to run another day and won the 400 meter event. Later, while in China as a missionary, he was imprisoned in a Japanese internment camp during World War II. He died there just before the war ended.

Vince Lombardi

David Maraniss, *When Pride Still Mattered: A Life of Vince Lombardi*, 1999.

Legendary football coach Vince Lombardi was the son of an Italian immigrant. He began his career as a high school football coach, staying for twenty years before moving on to Fordham, West Point, and then the New York Giants. Then at age forty-six, he got a chance to lead the struggling Green Bay Packers. The team won five world championships in nine seasons under his watch. He is still revered for his work ethic and obsession with victory.

David Millar

David Millar, *Racing Through the Dark: Crash. Burn. Coming Clean. Coming Back.*, 2011.

Scottish road racing cyclist David Millar was the 2007 British champion. He also won the Tour de France and wore the leader's jersey in all three Grand Tours. But before this, he was banned from the sport for two years for taking performance-enhancing drugs. In this memoir, he writes of how he went off track and fought his way back.

Max Mosley

Max Mosley, *Formula One and Beyond: The Autobiography*, 2015.

Max Mosley, former driver, team owner, and president of the FIA (the international motorsports governing body), writes of his prolific career. Over his half century in the business, Mosley turned Formula One into a multi-billion-dollar industry. But his private life is as interesting as the public one. As the son of the infamous couple Oswald and Diana Mosley, he has had to deal with his parents' scandals and his battles with the Murdoch press.

Joe Namath

Mark Kriegel, *Namath: A Biography*, 2004.

Joe Namath was one of the first celebrity pro athletes. Sports columnist and novelist Mark Kriegel narrates the NFL quarterback's rise from a blue-collar background to fame for his audacious football plays and playboy lifestyle off the field. In addition, Kriegel explains just why Namath had such a devoted following.

Jesse Owens

Jeremy Schaap, *Triumph: The Untold Story of Jesse Owens and Hitler's Olympics*, 2007.

In 1936, American participation in the Berlin Olympics was controversial. But the president of the U.S. Olympic Committee viewed the Nazi stance on Jews as irrelevant, and the team was sent, including Jesse Owens, the African American son of sharecroppers. Jeremy Schaap tells about the behind-the-scenes intrigue and maneuvering that aided Owens's success. His performance earned Owens four gold medals and terminated the purported idea of Aryan supremacy.

Jackie Robinson

Kostya Kennedy, *True: The Four Seasons of Jackie Robinson*, 2022.

One of the most influential athletes of all time, baseball's Jackie Robinson, opened the door for African Americans to participate in professional sports. In place of a traditional biography giving even treatment to Robinson's entire life, Kostya Kennedy focuses on four years of his life. Kennedy begins in 1946, when Robinson played for the all-White minor league team the Montreal Royals. Next, in 1949, Robinson won the Most Valuable Player award as a Brooklyn Dodger. In 1956, Robinson played his last season in the major leagues. In 1972, he died. Kennedy's narrow focus makes it possible to disclose information about Robinson not covered in previous biographies, making it especially valuable to fans.

Babe Ruth

Leigh Montville, *The Big Bam: The Life and Times of Babe Ruth*, 2006.

Babe Ruth, the baseball superstar, was later declared the twentieth century's most influential athlete. Using recently available materials, acclaimed biographer Leigh Montville tells of Ruth's youth in Baltimore to his ascendancy to cultural dominance in the 1920s. But there are many myths surrounding Ruth's life, and Montville strives to get to the bottom of them all.

Nick Saban

Monte Burke, *Saban: The Making of a Coach*, 2015.

The controversial coach of the University of Alabama, Nick Saban, changed college football forever. Monte Burke writes about Saban's well-known and wildly successful career. Covering Saban's early years in coaching, he also includes his stint with the Miami Dolphins. In addition, he shares Saban's often complicated relationships with other coaches and how he developed his "process."

John Thompson

John Thompson, *I Came as a Shadow: An Autobiography*, 2020.

After growing up in the Jim Crow South, John Thompson spent thirty years coaching college basketball and was the first Black head coach to win an NCAA championship. Thompson was tough, partly because his childhood was tough. He talks about his famous players and the origins of the phrase "Hoya Paranoia." But he also reflects on race relations and our culture at large.

Jim Thorpe

David Maraniss, *Path Lit by Lightning: The Life of Jim Thorpe*, 2022.

Called the greatest all-around athlete of the first half of the twentieth century, Jim Thorpe won gold medals in the 1912 Stockholm Olympics as a track runner, he played professional football in the NFL, and he played major league baseball for the New York Giants. But his heritage as a Native American, a member of the Sac and Fox Nation, made things difficult for him in many ways. After several setbacks, he turned to alcohol, had a series of unsuccessful marriages, and had money troubles. But no matter what life threw at him, he managed to survive.

Ted Williams

Ben Bradlee Jr., *The Kid: The Immortal Life of Ted Williams*, 2013.

Pulitzer Prize–winning journalist Ben Bradlee Jr. writes about one of the greatest hitters in baseball history, Ted Williams. The Boston Red Sox player set a record batting average in 1941 and the highest batting average in history, which is stunning considering he left baseball for five years at the height of his career to serve as a Marine pilot in World War II, then in the Korean War. But the passion that worked so well for him on the field hurt him off it in clashes with the press and at home. Bradlee presents this incredible athlete as the very talented and very human man he was.

Yao Ming

Brook Larmer, *Operation Yao Ming: The Chinese Sports Empire, American Big Business, and the Making of an NBA Superstar*, 2005.

Journalist Brook Larmer tells the story of the 7′6″ NBA superstar Yao Ming, who made his fortune in big-name sponsorships and changed pro basketball. Yao Ming's story begins in China, where the government was determined to raise a generation of athletes who would bring glory to the nation. By age thirteen, Yao Ming was playing professionally in China. When word got out about these athletes, the NBA and American sports companies like Reebok were determined to have them come here. While the story is about Yao Ming, it also profiles Wang Zhizhi, his less successful compatriot.

39

Outdoor Adventures

Peter Allison

Peter Allison, *Whatever You Do, Don't Run:*
***True Tales of a Botswana Safari Guide*, 2007.**

Australia native Peter Allison writes about his experiences as an African safari guide where adventure is plentiful. But while the wild animals he regularly encounters provide excitement, the tourists he deals with leave him rattled. He shares stories of the insane behaviors he's seen from the latter, while getting across his respect for the former.

Julie Angus

Julie Angus, *Rowboat in a Hurricane: My Amazing Journey*
***Across a Changing Atlantic Ocean*, 2008.**

Canadian biologist Julie Angus made history in 2005–2006 when she became the first woman to row across the Atlantic Ocean, with her fiancé Colin. For 145 days, she studied and documented the wildlife she observed. While this was gratifying, she also observed more pollution, particularly trash, than life. As if all that weren't enough, the pair also managed to survive four cyclones and two hurricanes that were so intense it's a wonder they and their boat survived.

Steven Callahan

Steven Callahan, *Adrift: Seventy-Six Days Lost at Sea*, 1986.

American author, naval architect, and sailor Steven Callahan recounts the seventy-six days he spent alone on an inflatable survival raft on the Atlantic Ocean. As the only person known to have survived more than a month alone at sea, his bestselling story is the model for many survival tales that followed it.

Jill Fredston

Jill Fredston, *Rowing to Latitude:*
***Journeys Along the Arctic's Edge*, 2001.**

Every summer for years, Jill Fredston and her husband, Doug Fesler, would paddle around the Arctic Ocean and the subarctic, just to explore the shore-lines. Over the years, their travels took them to Alaska, Canada, Greenland,

and Norway. They battled both fierce weather and polar bears while also experiencing sublime beauty and wonder.

Emma ("Grandma") Gatewood

Ben Montgomery, *Grandma Gatewood's Walk: The Inspiring Story of the Woman Who Saved the Appalachian Trail*, 2014.

When sixty-seven-year-old Grandma Gatewood left her Ohio hometown, with one change of clothes and less than two hundred dollars in her pocket, to "go on a walk," she next turned up on Maine's Mount Katahdin. Incredibly, she had hiked eight hundred miles alone along the Appalachian Trail to get there. Later, she became a popular press darling. The attention she garnered after hiking the neglected trail two more times possibly saved it from extinction. Journalist Ben Montgomery tells her story to answer the question, "Why did she do it?"

Eric Hansen

Eric Hansen, *Stranger in the Forest: On Foot Across Borneo*, 1988.

It took travel writer Eric Hansen seven months to walk across Borneo, a trip of nearly 1,500 miles. He was the first Westerner to ever make the trek. Traveling with him were members of the Penan, nomadic hunters indigenous to the island. They adopted Hansen and let him in on the secrets of their strange and eerie world.

Edmund Hillary

Sir Edmund Hillary, *View from the Summit*, 1999.

New Zealand mountaineer, explorer, and philanthropist, Sir Edmund Hillary wrote of his trek up Mount Everest and his history-making climb, which made him the first man to reach the summit, in May of 1953. He tells how he did it, while describing his other adventures, including a journey to the South Pole. This remarkable memoir, written decades after the event, is a page-turner from beginning to end.

David Kroodsma

David Kroodsma, *The Bicycle Diaries: My 21,000-Mile Ride for the Climate*, 2014.

After substantial time planning, climate researcher and journalist David Kroodsma rode his bicycle from his home in Palo Alto, California, all the way to the southern tip of South America. Calling his journey Ride for Climate, he used the trip to build global awareness of climate change and its effects on the landscapes he pedaled through. He got a lot of international media attention. He also met many wonderful people who helped him out.

Rick Lamplugh

Rick Lamplugh, *In the Temple of Wolves: A Winter's Immersion in Wild Yellowstone*, 2013.

Rick Lamplugh decided to spend a winter alone in the Lamar Valley, a remote corner of Yellowstone National Park. His plan was to watch the wildlife, including elk, bison, wolves, coyotes, mountain lions, eagles, and ravens. Using skis and snowshoes, he traveled around, recording what he saw and his conversations with experts. All the while, he wrestled with his own inner landscape.

Michael Lanza

Michael Lanza, *Before They're Gone: A Family's Year-Long Quest to Explore America's Most Endangered National Parks*, 2012.

After noting the changes to our national landscapes due to the changing climate, backpacker Michael Lanza decided to take his two children on a tour of threatened wilderness areas like Alaska's tidewater glaciers and Florida's Everglades. To Lanza, this was every bit as much a spiritual crisis as an environmental one. Nate, his nine-year-old son, and Alex, his seven-year-old daughter, visited as many of these places as they could in a year. He writes of the visits with his children and stresses that the world we leave them will determine their stories.

Sue Leaf

Sue Leaf, *Portage: A Family, a Canoe, and the Search for the Good Life*, 2015.

Beginning with a trip to the border lakes of the Boundary Waters Canoe Area Wilderness, biologist and birder Sue Leaf and her husband, Tom, with their four children, spent thirty-five years exploring North America's waterways together. They travel the paths of explorers before them, like Lewis and Clark and Jean Lafitte. Reminiscing about the places they've gone, Leaf shares memorable moments along the way, along with the natural and social history of each area.

Robert Macfarlane

Robert Macfarlane, *The Old Ways: A Journey on Foot*, 2012.

Acclaimed British writer Robert Macfarlane walks ancient roads and pathways in Britain to find an ancient network of routes around the British Isles and further afield. He shares the history of the places he goes and reflects on what they mean to the British people today.

Peter Matthiessen

Peter Matthiessen, *The Snow Leopard*, 1978.

World-renowned writer, naturalist, explorer, and activist Peter Matthiessen writes in the 1970s of a trip to Nepal, intending to study the Himalayan blue sheep found there. Hoping to catch sight of the rare snow leopard, he took his five-week expedition in the winter months. The result is this beautiful book about the wonders of nature.

Robert Moor

Robert Moor, *On Trails: An Exploration*, 2016.

For seven years, Robert Moor hiked trails all over the planet, from the neglected and nearly vanished to the grand and heavily used. He discloses what he discovered about the science, history, philosophy, and nature each path had to offer.

Trina Moyles

Trina Moyles, *Lookout: Love, Solitude, and Searching for Wildfire in the Boreal Forest*, 2021.

As a native of Alberta, Canada, Trina Moyles grew up hearing about the lookout observers, people who spent their summers alone at the top of hundred-foot-tall lookout towers scanning for signs of fire in the boreal forest. Despite her fears, she decides to try the job while working to sponsor her fiancé as an immigrant to Canada. With only a farm dog, labeled a domesticated wolf, Trina struggles to deal with loneliness and her dawning understanding of the crisis that is taking place in these wild places due to climate change.

Richard Proenneke

Sam Keith and Richard Proenneke, *One Man's Wilderness: An Alaskan Odyssey*, 1973.

Keeping journals as he went along, Richard Proenneke built a cabin and lived alone in the Alaskan wilderness. In this book, he shares his daily activities, his explorations of the area, and the natural events and creatures he witnessed. Many dream of such a life. Richard Proenneke lived it.

Aron Ralston

Aron Ralston, *Between a Rock and a Hard Place*, 2004.

One Saturday afternoon, twenty-seven-year-old mountaineer Aron Ralston decided to take a solo hike in Utah's Blue John Canyon. He was eight miles from his truck when, climbing off a wedged boulder, the rock came loose and pinned his right hand and wrist against the canyon wall. He was in that position for six horrifying days with little water or food and not even a jacket to keep him warm. He hadn't told a soul where he was going. As he confronted his predicament across the sleepless days and nights, he finally faced the desperate act he must perform to save himself.

David Adams Richards

David Adams Richards, *Lines on the Water: A Fly Fisherman's Life on the Miramichi*, 1998.

Canadian screenwriter, novelist, and poet David Adams Richards wrote this award-winning book about his membership in a community of fly fishermen. From the time he was four, fishing has been a passion of Richards's. While discussing the personalities of the fishing enthusiasts he has encountered, Richards also talks about nature, history, our changing world, and the lessons we can learn from them all.

John J. Rowlands

John J. Rowlands, *Cache Lake Country: Or, Life in the North Woods*, 1948.

As a child, John J. Rowlands dreamed of living alone by a lake. As an adult, when he was sent into the Canadian wilderness to survey land for a timber company, he found a quiet lake. He named it Cache Lake because he felt it had everything he would ever need, and he built a home there that he never left. In this narration, he tells how he survived, even providing instructions for making shoes, ovens, and canoes.

Antoine de Saint-Exupéry

Antoine de Saint-Exupéry, *Wind, Sand, and Stars*, 1939.

The twentieth-century author of the beloved fable *The Little Prince*, Antoine de Saint-Exupéry, was also a French pilot who first flew a plane at age twelve. In 1926 he began flying mail from Toulouse, France, to Dakar, Senegal. After leaving this position, he delivered mail for a time in South America. Trying to break a speed record flying from Paris to Saigon, he crashed in the Libyan desert. He crashed again attempting to fly from New York to Tierra del Fuego. This autobiographical novel tells of these adventures. Biographer Stacy Schiff has also written his comprehensive biography in *Saint-Exupéry: A Biography*.

Cheryl Strayed

Cheryl Strayed,
Wild: From Lost to Found on the Pacific Crest Trail, 2012.

At age twenty-six, Cheryl Strayed made the decision to hike the length of the Pacific Coast Trail from the Mojave Desert all the way to Washington State, alone. After losing her mother four years before, Strayed had struggled to find her footing in life. Even though she knew nothing about through hiking, she picked up some equipment and got going, figuring she had nothing to lose. Her adventures are by turns frightening, heartbreaking, and exhilarating.

Edward Whymper

Edward Whymper, *Scrambles Amongst the Alps*, 1871.

In the nineteenth century, when Edward Whymper began climbing the Alps one by one, he became a leader in the new field of mountaineering. It took him nine years to climb them all. In the process, he tried, and failed, to scale the Matterhorn seven times, before finally succeeding on the eighth, making him the first man in history to do so. But during the effort, he lost four comrades who fell to their deaths. He never got over the loss.

40

Animals and the People
Who Love Them

Joy Adamson

Joy Adamson, *Born Free: A Lioness of Two Worlds*, 1960.
Naturalist, artist, and author Joy Adamson wrote this classic story of a lion cub named Elsa who needed to transition from captivity to the wild. Adamson raised the cub and documented the experience with photographs. Her story was an international sensation. It has been used as a model for helping animals in danger from human development today.

Tony Angell

Tony Angell, *The House of Owls*, 2015.
Nature artist Tony Angell and his family observed pairs of western screech owls who lived in a nesting box the Angells provided outside their home window. For twenty-five years, Angell kept a journal of his drawings and observations of these creatures. Here he gives an overview of western screech owls and North American owl species.

Lawrence Anthony

**Lawrence Anthony, *The Elephant Whisperer:
My Life with the Herd in the African Wild*, 2009.**
While running the Thula Thula game reserve in Zululand, Lawrence Anthony was approached about taking in a "rogue" herd of elephants deemed a danger and destined for destruction. Anthony was their last chance. Against his better judgment, he took them in. Here he tells the story of the bond he formed with the herd and how he convinced them to stay within his reservation's borders. He says all the elephants have unique personalities and a strong drive to defend and protect their own.

Gwen Cooper

**Gwen Cooper, *Homer's Odyssey:
A Fearless Feline Tale, or How I Learned about Love and Life
with a Blind Wonder Cat*, 2009.**
Gwen Cooper, depressed over a romantic breakup and in need of a

higher-paying job, got a call from her veterinarian to tell her about the abandoned, eyeless, three-week-old kitten. She took it in, making it her second, and named him Homer. With Gwen, Homer grew and thrived. He made friends with every human who crossed his path, survived alone for days after the 9/11 attacks hit near his home, and fought off an intruder into his and Gwen's home. After a while, Gwen realized that Homer had done more for her than she could have done for herself, and her faith in life was renewed.

Sara Dykman

Sara Dykman, *Bicycling with Butterflies: My 10,201-Mile Journey Following the Monarch Migration*, 2021.

Monarch butterflies travel over 10,000 miles in their annual migration. The journey takes nine months. Sara Dykman details her odyssey as the first in history to follow them on a bicycle, which she assembled from used parts. While some supported her, many were unsympathetic to her efforts. But she keeps her sense of humor while helping us understand the migration's importance.

Charlie Gilmour

Charlie Gilmour, *Featherhood: A Memoir of Two Fathers and a Magpie*, 2020.

Charlie Gilmour rescued a baby magpie who had fallen from its nest and fell in love—naming the bird with starkly colored feathers Benzene. Charlie and the young bird formed a tight relationship. Shortly afterward, Charlie discovered that his father, the British poet Heathcote Williams, who abandoned Charlie when he was six months old, was dying. When Charlie found one of his father's poems about Heathcote's experience as a young man who rescued a young jackdaw that had fallen from a tree, he was startled by the parallels of his father's experience with his own. From this, Charlie finds the strength to become the father he never had.

Jane Goodall

Jane Goodall, *Through a Window: My Thirty Years with the Chimpanzees of Gombe*, 1990.

British primatologist and anthropologist Jane Goodall became one of the world's top experts on chimpanzees by living with them in the wilds of Tanzania for three decades. Her memoir recalling her time with them reads like a novel, with the chimps serving as fascinating characters. Theirs are stories of love, vengeance, motherhood, and war, much like ours.

Dave Goulson

Dave Goulson, *A Sting in the Tale: My Adventures with Bumblebees*, 2013.

British biologist and conservationist Dave Goulson takes us on his lifelong obsession with wildlife and his recent quest to save the short-haired bumble-bee. Once common in parts of Britain, it is now only found in the wilds of New Zealand as an invasive species. He details the life cycle of these rare bees and why we still need them in our world.

George Bird Grinnell

Michael Punke, *Last Stand: George Bird Grinnell, the Battle to Save the Buffalo, and the Birth of the New West*, 2007.

Once thirty million strong, the buffalo herds of the American West were decimated in the final three decades of the nineteenth century. Their demise was caused by a combination of the commercial value of their hides and a campaign by the U.S. Army to weaken the Indigenouos population by eradicating a primary source of their food. To fight their extinction, scientist and journalist George Bird Grinnell wrote stories in leading magazines, went to Washington, and traveled the West. It was the first environmental battle in the United States.

John Grogan

John Grogan, *Marley and Me: Life and Love with the World's Worst Dog*, 2005.

When journalist John Grogan was young, living an idyllic life with his wife Jenney, they adopted Marley, an adorable Labrador retriever puppy. It quickly became apparent that Marley would not be a calm pet after he was kicked out of obedience school. The family soldiered on when tranquilizers failed to mellow him, even when things got tough. But in the end, Marley won them over with his devotion to them. This heartwarming book was later turned into a major motion picture.

Jon Katz

Jon Katz, *Saving Simon: How a Rescue Donkey Taught Me the Meaning of Compassion*, 2014.

Author and photographer John Katz and his wife Maria reluctantly took in a neglected donkey named Simon. Severely malnourished and extremely weak, Simon began to thrive as John fed him by hand, read to him, and took him walking while talking to him as a friend. As Simon began to return his love, John was inspired to open his home to other abandoned and neglected animals.

Louise de Kiriline Lawrence

Merilyn Simonds, *Woman, Watching: Louise de Kiriline Lawrence and the Songbirds of Pimisi Bay*, 2022.
After the Bolsheviks murdered her husband during the Russian Revolution, Swedish aristocrat Louise de Kiriline Lawrence moved to a wilderness cabin in Canada, where she studied birds in the forest. Birder Merilyn Simonds met her in these woods decades later when Lawrence was elderly. Simonds becomes fascinated with this woman who has been called the "Canadian Rachel Carson."

Howard F. Lyman

Howard F. Lyman, *Mad Cowboy: Plain Truth from the Cattle Rancher Who Won't Eat Meat*, 1998.
Fourth-generation American farmer Howard F. Lyman spent decades raising dairy and meat products. But when he was diagnosed with a spine tumor, he vowed he would begin an organic farm if he survived. By 1990, he was a vegetarian. After researching mad cow disease, Lyman made an appearance on *The Oprah Winfrey Show* in 1996 to discuss the dangerous practices of the cattle and dairy industries. As a result, Oprah gave up hamburgers, and the cattle industry sued both her and Lyman. Lyman tells his incredible story here.

Mark W. Moffett

Mark W. Moffett, *Adventures among Ants: A Global Safari with a Cast of Trillions*, 2010.
Dubbed "the Indiana Jones of entomology," Mark W. Moffett travels the world to find out how species of ants live, build, and cooperate to survive. In some ways, their societies are like our own, only much smaller and moving on more rapid scales.

Farley Mowat

Farley Mowat, *Never Cry Wolf*, 1963.
As a young naturalist, conservationist, and author, Farley Mowat was sent to the Arctic alone to discover why wolves killed the arctic caribou. Here he describes the summer he spent there and how he came to love and respect the wolves. His memoir is now considered a classic in nature writing.

Ruth Padel

**Ruth Padel, *Tigers in Red Weather:*
A Quest for the Last Wild Tigers, 2005.**
A descendant of Charles Darwin, British poet and writer Ruth Padel traveled to a wildlife sanctuary in India. While there, she became enamored with the tigers and spent the next two years chasing them down in the eleven countries where they still roam free, all of which are in Asia. In talking with people who work with them, she learned shocking information: the United States has as many tigers in captivity as there are in the wild worldwide. By the end of her explorations, she is their passionate advocate.

Catherine Raven

Catherine Raven, *Fox and I: An Uncommon Friendship*, 2021.
Catherine Raven discloses how she fled her abusive father as a teen and got a job working as a ranger in the National Park System. She lived in her car or camped on a piece of land while she saved to buy it. She also worked through school, eventually earning a Ph.D. in biology. After building a house on a remote plot of land in Montana, she noticed a fox that came to her house every day at 4:15. Eventually, he sat near her as she read aloud to him. But even though they become friends, she cannot control the forces of nature.

Rin Tin Tin

Susan Orlean, *Rin Tin Tin: The Life and Legend*, 2011.
Rin Tin Tin was one of the most famous dogs in history. By 1927, he was Hollywood's number one box office star. Acclaimed writer Susan Orlean uses the life and the myths surrounding this American icon to examine the entertainment industry's relationship with animals and the changing role of dogs in American society.

Timothy Treadwell

**Nick Jans, *The Grizzly Maze: Timothy Treadwell's*
Fatal Obsession with Alaskan Bears, 2005.**
Award-winning outdoor writer Nick Jans tells the story of the famous "bear whisperer," Timothy Treadwell, who lived among the grizzlies in hopes of convincing others that they were not dangerous animals. In October 2003, Treadwell and his girlfriend were mauled. His story became the basis for the movie *The Grizzly Man*.

Alf Wight (aka James Herriot)

Jim Wight, *The Real James Herriot:*
***A Memoir of My Father*, 1999.**

Yorkshire veterinarian Alf Wight is beloved by millions for his books and the television series *All Creatures Great and Small*. All of these portrayed his real-life practice of animal medicine. For years, his son Jim Wight worked beside him. Here Jim talks about his beloved father and how he refused to allow fame to come between him and his work or his family.

Subjects of Biographies, Autobiographies, and Memoirs in *Library Lin's Curated Collection of Superlative Nonfiction*

Biographies, autobiographies, and memoirs about the following people are found in my first book. The page numbers on which you can find their books are indicated.

Index

Index

If you enjoyed this book, consider leaving a review!

Want to find even more biographies, autobiographies, and memoirs?

Check out *Library Lin's Curated Collection of Superlative Nonfiction*, available from Amazon, bookshop.org, Apple Books, Google Books, and Kobo.

You can also find the book and many other recommended books at librarylin.com. Join her email list to receive superlative award-winning titles from the previous year and receive "Lin's Top Ten," a monthly newsletter with ten curated, subject-specific titles.

Coming in 2025

Library Lin will present a curated collection of nature writing, from classic natural histories to current science and journalism about the state of the planet. Whether you love books about plants, wildlife, outdoor adventures, or philosophical observations of the natural world, there will be something here for you.

Stay up to date at librarylin.com

www.ingramcontent.com/pod-product-compliance
Lightning Source LLC
Chambersburg PA
CBHW041508120626
46551CB00018B/2353